PRAISE FOR TEMPESTA'S DREAM

*"The novel has enormous heart and a few times my eyes filled with tears. I was vividly involved with this young tenor, his dreams, and the wonderful old man who taught him. It is not an easy thing to convey the passion for song. However, the way the author did it, I could physically feel the young tenor singing and hear his voice."*
**-Stephanie Cowell, Author of** *Marrying Mozart*

*"The story holds charm and appeal. There is beauty in the depiction of the relationship between Giovanni and Isabella, as well as in the bond between Alfredo and the young tenor. Giovanni, Isabella and Alfredo will remain in 'memoria mia' for years to come."*
**-George Shirley, Tenor, University of Michigan Emeritus Professor of Music (Voice)**

*"I grant to you my warmest congratulations for your great work, which enhances the Casa Verdi and its guests."*
**- Antonio Magnocavallo, President of the Casa Verdi**

*"The author's contagious love of opera and his faith in human decency sing through this loveable page-turner of a story."*
   **-Susan Nicassio, Author of** *Tosca's Rome*

*"The story surprised me and involved me. The development of the book was very intriguing and moving."*
   **-Cecilia Gobbi, founder of the** *Associazione Musicale Tito Gobbi,* **an organization devoted to preserving and celebrating the record of her famous baritone father's contribution to opera**

*"A Powerful novel . . Tempesta's Dream is all about the music, it's all about the passion; and it's all about pursuing one's dream . . a moving, engrossing story."*
   *- D. Donovan, MidWest Book Review*

*"Within a very moving story of romance and friendship, the author has created a realistic portrait of a young singer's pursuit of an operatic career. This lovely tale allows one to acquire an understanding of and an affection for opera."*
   **-Audrey Schuh Redmann, Soprano**

*"This novel is a thorough pleasure."*
   **-Christina Vella,** *Author of Intimate Enemies, The Two Worlds of Baroness de Pontalba*

*"An intelligent and entertaining lyrical journey . . .A rare, beautiful story with passion and opera pulsating through each page. LoCoco has woven a unique novel with exceptionally developed characters, realistic dialogue and a well-balanced narrative."*
   **-Penn Book Review**

"What a story! Quite possibly, the best novel about opera I have ever read. The passion of opera pulsates throughout the entire novel. Highly recommended."

-John Gehl, Opera historian and the only American collaborator on *The Oxford Concise Encyclopedia of Opera*

"More than just a typical page-turner, Tempesta's Dream is many things at once, with something relentless and compelling between the book covers for everyone. . LoCoco takes the reader on an adventurous ride that combs the breadth and depth of all human experience, while touching upon Italian: geography, history, opera, food, and women."

-The Italian American Digest

"Adored this book and it is now added to my personal favorites."

- Literary Chanteuse

"This is a wonderful book, accurately written, that will give readers an in-depth knowledge about opera with its many performances, singers, and composers. It is a wonderful introduction to the world of opera!"

- Historical Novel Review

"True to the opera it honors, the book is full of strong emotions, heart, tears, love, ambition, friendship and an underlying decency. I enjoyed it and it had me turning to my opera recordings, which is always a good thing!"

- Italophile Book Reviews

BOOKS BY VINCENT B. LOCOCO

*Tempesta's Dream:*
*A Story of Love, Friendship and Opera*

---

BELLAFORTUNA SERIES

*A Song for Bellafortuna - Book 1*

*Saving the Music - Book 2*

# TEMPESTA'S DREAM

## A STORY OF LOVE, FRIENDSHIP AND OPERA

VINCENT B. "CHIP" LOCOCO

Cefalutana Press

*Per i miei bambini,*

**Matthew Vincent and Gabrielle Marie
LoCoco**

*Spero che la musica fará sempre parte della tua vita.
I wish that you will always have music in your life.*

# CONTENTS

"For me, music making is the most joyful activity possible, the most perfect expression of any emotion."

— LUCIANO PAVAROTTI, TENOR

# TEMPESTA'S DREAM

# PROLOGO

## MILAN, ITALY - MAY, 1962

*E*veryone doubted that he would ever return to her. After all, he was an American sailor, and it was a well-known fact that those sailors always had a different girl in every port. It was thought by others that she was just another young girl abandoned by her American sailor.

Yet, she thought differently. She had given up her own family and even her own religion to marry him. She always believed that he would come back to her. But time passed, and he had not returned.

As she sat on the floor of the living room of her sparsely furnished hilltop home, her blue-eyed, curly blonde-haired, three-year-old son, played with his toy model of an American ship. This was their child, but her sailor had no idea, as she discovered the pregnancy after he had left her side, not long after their wedding night.

While sitting with her son, her thoughts floated back to the night she married Lieutenant B. F. Pinkerton of the United

States Navy. They were wed, under the stars, on the hilltop overlooking Nagasaki harbor. She was so nervous that night, yet his tender, passionate words melted away all of her fears.

She always remembered with affection the words he told her that night as he pulled her close and kissed her. All of the doubters never heard what he told her as he held her tight. That was why they never believed he would come back to her. But she knew better. He loved her. He would return. He promised her.

She dreamed often of that *"un bel di"* (one fine day), when she would gaze down upon the harbor from her hilltop home and see her sailor's white warship, the *Abraham Lincoln*, enter Nagasaki harbor, flying the flag of the United States. Then her sailor, her husband, would walk up the winding uphill path to her little house, grab her in his arms and take her and their son back to America together.

He promised her he would return.

But that was three years ago. And he had not returned. She was now poor, abandoned by her family, and trying to raise her son. Her faithful maid, Suzuki, had stayed with her all these years. However, even Suzuki grew concerned for her mistress.

Suzuki tried to convince the young girl to return to her days as a Geisha. But the young girl defiantly stated that she would rather die than go back to the life she led prior to marrying her sailor. Those close to her were still trying to make her see that he would never return and that she should find someone else. Yet, she still waited; waited for his return.

Suddenly, her thoughts were interrupted by the thundering sound of a cannon shot from the harbor. Suzuki rushed into the living room where mother and son were and said breathlessly:

*Il cannone del porto!*
*The cannon of the port!*

The young girl sat motionless on the floor, as Suzuki ran toward the terrace and looked down toward the harbor. Suzuki quickly turned and came back inside the living room, saying with excitement:

*Una nave da guerra.*
*It is a warship.*

The young girl quickly got up from the floor, swept her son up into her arms, and scrambled toward the terrace. Suzuki followed closely behind.

For three years this is how it played out whenever a ship entered the harbor, as the young mother, holding tightly to her son, scanned the horizon to see the color and flag of the ship entering the harbor, only to have her dreams shattered once it was discovered that it was not her sailor's ship.

Standing on the terrace, the young girl looked down toward the harbor. As she saw the ship for the first time, she spoke out loud to her son, almost in disbelief:

*Bianca. Bianca.*
*It is White. White.*

*Il vessillo Americano delle stelle.*
*The American Flag with the stars.*

With her anticipation building, she put her son down and ran over to a telescope that was permanently set up on the terrace and which always pointed down toward the harbor. With Suzuki steadying her hand on the telescope, the young girl squinted tightly to get a better view of the ship.

The ship began to drop its anchor. The young girl strained to see the name of the ship. Unable to contain herself, she blurted out, as if she were commanding the telescope itself to speak:

*Il nome! Il nome! Il nome*
*The name! The name! The name!*

Looking through the telescope, she scanned back and forth until she was finally able to locate the name written on the side of the ship. As it came into view, she said:

*Eccolo.*
*Here it is.*

And then, with utter jubilation, she said the name of the ship:

*Abramo Lincoln!*
*Abraham Lincoln!*

Tears began streaming down her face. She fell to the ground and buried her face into her hands, overcome with emotion. Her young son got up and came over to her, grabbing her tightly from behind. She picked her head up, turned to her son, and then, as if in defiance of the last three years that she had waited, and with a feeling of vindication, she repeated, choked with tears:

*È giunto! È giunto! È giunto!*
*He has come. He has come. He has come.*

She then outstretched her arms, and exclaimed:

*Ei torna e m'ama!*
*He has returned and he loves me!*

---

As THE CHURCH bell from the nearby Duomo, the Cathedral in Milan, tolled midnight, Franco Tempesta stopped reading. Tears were running down his cheeks as he placed the libretto of Giacomo Puccini's opera, *Madama Butterfly*, on the nightstand next to his eight-year-old son's bed. Wiping the tears away, he said, "This is a good stopping point tonight, Giovanni."

Giovanni Tempesta loved how every night his father would take an opera libretto and make it into a bedtime story. Unlike other kids, Giovanni's father did not read nursery rhymes to his son at bedtime, but instead read opera librettos to him, relating to his young son the great stories and legends of operas written centuries ago. Young Giovanni quickly became fascinated with the stories his father told him. When his father reached a part in the libretto where an aria would be sung, Franco gently hummed the aria to his son.

Franco did not have a talent for music, but what he did

have was a love of music and a passion for opera that he passed to his son.

"Oh, Papa, finish telling me the story. I love the part when Madama Butterfly waits all night for Lieutenant Pinkerton to walk up the hill to her little Japanese house, only to become sad when he does return but with his American wife."

Franco replied, "Butterfly had given her entire life to Pinkerton. She had put all of her trust and love in him, but he threw it all away, without even a care of what it would do to her. When you fall in love, Giovanni, always respect that trust the girl places in you. You would only expect the same from her. For it is from that trust, that true love finds its roots. And love is what gives our life poetry. But Giovanni, it is late. Your mama is waiting for me. *Domani*. We will finish the story tomorrow. Perhaps we will even listen to the Di Stefano/De Los Angeles recording. The heartbreak in Di Stefano's voice is remarkable as Pinkerton finally realizes the pain he has caused." Franco then began to sing the opening lines of the aria, *Addio, fiorito asil*, where Pinkerton admits that he is a coward and cannot face Butterfly and runs from the home.

When he finished, Franco said, "Puccini's music is so emotional and wonderful. A singer who sings this music with passion can really touch your heart. So much so, that when a gifted soprano sings the line, '*Ei torna e m'ama!*'(He has returned and he loves me!), the crowd always breaks into a rousing round of applause. Giovanni, why do you think that is?"

"Because she hit the note," replied Giovanni, quizzically.

Franco answered, "No. It's much more than that. Puccini has magically weaved his music during the course of the opera into the very soul of every audience member. They feel for the character; they are living and dying with Butterfly. That is why they erupt in applause when her sailor returns. Their very own soul leaps with joy for her and, most importantly, with her.

"And that is what the power of opera can do, unlike any other art form. The composer has provided the canvas, yet the singer is the artist. He or she brings that creation to life. All of their training and their own life experiences are laid bare before the public. And we in the audience stand in awe before a human voice, a God-given voice, which brings this music to life, and which has the ability to reach down to your very core and grab hold of your soul. How a singer can do that is an amazing thing. Without a doubt, God blessed those singers with a gift. You see, we all have a voice, but God has touched a singer's voice. Giovanni, you have a beautiful voice. Pray that God blesses you with the gift to become a professional singer."

"I will, Papa. You know that since I was a little boy, I have always dreamed of becoming an opera singer. I want to bring the stories of opera to life on a stage."

Franco bent down and kissed Giovanni, saying, "And you will, with God's help. *Buona notte, Giovanni.*"

"*Ti amo, Papa.*"

Franco shook his head in agreement and replied, "*Ti voglio bene, mio figlio bellissimo.*" He then began to gently hum the famous humming chorus, the beautiful, wordless melancholy melody that ends the second act of *Madama Butterfly.*

As Giovanni Tempesta did every night, he fell asleep to the soothing sound of his father's voice, all the while knowing that his head would be filled with the passion of opera and the dream of one day becoming an opera singer.

# PART I

(17 YEARS LATER)

MILAN, ITALY
MARCH, 1979

# 1

# ANGELO'S RISTORANTE

*M*ost nights, as Giovanni Tempesta walked from his home past the *Teatro alla Scala di Milano* (La Scala), the world-famous opera house in his hometown of Milan, Italy, on his way to work, he would be filled with excitement as he thought about the performance going on inside the venerable old theater, and he would imagine himself singing on the stage in front of a packed house; but not tonight.

Tonight, March 3, 1979, was different. It was Giovanni's 25th birthday. This was a turning point for Giovanni. You see, he had always told himself that by his 25th birthday, his dream to become an opera singer had to be on a path to reality, or forever it would remain just that, nothing more than a dream.

Giovanni knew that he had a love and a passion for opera, unlike most young people his age. And, nurtured by his father, he had found and developed a voice, a tenor voice.

The more he sang, the more he came to believe that singing was his ultimate destiny. Both he and his father knew that God had given Giovanni this talent, and there was no doubt God wanted him to be a singer.

Even when his father passed away a few years back, Giovanni's burning desire to be an opera tenor remained strong. Yet, now at the age of 25, he fully realized that his dream to become a singer was finally coming to an end. He had no prospects for an operatic career. That was all Giovanni could think about this night as he continued walking toward Angelo's, the restaurant where he worked.

Angelo's was located in an old house at the corner of the *Via Victor de Sabata* and the *Via Verdi*, directly across the street from the right side of La Scala and not far from where Giovanni had lived his entire life. Angelo Basta was the proprietor. He was a fat, balding, jovial, little man who loved three things in life -- food, opera and women. Giovanni wasn't sure which was the correct order of preference of the three, but he knew Angelo indulged in them all.

On Thursday, Friday and Saturday nights, Angelo's became Giovanni's stage, his only stage. Giovanni would wander throughout the usually packed restaurant and sing arias and Neapolitan love songs. He also sang some Broadway tunes in English, a language that he, like many Italians his age, spoke very well. Sometimes he would take requests, and the people would stay to hear him sing until the wee hours of the morning. After he finished his performance, without fail, the customers in the restaurant would rise to their feet, cheer him, and tell him that he was better than what they heard at La Scala that night. They would proceed to tell him that he must get training, and if he did, people would speak of his career as they did of Caruso's. Then the customers would get their bill, sometimes leave a nice tip for Giovanni, and go about their lives, forgetting about the "Caruso of Angelo's", the nickname some regulars had given him.

Giovanni arrived at Angelo's the night of his birthday and, upon entering, was met by the Maenza brothers, the instrumentalists at the restaurant. The Maenza brothers, Mario, the piano player, and Jacopo, the violinist, were identical twins who had spent their entire lives in Milan. They were near seventy-six years of age and had never married. Both had white scraggly beards but with hair red as fire on top their heads, which gave them a very comical look.

Mario Maenza, standing by the bar near the front door of Angelo's, welcomed Giovanni when he entered, stating rather loudly, *"Ecco Giovanni Tempesta. Buon Compleanno!"* (Here is Giovanni Tempesta. Happy Birthday!)

*"Grazie, Mario,"* replied Giovanni.

Jacopo Maenza walked over and greeting Giovanni with a great, big hug also said, *"Buon Compleanno, Giovanni.* You're lucky since tonight should be an early night."

"Why?" asked Giovanni.

Jacopo responded back with a question, asking, "Did you not hear? Gluck's *Orfeo* is the opera being performed at La Scala tonight."

Giovanni replied, *"Si.* Rosa Papeto is singing the title role. It should be a great performance. She is a wonderful mezzo-soprano."

*"Ah, mio amico.* She is not singing," replied Jacopo. "Can you believe it? Papeto was the sole reason for the revival of this ancient opera."

"Why isn't she singing?" asked Giovanni.

Mario, with a wry smile, quickly responded, "She cancelled yesterday, claiming illness."

Giovanni asked, "Sick?"

Jacopo answered, "So she says. But the Milanese know the reason she cancelled was because of the events that occurred last year when she sang at La Scala in Donizetti's *Lucrezia Borgia* in the role of Orsini. She was booed by the throngs of people in the *loggione,* the standing room only area at the very top of the theater."

Giovanni replied, "Before my father passed away, he used to tell me stories about the *loggione* and the *logginisti,* the nickname for the opera fanatics who inhabit that area during the opera. He would always tell me that every singer who has ever sung at La Scala feared the *loggione.* As he put it, the *logginisti* could make or break a singer."

Mario said, "Well, the *logginisti* broke Signora Papeto. The raucous shouts coming from the *loggione* last year got so bad that by the third act of the opera, she couldn't be heard at all. With her cancellation this year, the *logginisti* have claimed yet another victim at La Scala."

Giovanni said with conviction, "Those people are tough."

"Indeed they are," replied Jacopo. "After Signorina Papeto withdrew from *Orfeo* this year, the management of La Scala signed a no-name singer to replace her. As a result, La Scala is half empty, which means Angelo's will not be crowded after the opera."

Mario, laughing while he spoke, said, "Which also means poor Angelo won't have a lot of women to pick from for his conquest tonight."

Jacopo agreed and said, "Because of all of this, there is no doubt that it will be an early night tonight."

"Good," replied Giovanni. He paused and then said, "I could use an early night."

There was a touch of sadness in the way Giovanni had replied. So much so, Mario picked up on it and asked if all was well.

Giovanni wanted to say to his friend that all was not well. The one thing he wanted more than anything else in the world he now believed he would never be able to achieve. For the first time, Giovanni began to feel that his entire life had been a waste by chasing an unattainable dream. But how could he say such things to anyone? There was no one he could tell that to. The only person he was close enough to have such a conversation with was his mother, and how could he really open up to his own mother and tell her that her son was a complete failure. Even though he loved Mario, he surely couldn't tell him his true feelings. Instead, he lied, and merely replied, "I'm fine, Mario. Just tired."

Mario said, "Go warm up, Giovanni. We should be starting soon. The opera will be over at La Scala, and the customers from the opera house will be arriving shortly."

Giovanni made his way to a small back office behind the kitchen. He always used the sparsely furnished room as his warm-up room as he prepared to sing at Angelo's. As he began to do his vocal exercises, the thought of turning 25 made the memories of his father come rushing in. His thoughts centered on how his father had taught him to love opera and had given Giovanni his early singing lessons. He remembered back to his days as a child and how, for hours, he would sit with his father, listening to opera recordings and quizzing each other on naming different singers from the past performing arias. Giovanni soon began to sing along with the great singers from the past while his father gave him advice on how to produce the perfect sound. Franco noticed early on that Giovanni had a special gift for singing and an uncanny knack for memorization. Over time, Giovanni developed a beautiful tenor voice, which had a rich sound and was dark in quality.

As Giovanni continued warming up on the night of his birthday, the memories of his father became too much to bear. Giovanni stopped in the middle of doing his vocal scales, and he sat down in the chair in the small office and cried hard. There was a mirror on the wall. Through the tears, he looked at himself. It was amazing how much he resembled his father, tall, lean, same athletic build with brown hair, and dark tan skin. The only real difference was Giovanni's uncanny blue eyes.

He was handsome like his father. Yet, at the age of 25, there was no woman in Giovanni's life. As he stared at the mirror, he thought about how his father had always taught him the importance of having someone to love.

For you see, not only had his father taught Giovanni about the romantic stories of opera, but he also passed down to Giovanni the belief that life without love is an empty life. This was the direct result of Giovanni's father and mother living their married life awash in love; the sweet comments, the whispered speech, the unspoken stares, the hidden, gentle touches, and the stolen, soft hugs between them. Furthermore, Giovanni's own life was enriched with all of the passionate love stories of opera. All of this made Giovanni understand the importance of love, and he came to strongly believe in the power and certainty of love at first sight, even though he had never personally experienced it in his own life.

Giovanni dated very little. He had great expectations when it came to women, and he wanted someone to give him the feeling as if being struck by lightning upon seeing her for the first time. Whereupon looking at each other, he would say, "It is she!" She would say, "It is he!" He likened his feeling to those of the characters in the operas he loved when the tenor sees a woman for the first time and falls immediately and passionately in love with her.

Giovanni was fully aware that he was a passionate romantic living in a very unromantic world, a world that was becoming even more unromantic day by day.

A knock on the door brought Giovanni back from his memories. Angelo Basta opened the door and said, "It's time, Tempesta. There is such a sparse crowd tonight for dinner. What the hell was La Scala thinking?"

Giovanni turned away, so Angelo couldn't see that he had been crying. "*Vengo,*" (I'm coming) replied Giovanni.

Angelo shut the door. Giovanni went down on one knee as he always did before singing at Angelo's. "For you, Papa," he said almost in a whisper. He then made the sign of the cross, wiped the tears from his eyes, and made his way to the dining room.

# 2

## ISABELLA MONTERONE

*A*s the customers began to trickle into the restaurant after the opera performance at La Scala, the Maenza brothers started to play operatic selections. As usual, the selections were some tunes from the opera that had been performed at La Scala that night. The first was the most famous aria from *Orfeo*, "Che fara senza Euridice?" The Maenza boys played it exquisitely.

Giovanni waited by the piano to sing. As he did so, he noticed a few regulars scattered among the small crowd. The restaurant had one large dining room. White Carrara marble tiles lined the floor. Angelo always took pride in telling the customers that the tiles used at the restaurant came from the same area in the Apuan Alps, where Michelangelo chose the blocks from which he carved his masterpieces, including the *David* in Florence.

The walls of the restaurant were filled with posters of operas and hundreds of pictures of the composers and singers who were made famous at nearby La Scala or who had eaten at the old restaurant. Giovanni loved walking around the restaurant, just taking in the photographs. Rumor had it that even the great Enrico Caruso as a young man had eaten at the restaurant after he had sung at the premiere of Giordano's *Fedora* in 1898.

The customers were sitting at tables, which were each adorned with empty Chianti wine bottles with a candle stuck in each bottle. Chianti wine, especially the wines produced by Ruffino, was Giovanni's favorite. When he was first hired a few years back, he insisted to Angelo that the tables be adorned with Chianti wine bottles instead of the Valtellina wines that are favored by the Milanese and which had been used at the restaurant since its opening. The candlelight, as it flickered off the photographs on the walls, and the melodic music gave the entire restaurant a romantic feel.

However, Giovanni was not feeling very romantic as he stood by the piano near the front of the restaurant. He was in a very reflective mood. His thoughts were interrupted when the music stopped. Mario Maenza, after accepting the applause of the crowd, nodded to Giovanni that it was time for him to begin to sing.

Giovanni, trying to forget his melancholy mood, walked over to Mario and said, "I want to only sing Puccini tonight. After all, these poor people had to just sit through three hours of Gluck."

Mario chuckled out loud. He knew how much Giovanni loved singing Puccini arias, his favorite opera composer. Giovanni started with the aria closest to his heart, 'E lucevan le stelle' (And the Stars were shining) from *Tosca*. The character, Mario Cavaradossi, sings the tenor aria before he is about to be executed. In the aria, he reminisces about meeting his love, Floria Tosca, in the garden of his villa, and then is shaken back to reality by the idea of his impending execution.

Jacopo gave the violin introduction and was soon joined by Mario on the piano playing Giacomo Puccini's gorgeous melody. When Giovanni began to sing, his remarkable tenor voice echoed off the walls of the restaurant and into the delighted ears of the patrons.

*E lucevan le stelle,*
*And the stars were shining,*

*ed olezzava la terra, stridea l'uscio dell'orto,*
*and the earth smelled wonderful, the garden gate creaked,*

*e un passo sfiorava la rena.*
*and a footstep brushed against the sandy path.*

*Entrava ella, fragrante, mi cadea fra le braccia.*
*She entered, all fragrant, and fell into my arms.*

At the words, *"Entrava ella, fragrante, mi cadea fra le braccia"*, Giovanni noticed her for the first time. At a table against the far wall, near the entrance to the kitchen, sitting between two people whom Giovanni guessed were her parents, he saw the most beautiful creature he had ever seen. She must have been no more than 18 years old, with jet-black hair, and piercing huge brown eyes. The candlelight from the Chianti wine bottle located on her table made her eyes sparkle.

Giovanni's mind started to wander. He was losing his

place and tempo in the aria. "Get a hold of yourself," he thought while staring at the unknown beauty. For the first time in his life, he felt as though lightning had struck him between the eyes. He had never felt like this before upon gazing at a woman.

He got back on tempo and sang the next line of the aria, all the time staring into her eyes.

*O dolci baci, o languide carezze,*
*Oh sweet kisses, oh sensuous caresses,*

*mentr'io fremente le belle forme*
*while I anxiously uncovered her beautiful*

*disciogliea dai veli!*
*form by removing her veils!*

At this point in the aria, the entire mood changes, as Mario Cavaradossi realizes that his life is coming to an end, and he reflects on his love. Giovanni closed his eyes as he made a fist with each of his hands, and he passionately ended the aria.

*Svanì per sempre il sogno mio d'amore.*
*My dream of love is gone forever.*

*L'ora è fuggita e muoio disperato!*
*The hour has fled and I am dying in despair!*

*E non ho amato mai tanto la vita!*
*Yet I have never felt such a strong love of life!*

When Giovanni completed the aria, the customers cheered him at once. Giovanni, slowly opening his eyes, stared at the young girl, until he finally bowed to accept the applause from the crowd at Angelo's. He came out of his bow, still with resounding applause throughout the restaurant. Mario and Jacopo started his next selection, an aria from *Le Villi*, Puccini's first opera. Giovanni turned toward the young lady and again sang into those eyes.

When he finished the aria, the crowd cheered again, while Giovanni slowly bowed toward his muse. Realizing that the singer was bowing to her, she shyly bowed her head from her seated position. Her father looked at her when she bowed back to Giovanni and then turned to him and snarled.

Giovanni sang a few more Puccini selections. Finally, Jacopo and Mario started to play the instrumental selection from Puccini's *Suor Angelica*, while Giovanni tried to make his way to this unknown beauty.

After being stopped by numerous customers at different tables, offering their congratulations, he finally reached her table. As Giovanni approached, her father rising from the table, met him. Her father was an imposing giant of a man who had a perpetual snarl on his face, which Giovanni thought made him resemble the evil police chief, Scarpia, from the opera, *Tosca.*

The man turned to his wife and said, "Let's go."

Giovanni, all the time looking at the young beauty, said to the man, "I hope everyone at your table enjoyed the evening?"

Gruffly her father stated, "*Si.* My wife and daughter had a wonderful time at the opera and have enjoyed our drinks and dessert, but we must be going." He turned to his daughter and said, "Get your coat," before he and his wife walked away from the table toward the front door.

Giovanni wanted to speak to the young beauty, but his nerves got the best of him. He had never approached a woman before to introduce himself. But something was telling him to speak to her. She fascinated him.

The young girl had stood up from the table, glanced at Giovanni, and started to walk toward the seat where her coat was lying. Giovanni raised his right hand and said, "*Aspetti, signorina*. Wait."

In Giovanni's mind ran the moment in Massenet's opera, *Manon*, when the tenor first meets the soprano. Giovanni always had music running through his head. Moments he experienced in life recalled for him scenes from operas. He would let the opera do his bidding.

Quickly, Giovanni grabbed the girl's coat off the chair and walked over to her. He spoke the lines from Massenet's opera *Manon* in a perfect imitation of his favorite tenor, Giuseppe di Stefano. Giovanni spoke the lines with great emotion.

*Fanciulla. Scusate!*
*Young lady. Excuse me!*

*Non so. . . Io non vi vidi mai,*
*I don't know you. . . I've never seen you before,*

*eppur, entro il mio cor, da lungo tempo siete,*
*yet, you have been in my heart for some time,*

*il nome vostro io so.*
*and it's as if I already know your name.*

The young girl smiled, but said not a word. She had never been spoken to like that before.

Giovanni asked, "*Come si chiama?*" (What is your name?)

She looked deeply into his blue eyes and then slowly said, "*Mi chiamo Isabella.*"

As Giovanni put Isabella's slender arms into her jacket, he whispered into her ear, "*Isabella. Bel nome.* (What a beautiful name.) *Mi chiamo Giovanni Tempesta.* I am a singer," he said with a smile. "Did you like my singing?"

"*Bèllo,*" she said with a lovely, soft voice.

Her father, who had made his way back toward the table, grumbled, "*Isabella, andiamo!*"

"I have to go," she said as she turned to leave.

Giovanni knew he had to act fast. "Can I see you? Where do you live?" he asked, hopeful for an answer, all the while staring into her huge brown eyes. He reached gently for her hand and just ever so lightly squeezed it. Her cheeks turned red at his touch.

She whispered to him very quickly, "I live at *Corso Magenta 24*, and I would love to see you. *Buona notte, Giovanni.*"

His heart jumped at once. As she left, Giovanni heard her father say, "Why were you talking with that café singer?"

After she had left the restaurant, Giovanni realized that he had not asked for her phone number, only her address. At least he was lucky enough to get that, considering he was so nervous. All of his thoughts were about Isabella. So much so, he didn't notice that the piano and violin music had stopped and that Jacopo was making an announcement. Suddenly, the entire restaurant was singing happy birthday to Giovanni, all except Angelo. He was too busy cursing the management of

La Scala for performing Gluck's *Orfeo* with a no-name singer on a Saturday, normally his busiest night.

Giovanni realized what was going on and thanked everyone for their kindness. He ended the evening by singing more selections of Puccini arias. Angelo asked him to wrap it up since the restaurant was half-full and he was losing money.

Giovanni ended the evening as he always did, with the aria "Nessun Dorma" from Puccini's last opera, *Turandot*. He sang the aria with great passion and hit the last *"vinceró"* perfectly. After the cheers from the crowd had died away, he prepared to go home with an *addio* to his accompanists, Mario and Jacopo.

Mario, as usual, was busy telling a patron about his late father, Constantino Maenza, who for many years was an oboist in the orchestra of the La Scala Opera House, and who performed at the premiere of Verdi's final opera, *Falstaff*, in 1893. Throughout the night, the Maenza boys told customers all about their father and that historic night at La Scala so long ago.

Giovanni said to him, *"Perdona l'interruzione.* Do you know the girl Isabella I was speaking to tonight? I've never seen her here before."

Mario excused himself from his conversation and told Giovanni, "Sure, that is the daughter of Pietro Monterone, the Judge. I hope you're not thinking you have a chance with her. Her family is one of the wealthiest in all of Milan, and her father is a real bastard."

*"No. Giammai,"* was Giovanni's response. "I was just wondering if you knew her."

As he left the old restaurant, his thoughts were only on

Isabella. He longed to see her, to talk with her, get to know her. The short walk to his home made him pass the front of La Scala for the second time that night. As he did so, he put his hands in the pockets of his jacket, due to the cool March air of Milan. He felt a paper rustle in his pocket. He pulled it out and read what he had written on the paper:

*Isabella Monterone Corso Magenta* 24

It was only 12:30 a.m., an early night for Giovanni when he was working at Angelo's. Thank God it was Gluck, he thought to himself. He very much wanted to see her. Why not tonight? He didn't have her phone number, so he would pay her a personal visit.

Since Giovanni lived fairly close to where he worked, he didn't own a car, only an old, used motor scooter. But tonight, like most nights, he had walked to Angelo's. He quickly started the long walk to *Corso Magenta 24.*

# 3

## JUST LIKE ROMÉO

The *Corso Magenta* was located to the west of the historic downtown area of Milan where Giovanni lived. The Magenta District was one of the wealthy sections of Milan. The most powerful and influential Milanese families resided there.

As Giovanni entered the Magenta District, he noticed that on either side of the street were many huge, gorgeous palazzi, each with an exquisite garden. He finally approached the home numbered 24.

He gulped hard when he saw it. It was a huge, two-story structure with windows across the front. An iron fence surrounded the home. On one side of the front door hung the flag of Lombardy, the province of Milan, and on the other side flew the Italian flag. Giovanni looked with awe at the size of the home and wondered how he would ever find Isabella.

He tried the front gate, but it was locked. So he did what

any young man would do when trying to see the most captivating girl in the world; he climbed the fence.

Once over the fence, Giovanni looked all around. The grounds of the home were meticulous. Every hedge was cut to perfection, and the garden had flowers of every color and style. Huge elm trees were scattered on the grounds. A crushed stone path led around the left side of the home.

Giovanni followed the path, which led to the back of the house. Little lights were arranged along the path, intermingled with flowers and plants. As he walked the path, he thought how stupid it was to walk all this way in the middle of the night and have no idea how he would find her. He called himself an idiot under his breath, *"Cretino. Cretino."*

He also questioned why this girl had so captivated him. The restaurant always had pretty girls in it at night, but he never before had felt compelled to approach any of them until tonight. He thought it was perhaps due to his melancholy mood, or was it something more?

As he rounded the corner of the back of the house, he stopped dead in his tracks. At the far corner, on the second floor, overlooking a swimming pool and statues in the backyard was a balcony. Standing on the balcony, in a flowing nightgown, was his beloved. The moonlight was beating down on her from above. She was leaning on the railing, looking out into the vast sky overlooking Milan.

Giovanni stood there in complete silence for a few seconds, mesmerized by her. He then left the path, moved closer and hid behind a hedge, all the while watching her.

Her long black hair moved ever so slightly with the gentle breeze. Her olive skin shone in the moonlight. Her breasts were silhouetted against her sheer nightgown. He couldn't believe that he had found her and that he was here now.

Through his mind ran one huge question: Now that he was here, what to do?

While he struggled to answer his own question, he continued looking at her on the balcony with the moon above. Doing so, for the second time that night, made Giovanni think of a moment from an opera. The moonlight beaming down on Isabella conjured up images of Puccini's *La Bohème*, and the awakening of love between Rodolfo and Mimi. Giovanni's question had been answered. Quietly he stepped from behind the hedge and in *mezza voce* started to sing 'O soave fanciulla' from *La Bohème*.

*O soave fanciulla!*
*Oh, lovely girl!*

*O dolce viso*
*Oh, sweet face*

*di mite circonfuso albar lunar.*
*surrounded by the light of the rising moon.*

*In te ravviso*
*In you I see the dream*

*il sogno ch'io vorrei sempre sognar!*
*I have always dreamed!*

Isabella jumped back upon hearing the song. She looked down but couldn't see in the darkness. What lovely words, she thought. She peered deeper into the darkness. Finally, as Giovanni stepped from the darkness and into the moonlight, Isabella quietly said, "Giovanni. *Zitto, zitto,* before my father hears you."

Giovanni was now directly below the balcony. He asked, "Can I come up?"

"*Si. Un momento.* My father would kill you and me."

Swiftly he scaled the latticework that led to her balcony. Once at the top, he swung his legs over the railing and came face to face with her and those wondrous brown eyes.

"I can't believe you came to see me," she said.

"I had to see you. I want to get to know all about you. I have never seen anyone like you before."

She smiled. He was so cute, especially those piercing blue eyes. Even his speaking voice sounded like he was singing. "You sing beautifully," she stated.

"You are beautiful," was his quick reply.

She smiled even brighter. Gently, Giovanni took her hand in his and kissed it. She had never been treated like this by anyone. He was a throwback to a lady's old romantic notion of how a man should act. With a touch of sarcasm, she asked, "Do you normally pick someone out of the crowd at Angelo's and come to sing to them later that night?"

Giovanni, without missing a beat, asked, "Do you normally allow on your balcony late at night men who serenade you?"

They both laughed heartily. Giovanni grew serious and said, "After I saw you and spoke to you tonight, all I wanted was to get to know you."

"I'm glad you came."

"I am too. Tell me about yourself," he said.

After they both sat down on the floor of the balcony, Isabella said, "Well, there's not much to tell. I just turned 18 and am a student in high school. I go to *Figlie di Christi*. I'm an only child, and I live with my father and stepmother. My father is very protective of me. My dream is to teach children one day. As I said, there is not much to tell. I live a fairly sheltered life. What about you, do you have any dreams?"

"I want to be an opera singer."

"Have you always wished to be one?" she asked.

"*Si*. My father loved opera, and I grew up with the voice of the great operatic tenor, Enrico Caruso, always being played around the house."

Giovanni, while mimicking his father's deep voice and mannerisms, quoted his father saying, "On the Victrola, that is the only way to listen to Caruso." Isabella laughed at how Giovanni had acted while imitating his father. Giovanni smiled and said to her, "God, I can still hear him say that. Whenever he played those Caruso records, he would always tell me that, while the extraordinary tenor voice of Caruso exploded out of the long, black horn, filling the room and my young ears with that wonderful sound."

She asked, "How did you learn to sing so beautifully?"

Giovanni went on to tell her how music played such an important part of his childhood and how his exposure to music, and opera in particular, began at a very early age, thanks in particular to his father.

Isabella, captivated by the story, said, "Your relationship with your father seems wonderful."

"It was. Those are all memories now. My father died in a car accident right before I was to graduate from high school."

Isabella reached out and grabbed his hand, and said, "That's awful."

"There's not a day that goes by that I do not think of him. I miss him so much. He wanted me to be an opera singer. There is nothing I would rather do with my life than to fulfill that dream of his and mine, but it is nothing more than a dream. After he died, I quickly realized that attending a university or music school was far too expensive, and I knew that I had to find a job to help my mother with the expenses of raising my younger sister, Gabriella.

"So, I took a job at a local pharmacy as a clerk. But, having a voice did allow me the opportunity to get a second job singing at Angelo's. Which I am glad that I did, as it allowed me to meet you."

She smiled and replied, "And I am glad you did. You really do have a beautiful voice. I am sure you will be a singer one day."

Giovanni shook his head negatively and said, "I have no prospects. I have been rejected by singing teachers all across Milan."

Isabella reassuringly replied, "Perhaps my father could help you. He has connections with musical people all over Italy."

Perking up, Giovanni asked excitedly, "Do you think he would help me?"

"If I ask him, I think he would," she told him.

Suddenly they heard a noise from inside. "It's my father. You must go," she said as they both stood up.

"Can I come by and see you tomorrow?"

"I would love that but come during the day, not in the

middle of the night," she said, holding his hand. "Perhaps then, I can talk to my father about helping you."

This was love! *Amore.* He couldn't take his eyes off of hers. She couldn't take her eyes off of his. Giovanni slowly leaned forward and was about to kiss her when her father burst onto the balcony.

"You, the waiter from Angelo's. Damn you! What gall to come here and seduce my young daughter," Judge Monterone bellowed.

Isabella yelled to her father that it was nothing, but her father only screamed louder at her to go inside. She refused.

"Judge Monterone," Giovanni stammered. "I mean no disrespect to you or your family. I just wanted to get to know your daughter. We were just talking."

"Get the hell off of my property. You scum! If you ever come near her again, I will have you thrown in prison. *Va! Va!*" he yelled.

Giovanni turned and started to climb down from the balcony. He heard the Judge tell Isabella, "You will never see him again, *capito.* He is a nobody, a nothing. I did not raise you and give you the best education so that you could marry some café singer."

"But father, you could help him start his singing career."

The Judge yelled back, "I wouldn't ask the local choir to give him an audition." Then the Judge, while leaning over the balcony to make sure Giovanni could hear, said very forcefully, "Take my word for it. He will never sing in Italy. He will never be a singer. He is nothing but poor trash. Trash!"

As Giovanni reached the bottom, he yelled back to the

Judge, "You will see, I will be a great singer, then you will take back your cruel words."

The Judge hurled down more insults at Giovanni and told him to leave or the police would be called. He then grabbed Isabella by the arm and harshly removed her from the balcony into her bedroom.

Giovanni was hurt by the remarks the Judge had made to him. He wasn't a nobody. He just needed a break in life, just one break. He walked by the pool and climbed the back fence of the property. Once on the other side, he looked back toward Isabella's balcony. Through the still-open balcony doors, he could see her sitting on the end of her bed crying. Giovanni would do anything to dry those tears.

On the other side of the fence, looking at the balcony from which he had just climbed down, Giovanni chuckled and thought to himself, "Just like Roméo." He quietly sang the balcony scene finale from Gounod's *Roméo and Juliette*, all the time watching Isabella.

*Va! Repose en paix! Sommeille!*
*Go! Rest peacefully! Sleep!*

*Qu'un sourire d'enfant*
*May a child's smile*

*ta bouche vermeille*
*come gently to rest*

*doucement vienne se poser!*
*on your rosy lips!*

*Et murmurant encor:*
*And still murmuring:*

*Je t'aime! à ton oreille,*
*"I love you" into your ear,*

*que la brise des nuits*
*may the night breeze*

*te porte ce baiser!*
*carry to you this kiss!*

As Giovanni sang the last word, he placed his hand to his mouth and blew her a kiss. He turned and started the long walk home, determined now more than ever to become a singer, no longer just for himself and his father, but now for her.

# 4

## ANNA TEMPESTA

*G*iovanni, with the bright March moon overhead, walked home down the winding streets of Milan that night. He heard the bells of the Duomo of Milan toll the three o'clock hour. He lived close to the Duomo and La Scala, which are both located within the *Cerchia dei Navigli,* which forms a ring around the historic downtown area of Milan and follows the outline of the former medieval walls that once protected the city. This area of Milan is the heart of the city.

As Giovanni made his way home down the *Via Manzoni,* he could see La Scala ahead. The opera house is situated on a splendid piazza. In the middle of the piazza stands a statue of Leonardo da Vinci, which faces the opera house. Across the piazza from La Scala is the *Galleria Vittorio Emanuele II,* a glass-enclosed gallery of upscale shops and restaurants. It was the first shopping mall ever created. Since its inception, the Milanese come daily to the *Galleria* to socialize, read their *Corriere della Sera*, and drink espresso.

A short walk through the Galleria leads to the spectacular *Piazza del Duomo,* and the famous Cathedral of Milan with its 135 pointed and chiseled spires. The piazza is always filled with pigeons, normally seated on the huge equestrian statue of *Vittorio Emanuele,* the first king of Italy. The Duomo dominates the entire area.

Occasionally, Giovanni would ascend to the roof of the cathedral, where he would be rewarded with a panoramic view of the snow-capped Swiss Alps, far off in the distance.

La Scala is the artistic center of Milan, while the Duomo is the religious center, with the *Galleria* separating the two. Giovanni grew up his entire life right in this vicinity, only a short walk away from the Duomo and La Scala.

The Tempesta home was a two-story structure on a crowded street called the *Via Umiltá*, very near the Duomo. The Tempesta home was not big, but it did have a nice-sized living room, a small kitchen, and three small bedrooms; one for Giovanni's mother, one for Gabriella, his much younger sister, and one for him. This was the house where he had been born and raised.

When he turned down his street, he realized the difference from the neighborhood where Isabella lived. The homes on his street were all run down, two-story homes. Clothes hung out the windows on clotheslines. The street itself was smaller. Yet, the neighborhood did have a peaceful tranquility about it, probably because the neighbors loved one another and looked out for each other and were happy with the little things in life.

The neighborhood did not have many young people

living in it. So the older couples looked at the Tempesta family as their own, especially since the death of Franco. Many times when Anna, Giovanni's mother, had to work late, they would watch Gabriella.

The old neighbors loved Giovanni and were well aware of the quality of his voice. They heard it almost daily as he was growing up, singing along with his old recordings. They were so well aware of it that on anniversaries, the husbands in the neighborhood were known to hire Giovanni to hide below the windows of their houses so that he could sing love songs to their wives while the husbands, standing in the street, mouthed the words, pretending to sing. Of course, the wives all knew who was doing the singing but always played along. When the time came for payment, Giovanni would always refuse to accept money from the husbands since they were all poor, but would finally consent to dinner one night at their home.

Without fail, he would go to dinner, the husband telling his wife that he invited Giovanni over because he helped the old man move something or fix something, keeping the real reason a supposed secret. Then when Giovanni was about to leave, the wife would always come over, kiss him on the cheek, and whisper into his ear, "Giovanni, *grazie*. You made my anniversary very special. You sing beautifully." He would smile, wish her many more happy anniversaries and take his extra food back to his family. Thus was life in the neighborhood.

Giovanni finally reached his house at *Via Umiltá 9*. He knew his mother would be sleeping lightly since he wasn't home yet. She often did this until his return from a long night at Angelo's.

His mother, Anna Tempesta, was a pretty, middle-aged lady who was a devout Catholic. She looked very Sicilian, with her dark hair, with streaks of gray, pulled back in a tightly wound bun. Her most prized possessions were her two children.

Anna was born in Cefalù, Sicily in 1930. At the age of 10, her parents, Vincenzo and Maria Tumminello, and her brother, Piero, moved to Milan, the business center of Italy, to find wealth and prosperity. Anna was still waiting.

At 23, she got a job as a seamstress at Babeto's, a ritzy clothing store located on the *Via Montenapoleone*, in the heart of the famous fashion district in Milan. Babeto's was a large store unique in that it offered an array of clothing by the great designers as well as signature collections by its young owner, Giorgio Babeto.

Giorgio Babeto expected his workers to work hard. Anna was a very good seamstress whom Giorgio trusted with the sewing of all of the outfits for his fashion shows, which he held twice a year. Although Giorgio was very difficult to work for, he paid his seamstresses well compared to the other stores in Milan. Giorgio was always impeccably dressed in suits of his own design and looked like a male model with his slicked back, wavy black hair.

It was at Babeto's that Anna met Franco Tempesta, nine years her senior. Franco, who was born in 1921 in Naples, moved with his family to Milan while in his teens, and later worked at Babeto's as a salesman. Franco and Anna fell madly in love with each other. Franco would always sing Neapolitan love songs to her, often hitting a sour note. But she loved it just the same. His nickname for her was Mimi, after the character in Puccini's *La Bohème*.

They married and settled into *"la bella vita"* (a beautiful life), but one without riches. Soon, they were blessed with Giovanni. "Your parents were right in moving from Cefalù. Giovanni is your prosperity," Franco would always tell Anna. Later, Gabriella followed. They were a poor but very happy family. Giovanni always was aware of how much love there was in his parents' relationship. Franco was a very romantic man who loved listening to operas and watching old Errol Flynn movies, dubbed in Italian, more so for the music of Korngold and Steiner than for the acting.

The family really never recovered from the loss of Franco many years before. Giovanni would never forget that night. His much younger sister, Gabriella, couldn't sleep at all. So Franco, as he sometimes did, put her in the car and took her for a drive at 2:00 a.m. around the neighborhood to put her to sleep. Giovanni was awakened when two Carabiniere officers showed up at the house and informed Anna that Franco had been broadsided by a drunk driver and had been killed instantly. Little Gabriella had been taken to the hospital for precautions. The loss of Franco was a devastating blow to both Giovanni and Anna. At the funeral, Giovanni played Caruso's recording of Handel's 'Ombra mai fu', one of his dad's favorite arias.

Anna would never remarry after the death of Franco since she still was in love with him and felt that he was the most wonderful, romantic man in the world. She devoted herself to her children and to her work at Babeto's.

Anna always supported Giovanni's dream to sing since she knew that was what he loved and what her husband would have wanted. However, since all she made was enough money to raise her family, all she could do was offer her prayers and encouragement to Giovanni. She had made the rounds to people of wealth that she knew, asking them to please hear her son and sponsor his training, but they would politely say no. Anna never really expected them to help anyway. Southern Italians, particularly the Sicilians, were despised by the Milanese. The locals referred to them as "*terroni*", a derogatory word meaning "people of the earth".

When Giovanni finally reached his house, he quietly went into the house, only to be met by the faint sound of his mother calling him, "*Giovanni, sei tu*? I'm glad you are home. You're late tonight. Must have been a busy night at Angelo's?" He nodded in the affirmative as he entered her small bedroom, keeping the real reason why he was late to himself. Anna asked, "Did you make papa proud?" This was her standard question whenever he came home from singing at Angelo's.

"*Si, Mamma.* I only sang Puccini. Papa would have loved it."

She hugged him, saying, "*Buon Compleanno, Giovanni.* I wanted to tell you that this morning, but you were sleeping when I left for work. Gabriella had to have a piece of your cake." Anna removed a small cake from her nightstand. A slice had been cut out of the cake. She sang happy birthday to Giovanni and cut him a small piece. "I got you a little something. I wish it could have been more."

Anna put her hand under her bed and fished out a bag. Giovanni recognized the red lettering on the bag immediately. It was the seal of La Scala. He quickly reached in the bag and pulled out his present. It was a pirated live recording of Puccini's *Manon Lescaut* with Clara Petrella and Giuseppe di Stefano, recorded in 1957 from Naples.

Anna said, "The lady at the La Scala gift store told me it was just released. Do you like it?"

"Mamma, I love it. I've been waiting for them to finally release this. It's supposed to be a great performance."

"Go get some rest, young man. Tomorrow is Sunday, and we will all go to church together." She kissed him goodnight, and Giovanni went to his room located on the second floor.

His room, of course, was littered with opera recordings. On the walls were posters of operas, especially the ones that he loved, which meant mostly Puccini operas. On his nightstand was a picture of his father, sitting in a chair next to the phonograph in the living room, a pipe dangling from his mouth, listening to an opera recording with a libretto in his hand. Giovanni loved that picture and looked at it often.

Before he got undressed, he took his new recording out and put it on the phonograph in his room. He just had to hear his favorite part, when Manon and Des Greiux meet for the first time. As he was getting into bed, the opera reached the part where Des Greiux sings about meeting Manon and the effect it had upon him; 'Donna non vidi mai'. Giovanni's thoughts immediately turned to Isabella as he sang the aria in his head along with Giuseppe di Stefano.

He again questioned why seeing her tonight at Angelo's had had such an effect on him. All he wanted was to be with her. But he knew that was impossible now because of her father. I must find a teacher, he thought. I am running out of time. This is my last chance. It is my only chance if I am to win her from her father. But how can I find one? Then he remembered.

He jumped from his bed and ran over to his desk. Buried under some papers was a box. He rummaged through it and pulled out three business cards. On the back of each one was the name of a different singing teacher.

A few times, when Giovanni finished singing at Angelo's, customers would come and tell him how great he was, and give him the name of a singing teacher who could help him. Giovanni had called the teachers to set up an audition with them but was rejected, usually without them even hearing a note.

However, since making those phone calls, Giovanni had gotten three new names from some patrons at Angelo's. Giovanni hadn't even looked at the names on the back of the cards before he threw them in the box in his desk. He feared being rejected by a teacher again. It had happened too many times in the past. But now he was willing to try anything, willing to risk the rejection. After Mass tomorrow, he would go see the teachers, sing for them, and get one of them to help him. For some strange reason, Giovanni felt as though it would be different this time. Perhaps one of those teachers would be willing to give him a chance.

Tomorrow he would find a teacher and start seriously training to become an opera tenor. And in so doing, he would get Judge Monterone's blessing to see Isabella. Slowly he drifted off to sleep.

# 5

# SIGNOR TOSCANO

he next morning, Sunday, Giovanni was awakened at 9:30 a.m. by his little sister, Gabriella. She was nine years old and looked very much like her mother. Giovanni was very close to his sister.

Gabriella, who had climbed into bed and on top of Giovanni's chest, said, "Mamma said to get up. We are all going to Mass."

After wrestling with her in bed, Giovanni arose and took his shower. He got dressed, making sure to put the three business cards into his pocket. Then he went to the kitchen to get a bite to eat where his mother met him. She said, "After Mass, we have been invited to dinner over at the Amatos' house."

Giovanni asked, "Would it be alright if I skipped? I have something very important to do today." His mother told him that would be fine and quickly got Giovanni and Gabriella out of the house on the way to the Duomo for Mass. Giovanni drove his motor scooter over to the cathedral and met his family there.

Ever since he was born, his family had always attended Sunday Mass at the Duomo. It was from this church that his father had been buried. But, as he walked into the piazza on this March day, Giovanni thought of Isabella.

While he was in Mass, Giovanni said the 'Our Father' over and over again. "Please let me find a teacher. Please help me." He called upon God and his father to help him. He was sure his prayers were about to be answered.

After Mass, he kissed his family goodbye and told them to have fun at the Amatos. As he walked away from the cathedral, he pulled out the three business cards. He had looked at the addresses before he left home, mapped out the locations, and had planned where to go first. He was hoping the music teachers would all be home on this Sunday morning. The weather was gloomy, yet Giovanni was upbeat. All of the teachers lived in the same general vicinity in the Northwest section of Milan. He got on his motor scooter and made his way out to that part of town.

Signor Federico Toscano was his first stop. Giovanni had heard of the great Maestro. Signor Toscano had conducted all over the world and at La Scala. He had even been a student of the greatest Maestro, Arturo Toscanini. But Signor Toscano had retired early in his career to make a fortune teaching young aspiring singers.

Signor Toscano lived in an upper apartment in a four-story building, which overlooked Piazza Buonarroti. Giovanni found a parking spot for his motor scooter across the piazza from Signor Toscano's apartment building.

Giovanni had never been to this part of Milan, at least on

foot. As Giovanni walked through the piazza, he looked at the business card one last time and got the name of the person who had recommended Signor Toscano to Giovanni.

Giovanni approached the front door to the building, and nervously rang the doorbell. A commanding voice came over the loudspeaker and said, "Toscano."

"Signor Toscano, my name is Giovanni Tempesta. I am a singer in need of a teacher. Your friend, Signor Preziosa, gave me your name. *Posso parlare con voi*?" (May I speak to you?)

Signor Toscano asked quizzically, "A singer, huh? I will buzz you in. I'm located in the upper apartment."

Giovanni was buzzed in and took the elevator to the top floor. The door to the apartment was open, so Giovanni walked in and looked around the apartment.

Signor Toscano was nowhere to be seen. The room Giovanni was standing in was huge. To his left was a giant window that overlooked the piazza down below. An old three-story building faced Signor Toscano's apartment from across the piazza, very near to where Giovanni had parked.

A grand piano was located next to the window. Giovanni tried to imagine himself coming here every day, vocalizing, as Signor Toscano sat at the piano, training Giovanni to become a world-class tenor. Pictures of Signor Toscano's students, as well as singers whom he had conducted in operas over the years littered the wall by the piano. Perhaps Giovanni's picture would be up on the wall one day.

"I am a busy man," Signor Toscano said as he walked out of the kitchen. "I do not have time to hear every bird that thinks he can chirp."

The presence of Signor Toscano startled Giovanni. Signor Toscano was a gentleman not yet 70 years old, with long white hair that stood straight up on his head, which must have made quite a sight when he conducted.

Giovanni looked directly at Signor Toscano and responded, "God gave me a gift, my father gave me the passion, and my love gives me the desire. I need to sing. *Credo al destino.*"

Signor Toscano laughed and said, "*Destino?* No. The cemetery is filled with people who chased a dream, a destiny, which they never could achieve. Don't do the same. You will only waste your life away. How old are you?"

"*Ho venti cinque anni,*" Giovanni responded.

"You are 25. Yet, you have no teacher? Are you studying music in school?"

Giovanni shook his head no and said, "I am poor. I have no teacher and am not in school. I sing at Angelo's at night, the restaurant close to La Scala. I am very good. I am self-taught, but I know to start my career, I need a teacher, both for the development of the technique and for the connections a teacher can provide. I know it will take hard work, but I'm willing and able."

"You are very wise, Signor Tempesta. You understand what it takes to become an opera singer. But being wise, you know a person with my credentials cannot take a singer from a café as a student. I would be the laughing stock of Milan."

Giovanni spoke louder, "What does it matter where I come from? It is the voice that counts."

Signor Toscano said, "If you were younger, perhaps you would be correct. But you are old, as students go, and you have no training. Even if I took you in, you would never be able to have a career. Who in Milan or all of Italy would pay to see a boy who started singing at Angelo's? They would think I was a crackpot. They would say Toscano is ready for Verdi's *Casa di Riposo*," as Signor Toscano gestured his finger to the old three-story building across the piazza.

Giovanni felt his chest muscles tightening. Signor Toscano's words were like an arrow piercing through his heart. His mind was awash. He wanted to leave. His dream was being torn to shreds. Signor Toscano continued, "Go get a real job, find a wife, and make your mark on life that way. Give up trying to become a singer."

Giovanni said emphatically, "But I want to sing. If you won't, do you know of anyone who would help me?"

"Not at your age and with no training. In addition, you said you are poor. Teachers are expensive. There is not one single voice teacher worth anything in all of Milan or Italy for that matter who would support you. Heed my words. Move on. Give up your dream."

Giovanni, completely dejected, tried to hold back his tears. He asked Signor Toscano if he would at least hear him sing to see if he believed Giovanni had any talent.

Signor Toscano shook his head no and said, "I can tell just by looking at you, you have no chance of becoming a singer. You are not built like one. Don't chase a fantasy. You will end up unhappy." As Giovanni turned to leave, Signor Toscano spoke out, "Oh, but if only my students had half your drive and passion."

Giovanni received no satisfaction from that. He left Signor Toscano's apartment, took the elevator down to the bottom, and left the apartment complex.

Once outside, he reached into his pocket and pulled out the two remaining business cards. With all the rage he could muster, he tore them to shreds.

In a daze, he walked across the piazza toward his motor scooter. He was devastated. His dream was finished. God had not helped; no one cared. Even his father had let him down. He would no longer subject himself to this rejection anymore.

A brisk wind began to blow. The sky turned dark, and the clouds were laden with rain. The piazza was empty as people went scurrying inside to avoid the gathering rainstorm. The weather matched Giovanni's feelings at that moment.

As Giovanni reached the opposite side of the piazza, he heard the faint sound of a piano and a singing voice coming from the old, Venetian-style, three-story palazzo that faced Signor Toscano's apartment complex. Someone was singing 'De' miei bollenti spiriti' from Giuseppe Verdi's *La Traviata*, in a beautiful, yet old tenor voice.

For a moment, Giovanni forgot about Signor Toscano, and he just listened. The voice was extraordinary. Giovanni thought that the voice had to have been professionally trained.

As Giovanni stood and listened, he noticed, high above the door, at the very peak of the top of the building, the name of the place written in marble. It read:

*Casa di Riposo per Musicisti,*
*1902 fondata dal Maestro Giuseppe Verdi*

This was the building that Signor Toscano had mentioned. Giovanni knew of the *Casa di Riposo*, but he had never visited it. He walked up the stairs and entered the old building.

# 6

# CASA VERDI

*U*pon entering the building, Giovanni walked into an attractive foyer. A huge grand staircase was at the far end of the foyer, which led to the grand music salon located on the second floor. The sound of the piano and the tenor voice, coming from the salon, wafted throughout the building. The foyer had a few chairs in the waiting area and a counter located against a far wall. Potted plants were arranged neatly amongst the chairs. But what caught Giovanni's attention immediately were pictures located on the wall to the right of the entrance door. They were of different people, all on the stage of the La Scala Opera House, in costumes from operas. Above the photos was a sign that read, "Our residents in the glory of their careers." Giovanni recognized the names of a few of the singers.

A middle-aged lady was hard at work behind the counter. She picked her head up slightly from her desk and shot a glance at Giovanni as he was peering at the pictures on the wall. She asked Giovanni, "Signor, are you family to a resident here?"

"No, I was just looking around."

She stood up from the desk and said, "Well, there are no tours given on Sundays. We are open for tours only Tuesday through Friday between 10:00 a.m. and 4:00 p.m."

Giovanni asked, "Tours? You give tours here?"

"*Si*. This is the *Casa di Riposo*, the rest home that was established by that great opera composer, Giuseppe Verdi, for retired musicians."

Giovanni asked, "These pictures of people on the wall, they are residents here?"

"That is our wall of glory. Those are pictures of our residents, both those who have left us for their eternal reward and those with us presently when they made their La Scala debut. You know, the opera house here in Milan."

"Oh, I know," he replied, looking at the pictures even more intently. "Does every resident have a picture up here?"

"No. Some of our residents are instrumentalists, not singers. Others are chorus members while some of our residents are family members of musicians and, of course, never sang. And some of our residents did sing and had an operatic career, but never sang at La Scala."

Giovanni asked her, "Do you think I could look around this place?"

"Well, the administrator is very emphatic that no one tours the facility except during visiting hours." While she was speaking to Giovanni, she looked harder and harder at him. She finally asked, "Do I know you? You look very familiar. Where do you work?"

"I work at Roberto's pharmacy, and I sing at Angelo's Restaurant."

"*La conosco.* That's it, the 'Caruso of Angelo's'. My husband and I eat there on occasions, and we love to hear you sing. My name is Lydia Trepidoro. Look, since you have given us such joy at dinner, I will do you this favor; have a look around. If anyone asks why you are here, tell them you are a relative of Alfredo del Monte. He's the nicest resident here, and he always plays along whenever I send someone to him. He is the gentleman playing the piano and singing in the salon on the second floor. Tell Alfredo that Lydia sent you, and then proceed to wander around."

Giovanni listened and heard Signor del Monte now singing 'Ah sì ben mio' from Verdi's *Il Trovatore.* He had a captivating voice. Giovanni asked Lydia, "So, I just go up these stairs to see Signor del Monte?"

"*Sì,*" was her reply. Before he left, he asked Lydia if she could point out Signor del Monte's picture of his debut at La Scala.

A sad look came across her face. "He is one of the residents who never sang at La Scala."

Giovanni thanked Lydia for her kindness and then turned toward the staircase to make his way to the salon and Signor Alfredo del Monte.

---

THE STAIRCASE LED to the enticing grand music salon on the second floor. The room had numerous sofas and seats, with potted green ferns throughout the room. It had a very open and airy feel to it with a lot of windows. The room reminded Giovanni of the second act set of Verdi's *La Traviata*. Along the walls were bookcases filled with books. On the walls were posters of many Verdi operas. Throughout the room were cabinets, which held medals and papers. In one corner was an old piano, roped off from the rest of the room, with a picture of Verdi on the top of the piano. On the opposite side of the room, Giovanni saw another, newer piano, with an elderly gentleman sitting at it. No one else was in the salon.

The old man was nearing the end of the aria from *Il Trovatore*. His back was to Giovanni. When he completed the aria, Giovanni cleared his throat. The old man turned slowly from the piano. Giovanni addressed him, "Signor Alfredo del Monte? Lydia said to tell you that she sent me."

As Alfredo turned completely around, he said with a laugh, "Oh, she did. She often sends to me my long lost relatives. What would you like to be, a cousin or a nephew?"

Giovanni didn't know how to respond. "Nephew," he said pensively. He guessed Alfredo had to be from Sicily since his accent sounded very much like his mother's.

"*Bene*. It's nice of you to come see your *zio*," Alfredo said with a laugh.

For the first time, Giovanni noticed that Signor Alfredo was totally blind. His eyes were open, but it was obvious that he could not see out of them. Giovanni couldn't tell how old Alfredo was; he guessed he had to be over 70. His face was worn; his eyes were dead, yet his face had a look of compassion touched with sadness. But when Alfredo smiled, his whole face lit up, making him look much younger and happier.

Giovanni told Alfredo, "I've never been here before. I

happened to be in the neighborhood, and I heard you singing from outside."

"This is a retirement home for old coots like me. You may go wander all around this place. Just tell anyone who asks if you belong that your *zio* is in the salon. I will cover for you. Go, have a nice look around."

"You have a beautiful voice, Signor Alfredo. Did you ever sing in the opera?"

Alfredo sat quietly for a moment, thinking, then said, "Oh yes, a long, long time ago. Those are just faded memories. Now I am a resident here. I just come in the salon and reminisce. May I ask who I am talking to?"

"My name is Giovanni Tempesta. I am a singer."

"Oh, and what do you sing, Signor Tempesta?"

"I am an opera tenor or at least trying to become one," Giovanni responded.

"So, you like opera? Who is the greatest composer of all time?"

"Puccini," shot back Giovanni.

"*Io sono con un pagano,*" (I am with a heathen) Alfredo yelled. "Giuseppe Verdi is the Maestro. He is the greatest. He changed all of opera and music in general, and everyone that followed him was merely carrying his torch. His name still is revered. He even provided care for us old singers, like me. Do you know about this place?"

"I know it's an old folks home that Verdi established for musicians."

Alfredo laughed and said, "That my young friend is only half the story. It's like saying St. Peter's is just another church in Rome." Giovanni sat down on one of the sofas as Alfredo continued and said, "When Giuseppe Verdi was nearing the end of his career, he became concerned that there were numerous musicians who faced old age with nothing more than memories. Therefore, he wanted to provide for their care when they grew old. The memory of Mozart being buried in a pauper's grave was a driving force behind his idea.

"In 1889, he secretly bought this plot of land where we are today. The only people who knew about his idea at the time were his wife, Strepponi, who was a retired singer, Ricordi, his publisher, Arrigo Boito, his librettist for *Otello* and *Falstaff*, his final operas, and Camillo Boito, the brother of Arrigo and an architect. Verdi commissioned Camillo Boito to draw up the plans. Verdi took an active role in the plans. For example, the first set of plans put the sleeping quarters in dormitories, but this struck Verdi as too institutional. Verdi wanted only two residents per room and thought that by doing so, the residents could help each other at night, yet still have privacy. Boito's plans called the facility an asylum. But Verdi thought that too harsh. So he came up with the name, The House of Rest for Musicians.

"Verdi wanted the home to be large enough to hold 100 musicians with the stipulation that the ratio be sixty men to forty women and that the residents all had to be Italian citizens who had reached the age of 65 and had practiced the art of music professionally. Verdi also set up a priority for admission, with, of course, composers being first."

Giovanni chuckled out loud at that comment.

Alfredo continued, "He continually watched the construction of his beloved *Casa di Riposo*. He said that even taking into consideration all of his operas that he wrote over the course of his long career, the *Casa di Riposo* was his greatest life's work.

"Verdi's wife died in 1897 and he turned his attention completely to his project. In January 1901, Verdi lay dying at the Grand Hotel of Milan. He had achieved so much respect that the citizens of Milan put hay on the street outside of the hotel to lessen the sound of the carriages passing by his window.

"Verdi died on January 27, 1901 at the age of 87. He was buried next to his wife at a cemetery on the outskirts of Milan, the *Cimitero Monumentale*. In his will, he directed that his property go to different people and institutions. To the Casa Verdi, as it is regarded today by the Milanese, he left all of his royalties from his operas. Verdi also left to the *Casa* his very first piano, a spinet, that his father had given him in 1831." Alfredo pointed to the old piano in the corner. "That's it in the corner over there, with the picture of Verdi on it."

Giovanni looked at the old piano in awe.

Alfredo continued, "He also left all of his decorations and memorabilia, which are also found throughout the room."

Giovanni was like a child in a toy store.

"When Verdi died in January, he had requested a small ceremony, which was followed. However, in February, under the terms of the will, his body and Strepponi's were removed and brought here to be buried in the chapel at the *Casa Verdi*. All of Milan turned out for the spectacle. Toscanini conducted the La Scala Orchestra on the steps of the cemetery chapel in the chorus of the Hebrew slaves, 'Va, pensiero' from Verdi's *Nabucco*, as the carriage led by black horses made its way down the streets of Milan. Huge black banners hung off of every balcony. Two hundred thousand people lined the streets. A huge throng walked with the bodies to the *Casa Verdi* to lay them to rest. All the great composers, Puccini,

Mascagni, Giordano, Leoncavallo, walked behind the casket as well as heads of state from all over the world. And it is here that he now sleeps, with us, the people he cared about."

Giovanni was fascinated by the story and the knowledge of Signor Alfredo del Monte. Giovanni loved how Alfredo seemed to have a natural talent for telling stories. Giovanni asked excitedly, "Can you take me to see where they are buried?"

Alfredo rose from his piano. "As you can surely see, I am blind. Grab my hand and lead me back to the first floor from where you came in, and I will show you."

Giovanni slipped his hand into the elderly hand of Alfredo, who said, "*Andiamo,* Giovanni Tempesta. The Maestro awaits." They both left the salon down the stairs to the first floor.

# 7

## ALFREDO DEL MONTE

*G*iovanni held Alfredo's hand all the way down the stairs. On the stairs, they passed another resident who was making his way to the music salon. Giovanni thought it strange that the resident brushed pass Alfredo without even acknowledging his presence.

At the base of the stairs, Giovanni noticed Lydia again. "Signora Lydia, thank you for showing me where my *'zio'* was sitting." Lydia laughed from behind her workstation, and she told Alfredo what a wonderful voice Giovanni possessed.

Alfredo and Giovanni cut across the first floor to a door that led to an inner courtyard. The grassy courtyard was filled with flowers and lined with perfectly trimmed shrubs. It was a very peaceful place. At the other end of the courtyard was the two-story chapel.

"Straight ahead is the chapel," Alfredo said, as a few raindrops pelted them as they made their way through the courtyard. Across the courtyard, Giovanni noticed the chapel entrance with three stained glass windows located high above it.

A small stairway at the entrance led down to the tomb. Giovanni could hear music being played very softly. It was Verdi's *Requiem*, the Mass for the dead. He loved that work and immediately recognized the voices of Maria Caniglia and Beniamino Gigli, singing the 'Hostias' section.

As Giovanni reached the landing, he looked and was awestruck. The entire interior of the tomb was lined with marble. Laid side by side, with a huge lit candle between them, were two tombs. The light coming through the stained glass windows above illuminated the mosaic angels that overlooked the tombs. On the tops of both tombs were written just the simple names of two people, Giuseppe Verdi and Giuseppina Strepponi. Here, laid to rest, were the Maestro and his wife.

All was quiet except for the music. Giovanni had so many thoughts running through his mind. He wondered if his father had ever been to this place; if he had ever visited the tomb.

His thoughts were interrupted when Alfredo asked, "Signor Giovanni Tempesta, the boy who wants to be a famous opera tenor, do you know why you want to sing?"

Giovanni said, "*Il mio Padre*. My deceased father wanted me to be an opera singer. He believed that I had the talent to be one. I came to believe that myself. I have worked hard, teaching myself how to sing. My father made me believe that God had given me this talent. I have come to the belief that I want to sing because that is what God wants me to do."

"Your father was a wise man, Giovanni. The talent to sing

or to compose music does indeed come from God. But do you know why God gives certain people this talent? Why he wants artists in this world?"

Giovanni asked in reply, "Why?"

"The first is personal to God. People like Verdi, your Puccini, Caruso, all the great artists and composers who have come before us, God put people like that on this earth so that through music, we see Him. What a gift that is, Giovanni. Just think about that. God chose an individual, a fellow human being, to be blessed with a special talent, which ultimately, through that talent, brings people closer to Him. Sure, people can perfect their voice by training, but God must touch the voice first with talent. And that talent only comes from God. I was blessed with such a gift, and I had the opportunity to become a singer to fulfill this destiny, to allow people to see God through music."

"I wish for the same opportunity, Alfredo."

"The other reason for God putting artists in this world is for all of us. It gives passion to our lives, Giovanni. And passion is what gives to our life a purpose. What we as humans need in order to live life fully is passion. Passion is, or at least should be, the heart and soul of our life. Passion provides people a different perspective on this mundane, hard life."

"And music provides joy to the person listening," replied Giovanni.

Alfredo smiled and said, "It is true music brings joy to people, and they forget about this hard life while they are listening. However, most of the people return to their life, forgetting music and the way it made them feel. Joy alone,

Giovanni, does not bring passion. But, when one lives with what I call background music, passion can be found."

"What do you mean by background music, Alfredo?"

"Let me explain it this way. When you go to a movie, the background music enhances the story and adds passion and romance. Sweeping musical scores that let the listener feel the emotion of the character. Our lives outside of the theater need background music as well. When I am in a situation in my life, be it happy or sad, I have music running from operas and movies throughout my head. That is what I mean by background music."

Giovanni was stunned. This blind old man had just stated exactly how Giovanni had lived his entire life. He said, "Signor Alfredo, since I was 11 years old when I attended my first opera, I always wanted to sing. But more than that, every situation that comes up in my life, I think of it in terms of music. If I see a girl, I have a part of an opera playing in my head or a piece of music from a classic movie. Moments in my life are lived with music in my head. I know my father did the same thing."

Alfredo said, "Based on how life is today, not many people hear background music in their heads. You, *amico*, you whom I have known only a short while, I know you hear it. Your life is enhanced with music. And even more importantly, you have been touched by opera. With opera, it goes beyond mere background music. The wedding of word and music goes to the very pulsation at the core and heart of all existence."

Giovanni was mesmerized by the ability of Alfredo to describe the importance of opera. Alfredo continued, "Opera is the greatest art form. As the composer, Vincenzo Bellini, said, 'When you sing, it must make the audience weep, shudder and die'. That is what the power of the human voice can do when God touches it with this talent. A singer, through the composer's music, can bring passion into a person's life."

Giovanni said, "My father passed his love of music on to me, and now I want to pass it on to others. I want to sing to tell people the stories of operas. And I want to let people see my passion for this art form."

Alfredo interjected and said, "And you want to 'touch their soul'. That is why you should sing, Giovanni. That is why God wants you to sing. He wants you to bring this gift to others. He wants you to provide passion to their lives. God willed it."

Giovanni replied, "You have summed up for me my destiny." And then with a touch of sadness, he added, "A destiny that I cannot fulfill."

Giovanni became quiet. Alfredo, moved by the words of this young boy, was also quiet for a few moments before asking, "Well, what do you think of the *Casa di Riposo*?"

Giovanni, getting control of himself, responded, "I think this is a special place, but to be honest with you, Puccini is a better composer."

Alfredo gave out a huge laugh and said, "Do you know that when Puccini was still alive, he would send to the residents of the *Casa Verdi* game that he had shot while hunting at his beloved *Torre del Lago*."

"I didn't know that, but it makes sense because he loved to hunt."

"They take good care of us here. The staff is very attentive. And they provide us with entertainment. Just two weeks ago, the La Scala Orchestra, under the baton of its director, Maestro Massimo Torcelli, performed a concert here. La Scala has been doing that tradition here at the Casa Verdi since the conductor, Arturo Toscanini, started it. And from time to time, other singers will stop by and give us free concerts."

Giovanni asked, "Do you go to the opera a lot?"

"Well, not anymore. However, occasionally La Scala offers the Royal Box for a performance, and a number of the residents go to the opera."

"Do you go?"

"No, Giovanni. It has been some time since I have been to La Scala. I do know the crowd at La Scala always welcomes the residents with a standing ovation. It warms their hearts as they relish in the glow of their memories."

Giovanni had so many questions for Signor Alfredo. He felt like he could speak to him for hours. "Signor Alfredo, tell me about yourself, and when you started to sing?"

Signor Alfredo reached down with his right hand and felt for the stairs. He then sat down on one of the steps, which led directly to Verdi's tomb and said, "I was born in Catania, Sicily, the hometown of the great playwright, Giovanni Verga, the opera composer, Vincenzo Bellini and the great tenor, Giuseppe di Stefano."

Giovanni said excitedly, "He is my favorite tenor of all time. My deceased father loved Caruso. We would argue for hours over who was the better tenor."

Alfredo said, "Di Stefano was great, but I would probably have to vote with your father. As a young man, I knew I had a beautiful tenor voice and soon found myself being taught by the handsome baritone, Luigi Montesanto, who by the way was the first Michele in Puccini's *Il Tabarro* at the Met and who also later taught di Stefano."

Giovanni said emphatically, "Signor Montesanto sang in a *Pagliacci* with the great Caruso in 1915 here in Milan. Someone who sang with Caruso taught you? *Gran Dio.*"

"Giovanni, you really do know your opera. I would always make my teacher describe to me what Caruso's voice sounded like in person. 'The most glorious sound he ever heard' was the way Signor Montesanto described that voice."

"My father would have given anything just to hear that voice one time, live."

Alfredo said, "Me too. He was the greatest. My career started slowly, singing the minor roles, but soon I started singing the major roles. My career took off when I sang for an indisposed Beniamino Gigli in *La Forza del Destino* at the Arena in Verona. From there, I sang at some of the major opera houses in Europe. My career was well on its way, but it ended during WWII. After the war, my career was officially over. And as you can tell, I am now blind and live here where the staff cares for me."

Giovanni asked Alfredo, "Signora Lydia told me that the reason your picture is not on the wall in the lobby was because you never sang at La Scala; why didn't you?"

"Giovanni, life doesn't turn out the way it always should. Now, it's time for tea. I hope you have enjoyed your tour of the Maestro's tomb."

"Oh, I have. I would love to come back and see my '*zio*' again and talk opera."

"I would like that very much. Come anytime you wish."

As they began to leave, Giovanni turned and looked at the

tomb one last time. Imagine, the great Verdi was resting right here. He then looked at Alfredo, standing next to him.

Speaking with Alfredo about opera reminded Giovanni of all his talks with his father years ago. He missed those times so much. Suddenly, a thought came leaping into Giovanni's head. He blurted out, "Signor Alfredo del Monte, my name is Giovanni Tempesta. I am a singer in need of a teacher. Singing is my destiny. *Credo al destino*. Will you teach me?"

A smile came across the old man's face. "Singing is my destiny" were the same words he had told his teacher, Luigi Montesanto, when he met him for the first time. But Alfredo was old. Years of tragedy and regret had taken their toll on him. He couldn't teach. He never had. Why start now? Yet, there was something special about this boy. Why not give it a try? It would be nice to have someone around, someone to discuss opera with on a daily basis. Without even hearing him sing one note, Alfredo decided that he would.

Nodding his head with an air of understanding, Alfredo said, "*Destino*? *Credo destino*? I will help you follow your destiny, Giovanni. Lydia said that you have a beautiful voice. I trust her. We start tomorrow. What time can you come?"

Excitedly, Giovanni responded, "I get off of work at four in the afternoon. I can be here by 4:30 p.m."

"Good. I'm an old man. I expect you to be prompt and work hard."

Giovanni asked pensively:

> *Quanto? Il prezzo?*
> *How much? The price?*

Alfredo laughed, recognizing the line from Puccini's *Tosca*.

"Don't worry, my young tenor. I don't want Scarpia's payment. My price is your company and an invitation to your debut at La Scala."

Giovanni smiled and uttered a thank you to his new teacher. As he left the resting place of Verdi, he thanked God and his father. Of all the possible places, down in the tomb of Giuseppe Verdi, he had finally found his teacher. There was no doubt his father had played a role in lining that up, he thought.

As he left the *Casa di Riposo*, his thoughts turned to Isabella. He would go to see her tonight, even though he was warned not to by her father. He made his way out the front door and into the rain.

# 8

## LA NOTTE É BELLA

*G*iovanni waited until 10:30 p.m. that night before he made his way to Isabella's home. He was ecstatic about the events of earlier that day. He finally had a teacher. He parked his motor scooter on the street behind Isabella's house and jumped the fence near the swimming pool. He made his way directly to the balcony.

The rain from earlier that day had stopped, and a light fog had taken over the city. The moon, covered by the fog, was not as bright as last night, which gave Giovanni some comfort in perhaps avoiding Isabella's father.

There was no sign of life, except for a light coming from the balcony double doors to Isabella's bedroom. He climbed up to the balcony and then gently rapped on the double doors to her room. "Isabella, are you there?"

The door opened suddenly, and Isabella swiftly came onto the balcony, closing the doors behind her. She was dressed only in a nightshirt. Giovanni looked at her attractive thin legs and the outline of her underwear under her nightshirt. He then looked into those wondrous brown eyes.

"Giovanni, I was hoping to see you again. I knew after the run-in you had with my father last night that you wouldn't come today, but you are here now."

"I had to see you."

"My father has forbidden me to see you or talk to you. However, he has gone out for the night with my stepmother."

"Your father will not separate us. I will see you and will not be stopped by him," Giovanni said with determination. And then, suddenly speaking tenderly, he said, "You are everything I have ever dreamed of. I can't stop thinking about you, and all I want to do is be with you.

Dejectedly she said, "But you don't understand. He will not let you see me. Are you willing to see me if you have to hide and not be seen? You can't call me on the telephone. You can't be seen with me. If my father found out, he . . ." She stopped in the middle of her sentence.

"He won't find out," Giovanni said, trying to reassure her. "I want to be with you."

"I want to see you, Giovanni, but I cannot stand up to my father."

Giovanni gave her a look of understanding and then said very passionately:

> *Resta vicina a me! La notte é bella!*
> *Stay with me! The night is beautiful!*

"Is that from an opera?" she asked.

"Yes, it is. It is a very meaningful opera to me today. Those words are from Puccini's opera, *Il Tabarro*. Today, I have found my teacher. The baritone who sang at the premiere of that opera in 1918 taught him. He is very knowledgeable about opera. He is willing to give me a chance."

He went on to tell her about his visit with Signor Toscano and how he came upon the *Casa Verdi* and his meeting with Signor Alfredo del Monte.

When he finished talking, Isabella looked sadly in his eyes and said, "What are we to do about my father?"

"Today, I found my teacher. Tomorrow I begin my training to become a singer, and the day I sing at La Scala, your father will be there, sitting next to his daughter, my wife, with a look of pride on his face."

Her heart jumped at the words, my wife. As Giovanni pulled her close, she leaned her face forward toward his. He smiled as he gently stroked the side of her face. His heart began to beat faster and faster. With her eyes, she drew his lips to hers. As Giovanni closed his eyes, they kissed. Their kiss was soft and awkward at first, but as she slightly opened her mouth, their kiss grew in intensity, and Giovanni pulled her tight against him. She then let her mouth find his neck as she gently kissed it. Their lips then found each other again, but this time their kiss deepened. Their hearts raced even faster.

Their kiss was a miracle, both tender and passionate, a kiss of youth, and of love. He now knew for certain that "It is she". He also knew that for Isabella, "It is he". There was no need to ask Isabella if she wanted to date. The answer was in her kiss. Slowly but surely, the seeds of true love were being planted.

Before Giovanni left Isabella that night, he asked her, "Can I see you next Sunday? I would like to take you somewhere."

Isabella asked, "Sure. Where?"

Giovanni said, "Wait and see. It's a very special place to me. I only have a motor scooter. If you have a car, can we take it that day?"

"*Si*. What time and where?"

Not wanting her to see the poor section of town in which he lived, he said, "Pick me up by La Scala at 10:00 a.m. We won't be back until dark."

"*Ci vediamo presto, Giovanni*." (I'll see you then, Giovanni.)

# PART II

MILAN, ITALY
MARCH, 1979

# 9

# A TEACHER AND HIS STUDENT

*M*onday was a spectacular March day in Milan. The cold winds coming down off the Swiss Alps were not as prevalent as the Milanese anxiously awaited the arrival of spring.

It was said by the southern Italians, especially the Sicilians, that the Italians who lived in the north worked hard and played little. The southerners said that for every church found in Rome, there was a bank in Milan. They believed that the reason why the Milanese worked so hard was because they were really part of Switzerland and not Italy, and therefore, the Milanese didn't know how to take it easy and enjoy life like the Sicilians but instead stayed indoors counting their money.

Giovanni, having Sicilian blood, knew how to enjoy life. He worked hard but enjoyed his time away from work as well. Therefore, it didn't come as a surprise to Signor Roberto Casa at the pharmacy when Giovanni asked to get off a little early on that Monday. All-day Giovanni looked at the clock, counting the hours till he could meet Signor Alfredo for his first lesson. He was finally going to officially start his training.

By 3:30 p.m. that afternoon, he was on his motor scooter heading out to the Northwest corner of Milan. He arrived at the *Casa Verdi* at 4:00 p.m. and entered the old building.

With no one singing, the home was quiet. Sitting at her usual spot in the foyer was Lydia. "Signor Giovanni, you have come back to see your 'zio' so soon, how nice," she said.

"Yes, thank you again for your help yesterday. You don't know what it means to me."

"Well, I'm sure Signor del Monte will be happy to see you. He never gets any visitors. I believe he is in the cafeteria having an espresso."

Giovanni said *addio* to Lydia and followed her directions to the cafeteria. While he walked the hallway leading to his destination, in his mind ran a picture of Giuseppe Verdi, walking these same hallways while the construction was going on. Giovanni noticed that every doorknob to the residents' rooms was harp-shaped. He looked at the names on the doors of a few of the residents' rooms. Every so often, he came across a name that he recognized from an opera recording he had at home.

As he entered the cafeteria, the smell of strong espresso hit him at the door. The room was filled with about 40 to 50 residents. Playing over the loudspeakers was the love duet from Verdi's *Un Ballo in Maschera,* with Tebaldi and Pavarotti. The residents were all sitting around laughing, talking and drinking their espresso.

Giovanni looked at all of the old faces of the residents and wondered which of them had sung at La Scala in their life. In the back corner, sitting at a table by himself, he noticed Signor Alfredo del Monte. He was sipping his espresso and enjoying the music.

"Signor Alfredo," he said as he approached. "I am ready to begin my first lesson."

Alfredo smiled when he heard Giovanni's voice. "You must be eager to begin. You are early. Let me finish my espresso, and then you can lead me to the salon so that we may begin our training."

Giovanni sat down next to Alfredo and answered questions about his family while Alfredo finished his drink. As Giovanni did so, he couldn't help but overhear the heated discussion between three residents sitting at the table next to them.

The three were arguing over the opera, *Un Ballo in Maschera*, which was being played. Two of the residents, a male and female, stated that the opera is better when it is performed, as it was done at the premiere, with the story taking place in America. The third resident, a male, argued that the censors, who forced Verdi to move the locale from Sweden to America, had hurt the opera. To get his point across, he said with a booming voice, "When I sang at La Scala with the great Maria Caniglia, the opera was changed to Sweden. *Magnifico*."

The other man yelled back, "In the '50s, when I sang it at La Scala with the great Leyla Gencer, it was performed with the American locale. *Magnifico*."

The woman acted as a referee until the argument got too heated and the two men stormed out of the room. Alfredo laughed as he heard the men leave and said, "An argument like that can only take place at the *Casa Verdi*."

Giovanni asked, "They both sang at La Scala?"

Alfredo said, "*Si*. If you would ask them, they would tell you all about it. You see, Signor Tempesta, the competitive spirit runs rampant throughout these halls."

Soon, Alfredo and Giovanni were making their way to the grand music salon. As they did so, they passed a row of rooms from which Giovanni heard a flute and a piano being played. Giovanni asked, "What are these rooms?"

Alfredo said, "Those are practice rooms. Some of our residents still vocalize every day. Others, like me now, give voice or music lessons and use these rooms for their students. But, we won't be needing those rooms just yet."

Giovanni and Alfredo entered the grand music salon. There was only one resident, an elderly woman sitting on a far sofa reading a novel. She glanced quickly over at the two of them and then put her head down without acknowledging them.

"Giovanni, have a seat over by Verdi's piano." Giovanni sat on a chair right next to the piano, while Alfredo sat on a sofa directly across from him. Alfredo settled into his seat and then started to speak. "Today, you begin your training. You must trust me when I tell you the key to singing opera is to learn from the past. And the way opera singers can learn from the past is to listen to those who came before them. In that way, you can get a feel for the technique. You can find different ways to phrase a line or sing a special part of an aria. Get different interpretations from different singers, the great singers."

Giovanni was beset with anticipation. He could hardly

contain himself. He finally blurted out, "Signor Alfredo, would you like me to sing an aria for you?"

Alfredo shook his head no and said, "Giovanni, you must first listen before you can learn."

Giovanni settled back into his chair.

"I'm sure you have heard of the great conductor, Tullio Serafin."

Giovanni spoke up and said, "Sure. He was an assistant conductor at La Scala for Arturo Toscanini and eventually took over control of La Scala in the '50s."

"Giovanni, you have an excellent knowledge of opera. Tullio Serafin was asked one day about singers. His comment was, 'I have heard all the great singers in my life and have conducted most of them, but there have only been three miracles, tenor, Enrico Caruso, soprano, Rosa Ponselle and baritone, Titta Ruffo.' "

Giovanni loved chatting with Alfredo. The stories he told, Giovanni had never heard.

Alfredo continued, "I'm sure you have heard of the great sopranos, Lotte Lehmann and Geraldine Farrar."

Giovanni jumped at the chance to show his knowledge. "I have heard of them and have some of their records. Signora Farrar sang in the world premiere of Puccini's *Sour Angelica*."

Alfredo laughed at the mention of Puccini and said, "I should have guessed you would have gotten that one. One day, Signora Farrar asked Signora Lehmann to categorize opera singers. Signora Lehmann said that 'before doing so, you have to take Caruso and Ponselle, put them aside and then you may begin.' Signora Farrar continued and asked Signora Lehmann, 'How do you even attempt to sing like those two?' Signora Lehmann looked right at her and said, 'By special arrangement . . .with God.'

"My dear Giovanni, Caruso, Ponselle and Ruffo had the gift from God. Before you can even begin to become a singer, you must learn from them. I have recordings of all three singers. You will study their inflection, phrasing, breath control, power, and interpretation. After you listen to a few arias, we will discuss in detail everything about that singer and how they produced the sound. From them, you will learn. You will not imitate them, but seek inspiration from them. They will be your teachers. I will be their assistant. And in so doing, hopefully, by special arrangement with God, you will be touched with the gift, a gift I never did have; a gift very few have ever had; to be the best. Now go by the record player over there, and let's begin with Caruso. Lydia put the recordings we will listen to in a bag next to the phonograph. We will begin with the bel canto operas of Bellini and Donizetti to learn complete breath control. Let us begin."

As Giovanni went to put the record into the phonograph, Alfredo said, "Caruso is the greatest tenor who ever lived. The proof for us lies in the performances he left on disc at the dawn of recording. The gramophone was in its infancy. The Gramophone & Typewriter Company thought that in order for the recording industry to take off, it needed top-notch singers under contract to record. But, almost every singer that the company approached refused to be recorded by a 'toy'.

"In 1902, Fred Gaisberg, a recording technician for the company, heard a young rising tenor make a sensation at La Scala in Franchetti's *Germania*. Gaisberg immediately inquired if the young singer would record and what his fee would be. The virtually unknown singer's name was Enrico Caruso.

"Caruso's agent, Salvatore Cottone, informed Gaisberg that Caruso would sing for 100 pounds and that he would record ten sides, with the session lasting only two hours. Gaisberg sent word to his bosses in London, urging them to agree. His bosses wired back, 'FEE EXHORBITANT. FORBID YOU TO RECORD.'

"In a move that the company would later thank Gaisberg for the rest of his life, he disregarded the cable, and on April 11, 1902, he transformed his suite on the 3rd floor of the Grand Hotel here in Milan into a recording studio. He had a piano brought in for Salvatore Cottone to accompany Caruso. For two hours, Caruso's voice was put on disc for the first time. He made ten sides.

"The records were rushed into production and became an instant success. The company's executives first goal after that was to lure Caruso back into the recording studio. Other singers soon flocked to get under contract to record. Caruso had given the gramophone respectability. Those ten sides recorded that day made millions for the company. Caruso went on to record more and entered into a very lucrative recording contract. Now let us listen to an early record that he made."

The first selection was Caruso's recording of 'Una furtiva lagrima' from Donizetti's *L'Elisir d'amore* with piano accompaniment. Caruso had recorded it in New York on February 1, 1904 in room 826 at Carnegie Hall. It was the first time he had recorded outside of Milan.

The record started, and a voice blazed out of the loudspeaker. Giovanni grew up with that voice and recognized it immediately. He thought of his father as he listened. The technical ability of Caruso was exemplary in the recording. At the end of the aria, Caruso sang a note *mezza voce*, and then swelled the note into a chest note, all in one breath. Giovanni and Alfredo listened to that final note about 10 times, each time discussing the technique that was used.

Into the evening, Giovanni and Alfredo sat in the salon, playing different arias sung by the three miracles, dissecting each singer's technique. They listened to Ruffo in *Lucia*, Ponselle in *Norma* and *La Vestale* and Caruso in *La Favorite* as well as many other selections. Sometimes, Alfredo would make Giovanni replay a certain part of an aria over and over again, to get a certain phrase or styling embedded into his head.

Finally, at midnight, Alfredo said that was enough for the day, and Giovanni was to come back tomorrow. Before Giovanni left, he told Alfredo, "Thank you for taking me on as your student."

Alfredo patted him on his back and said, "Keep working hard. I will do whatever I can to teach you."

Giovanni left for home very pleased with his first day of training.

GIOVANNI TRAINED with Alfredo the rest of that week in the same manner. Giovanni went to the *Casa Verdi*, after working at the pharmacy, and listened to recordings of the three miracles. Except for the nights he had to leave early to sing at Angelo's, he stayed at the *Casa Verdi* into the late hours of the night, discussing the technique of each singer.

Alfredo spoke at length with Giovanni about the different parts of vocal techniques such as *legato, portamento, vibrato, tessitura,* and *fioritura.* Alfredo used the three miracles to give examples to Giovanni of how a singer used all of these to enhance the technique.

As the days passed, Alfredo and Giovanni moved from listening to the bel canto operas of Bellini and Donizetti, to the operas of Verdi, Giordano, Leoncavallo, Mascagni, Ponchielli, and of course, Puccini. Giovanni was very impressed with Alfredo's knowledge. He very much wanted Alfredo to hear him sing and get his true opinion of his voice.

But Alfredo believed that the study of great singers and an understanding of their techniques had to come first. Of course, that didn't stop Giovanni from trying on his own.

During that first week of training, when Giovanni was at home, he incessantly sang and worked on the different techniques that Alfredo had spoken about during their training. Giovanni stood in front of the mirror in his bedroom, trying desperately to perfect the technique, as described by Alfredo. To Anna, it was as if her husband was alive again, teaching Giovanni to sing as her son's voice filled the home, vocalizing.

As Giovanni walked home from Angelo's that Saturday night with the first week of training with Alfredo complete, he was ready for a break. As he turned down his street, he remembered that he would be seeing Isabella tomorrow. His thoughts turned away from singers, opera and Alfredo, and he only thought of her. He finally reached his house, went in to sleep, and dreamed of Isabella.

# 10

## IL CIELO DI TOSCANA

*G*iovanni awoke early on Sunday morning and went to Mass at the Duomo. By 9:30 a.m., he was standing in front of La Scala, eager with anticipation about spending the day with Isabella. Right by the front door of La Scala was a poster for the previous night's performance of Donizetti's *L'elisir d'amore.* Blazed across the poster were the words, TONIGHT'S PERFORMANCE SOLD OUT! As usual, he thought.

He read the cast list for that performance; Mirella Freni, Luciano Pavarotti and Leo Nucci. Everyone at Angelo's last night after the performance raved about it and said how wonderful Pavarotti had been in the role of Nemorino. It would have been a good one to see, he thought. Suddenly, the bells from the Duomo tolled the ten o'clock hour.

He looked out toward the *Via Manzoni*, the street which runs in front of La Scala, and saw, coming around the corner, a red Ferrari convertible, being driven by Isabella. She looked stunning, sitting behind the wheel, with her sleeveless shirt and her sunglasses sitting on top of her head, which was holding her hair in place in the open convertible. She pulled in front of La Scala.

"*Buon giorno*," Giovanni said as he approached the passenger side of the car.

She replied, "*Buon giorno, Giovanni*. You can drive since you know where we are going."

"No way. Are you nuts? *Sei matta*."

As she stepped out of the car, she said, "I want you to." She came around to the passenger side and gave Giovanni a big hug and a kiss. Giovanni opened the car door and let her in, walked to the other side, put a basket in the back seat, climbed in, and pulled away, startled by the power with which the car surged.

"Where are we going?" she asked as they pulled away and drove along the *Via Manzoni* toward the *Corso di Porta Romana*, which led south out of Milan.

"I thought we would go for a picnic in the countryside. It's such a beautiful day."

"I like that. You made a good choice."

After about thirty minutes, Giovanni and Isabella left the traffic of Milan and were out on the country roads, heading south. They talked the entire time.

At one point, Giovanni said, "I love this car. Is it yours?"

"Yes, it's mine. My father bought it for me when I turned 17. It's to make up for the fact that he wasn't around much for me when I was growing up. I guess it was to let me know how much he loves me."

Giovanni didn't know how to respond, and Isabella could

tell, so she changed the subject and asked, "Where in the countryside are we going?"

"Vicopelago. A town located at the start of the Tuscan hills."

She said, "I've never been there. Is it nice?"

"It's the most beautiful place in the world."

They drove for another hour and a half toward Tuscany. The landscape soon changed to the vineyard filled lands, rolling hills and the cypress trees of the heart of Italy. Their conversation never did stop. Finally, they reached the area of Vicopelago, at the beginning of the Tuscan hills and Chianti wine country.

Vicopelago, a typical Italian hill town, is passed by thousands of tourists every day traveling on the busy highway en route to Florence, with hardly a look at the little town dotting the countryside. If only they knew the treasures they missed.

Giovanni turned off the main highway and headed to the small, quaint Italian town. The town of Vicopelago sat halfway up a hill, with a lake at its base. A single road ran from the town to a building at the very top of the hill. Giovanni said, "That old building up above is where we are going," as he started the climb to the top of the hill.

When they reached the front iron gates of the building, Isabella noticed a huge crucifix at the top of the gate. The place was deserted and looked like no one had lived there for some time. As they exited the vehicle, Isabella asked, "What is this place?"

"This is an old, abandoned convent." Giovanni took his basket out of the back seat and walked into the convent.

The front gate led directly into the inner courtyard. On the left was a chapel, and on the right was the cloister. In the center of the courtyard was a fountain surrounded by cypress trees and a cross. The entire inner courtyard had the look of a captivating, enclosed garden. A few flowers still grew around the fountain. At the back of the courtyard was an iron gate that led to a cemetery right on a gentle southerly downslope at the top of the hill.

Giovanni placed his basket by the fountain and, with the help of Isabella, spread a blanket on the ground. He also took out wine glasses and some cheese. After their picnic spot had been set up, he told Isabella to follow him but asked her to close her eyes. Holding hands, they walked to the iron gate by the cemetery.

When he reached the back gate, he said, "Isabella, open your eyes and welcome paradise." As she opened her eyes, Giovanni pointed out beyond the back gate and the cemetery and said, *"Ecco, il cielo di Toscana."* (Behold, the skies of Tuscany.)

Isabella gasped at the view. The whole of Tuscany lay before her. Vineyards stretched for miles with their little country homes situated nearby. Down in the valley below, there were also beautiful olive groves. The Tuscan hills loomed in the background, with every color of the rainbow reflected on them. Cypress trees grew in abundance throughout the countryside. A few sparse clouds hung overhead. *"Paradiso,"* she said, almost as if in a trance. "This is the most fantastic view I have ever seen. How did you ever find this place?"

"My father and I would come here when I was a little boy, and I would run all over the place while he listened to his operas on his battery-operated phonograph, as he sat right there in the middle of the square by the fountain."

Isabella ventured out into the cemetery. She asked, "Are these the nuns who once lived here?"

"Yes, they all lived here at the convent, but the convent was finally closed a few years ago. The remaining nuns moved to another location."

"With this view, I may have even considered becoming a nun," Isabella said with a laugh.

Giovanni, laughing, said, "But you don't look like a nun."

Isabella walked among the tombstones until she came across a huge crucifix sitting on top a lovely tomb. The words on the tomb read, "Laid to rest with all of our love, October 1922, our beloved Mother Superior, Suor Giulia Enrichetta, Iginia Puccini."

"Giovanni, look, here is the head of the nuns."

"You don't know who that is, do you?"

Isabella shook her head no.

"Iginia Puccini was the sister of Giacomo Puccini, the greatest opera composer who ever lived. She was the Mother Superior of this convent. Puccini visited this place very often, especially when he was working on his opera, *Suor Angelica*. That is how my father and I found this place."

"I've never heard of that opera," Isabella said with a shrug. "But then again, I haven't heard of a lot of them."

Giovanni was standing right by her now in the middle of the cemetery and said, "To me, it's the most touching of all of his operas. It is an opera written for an all-female cast. In the story, Suor Angelica is a young girl from a rich family. She had a child out of wedlock, and because of her sin, her family put her away in a convent. After seven years with no news of her son, she is visited by her cold-hearted aunt, who unemotionally tells her that the boy died. Angelica becomes overwhelmed by a deep and tragic sadness. In her uncontrollably depressed state, she takes poison so that she may be with her son. However, she realizes that because suicide is a mortal sin, she will not be with her son in heaven. Frantically, she prays to the Virgin Mary, who appears in a vision with the child to lead her to paradise.

"When Puccini finished composing the opera, he came to the convent and played the entire opera for the nuns in the cloister over there on their piano, a piano donated by Puccini himself. By the end, all of the nuns were crying, and Puccini was embarrassed for talking about Suor Angelica's sin in front of them. After Puccini finished, the nuns quickly ran to the chapel and prayed for poor Suor Angelica."

Isabella asked, "You really love opera, don't you?"

"I always have. The stories they tell are to me the equivalent to the novels that people read today. But mine have much more passion. That is why I want to sing, to tell these stories through my voice."

"What was the first opera you ever attended?"

"The first time I attended an opera was with my father at La Scala, the night I turned 11 back in 1965. For my first visit to La Scala, my father had purchased standing room only tickets, which meant we would watch the opera from the top gallery of the auditorium, the *loggione*."

Giovanni went on, describing to Isabella his first experience of seeing an opera at La Scala.

As GIOVANNI and his father entered the delightful lobby of the theater that night, they were met by four full-length statues of the great opera composers from the past; Rossini, Bellini, Donizetti, and Verdi. His father pointed to the statues and said, "These are the sentinels and muses of La Scala." Franco then opened the gold-framed, mirrored glass door inside the lobby and led Giovanni into the theater.

Once inside, Franco bent down and told Giovanni, "This is the sacred temple of opera. To be considered a great singer, you must perform here. La Scala is the most important and famous opera house in the world. It has the best acoustics of any opera house. Singers say the acoustics are that way because when you are on the stage, the ghosts of singers past help carry your voice to the audience."

Giovanni was astonished at the captivating interior of the house, the dark red colored curtain with gold trim; the gorgeous boxes above the lavish red seats; the royal box situated in the middle of the theater; and the stunning chandelier hanging over all.

The *mascherine* (ushers) showed Giovanni and his father the way to the *loggione,* up a long flight of stairs. Giovanni, out of breath after the climb, finally walked through a small doorway and came out into the standing room only area at the very top of the theater. The top gallery had a bench around the curved back wall, which allowed one to sit during intermissions.

Franco and Giovanni found a spot to stand and awaited the start of the opera. Down below, Giovanni noticed the *platea* (orchestra section) where the elegant people were seated.

Verdi's *Aida* was the opera that night. It was a wonderful

production by the famous opera and film director, Franco Zeffirelli. The role of Aida was sung by Gabriella Tucci, Amneris by Fiorenza Cossotto and Amonasro by Piero Cappuccilli. Gianandrea Gavazzeni was the conductor.

When the curtain rose, and the orchestra started playing, little Giovanni was transfixed. Here for the first time, the stories that he was told as a little boy came to life. Giovanni, who had never been anywhere outside of Milan and its surrounding areas, suddenly was transported to ancient Egypt. The opera tells the story of the Ethiopian slave, Aida, who falls in love with the commander of the Egyptian forces, Radames, who are at war with the Ethiopians.

But what affected Giovanni most of all was watching and listening to the tenor, Carlo Bergonzi, singing the lead role of Radames. Bergonzi sang with unbridled passion and ardor, and the audience went wild at the notes that came out of his throat.

In the *loggione,* the Bergonzi supporters were silencing the people who were screaming their support for Franco Corelli, a rival tenor who also sang at La Scala. Even with Giovanni standing at the very top of the theater, Bergonzi's voice sounded as if he was standing next to him, singing into his ear. Giovanni got a shudder through his spine as he remembered his father telling him about the ghosts of singers past carrying the man's voice to him.

Giovanni was moved to tears at the end of the opera when Radames was sentenced to death for treason, and Aida, because of her love for him, secretly joined him in the tomb to be buried alive. As Giovanni cheered during the curtain calls, he remembered that this opera had a huge effect on an opera composer whom he loved, Giacomo Puccini.

Puccini, while still a young musician growing up in Lucca, walked to nearby Pisa one night to attend a performance of *Aida*. Puccini credited that performance as the one that opened a new door to him. He always said, "At that moment, God touched me with his little finger and said to compose operas." Puccini became one of the greatest composers Italy ever produced. He was Franco and Giovanni Tempesta's favorite composer.

After seeing *Aida* that night, Giovanni felt like a door had been opened for him. He wanted to become an opera singer and tell with his voice the stories that he loved. He felt he had been given a gift and that God wanted him to be an opera singer. He was born, baptized, bred and conditioned to do it.

---

AFTER RELATING his remembrance of his first visit to La Scala, Giovanni said to her, "After the death of my father, really any chance of my becoming a singer went down the drain. But, I now know his death made me strive more and more to achieve a career in opera. And thanks to meeting you and making me do whatever I could to find a teacher, I met Alfredo."

Isabella pulled him close and gently kissed him.

Giovanni then grabbed Isabella's hand and led her to the basket by the fountain. They sat down on the blanket and started to eat cheese as Giovanni pulled out sandwiches and poured the vino, a nice Ruffino Chianti. It was a perfect wine to complement their salami sandwiches on focaccia bread.

Isabella said to Giovanni, "I don't know much about opera. I've only been to a few of them at La Scala and slept through most of them. But the way you talk about it and the way you tell these stories, you make me want to see more. You have made me see things I never knew even existed. This place is so beautiful, and the story you told about *Suor Angelica* is so moving."

"Isabella, opera is more than music. It's a story told through the use of music. The aria, 'Senza mamma, o bimbo, tu sei morto' (Without your mother, dear child, you died) that Suor Angelica sings when she finds out that her son died is perhaps one of the most melodic and moving arias in all of opera. You must hear it sung with the music one day, and then you will understand the power of opera. I often thought that people who don't believe in God should have to listen to this aria. They would know God does indeed exist. And with Puccini, you get the king of melody. Whenever I come up here, I am reminded of a statement Puccini once made.

"One day, Puccini was attending a rehearsal of *Suor Angelica*. The wonderful soprano, Maria Jeritza, was singing that day. After she sang 'Senza mamma', Puccini made his way up to her. He wanted more from her. He wanted her to attain something almost spiritual. He whispered to her delicately, but urgently, 'Carissima mia, when you sing, you have to walk in the clouds of melody.' That is where Puccini lived his entire life, in the clouds of melody."

Isabella turned her head and looked around the convent. She asked, "Puccini came here and got ideas about this opera?"

"Yes, he would speak to the nuns and would try to put the atmosphere from this place into his opera."

Isabella asked, "Do most composers visit the area they are trying to portray in the opera?"

"No. Puccini was the master in providing atmosphere in his music. My father loved telling me that when Puccini was working on *Tosca*, he climbed to the top of *Castel Sant'Angelo* in Rome at dawn so that he could hear how the bells of St. Peter sounded as they tolled in the morning above the city. He then put that sound into his opera."

She asked Giovanni, "You were very close with your father, weren't you?"

"Yes. When he died, a part of me died. He wanted me to be an opera singer, and I am determined to be one. Ever since I was little, we listened to music together and spoke about opera. I miss him so much."

Isabella replied, "You were lucky to have a good relationship with your father. I have none. My mother, Angelina, died of cancer when I was twelve. Sitting here in this courtyard reminds me of her. She would have loved this spot. For hours she would work in the garden at our house. Next to me, that garden was her pride and joy. I loved her very much. Not a day goes by that I do not think of her. She was very beautiful and kind. But cancer took her away from me, and she died a horrible death. I watched her grow weaker and weaker every day."

Giovanni thought to himself how alike he and Isabella were. Both had the same life experiences. He asked, "How was your mother's relationship with your father?"

"She loved him. But, when he became a judge, he changed. The power corrupted him and killed his relationship with his wife. She turned to raising me and taking care of her garden, although she still loved the man she married. The last words she told me before she died were to take care of him."

Isabella began to cry. Giovanni put his arm around her as she said, "I tried to make life easy for my father after she died. But we had no relationship. Soon he married my stepmother, who wants me out of their life. I just can't leave him and forget about him. I try to remain close to him because I know that is what my mother wanted. But he just doesn't understand me. He wants everything his way. My father wants me to be a lawyer. He wants me to go to Bologna to study pre-law. I want to teach children. But, he won't hear of it. I love him, but he just doesn't understand me."

"You would be a great teacher. You must be wonderful with children," he said.

"I love being around children. I volunteer two days a week at a grammar school tutoring children. I don't want to be anything else except a teacher."

"Isabella, the calling to be a teacher is one of the most rewarding because of the impact you can have on a child. By becoming a teacher, you are helping people."

"*Grazie, Giovanni.* I wish you could make my father believe that. He believes my becoming a teacher is a waste of the education he provided for me. He wants me to be a lawyer so that I can continue to live the lifestyle that I am accustomed to."

Giovanni said, "I believe we must follow the path that would make us most happy. For me, it's opera. If teaching is the path for you, then follow your dream. Your father will understand as long as he sees that you are indeed happy.

"He will never understand, Giovanni."

Giovanni and Isabella continued eating and talking throughout the afternoon. They walked all over the grounds of the old convent and even peered into the chapel. Giovanni pushed the chained front doors to the chapel just wide enough so that Isabella could look in.

The chapel was small but lovely. It had ten rows of pews. It was obviously still well kept. Unlit candles were arranged by the altar. Along the chapel walls were the Stations of the Cross. Between each scene were stained glass windows. But the thing that caught Isabella's eyes the most were three huge clear windows located directly behind the small marble altar. The entire Tuscan landscape and hills were visible off in the distance. The beauty of the place awed Isabella. She asked, "It's all so delightful. Does someone still care for it all?"

"A priest from the town of Vicopelago comes here and cares for the grounds. His name is Padre Guardiano. When I came here with my father, we used to see him here, weeding the garden around the fountain and cleaning the graves of the sisters. He used to say Mass for the sisters when this was still an active convent. We got to know Padre Guardiano very well. When my father died, he said the funeral Mass at the Duomo back in Milan."

Giovanni and Isabella continued to wander around and talk. Finally, at around six o'clock, as the sun began to set, they packed the basket and started toward the car. Isabella took one last look, pass the cemetery gate of the old convent. The view was even more spectacular as the sun was setting.

"Giovanni, I love this place. I would like to come back here again. It's our little secret garden," she said, smiling at him. "You made an excellent choice for a date spot."

Standing there, looking at her with the sunlit hills gleaming in the background, Giovanni grabbed her hands and said, "*Ti amo, Isabella.*"

"*Ti amo, Giovanni,*" she responded.

He pulled her toward him, and their lips connected, passionately. Isabella pressed her body into his. When they finished kissing, they both silently stared into each other's eyes. With her heart racing, she placed her hand on the back of his head and pulled him toward her as their lips met again, but this time much more aggressively. They pressed their bodies together in an even tighter embrace. His heartbeat soon matched hers as his hand brushed the front of her shirt, and he felt her hardening nipples through her shirt. She opened her mouth wider, and their tongues met, making her tremble and providing her with sensations she never knew she was capable of feeling. She felt his excitement, and pulled her mouth away, as she whispered into his ear, "*Mi piace come mi baci.*" (I like how you kiss me.)

Giovanni smiled at her and replied, "*E' stato grandioso, facciamolo ancora!*" (It was great, let's do it again!)

Their lips met again as they kissed even more deeply than before, until she turned around in his arms, allowing him to hold her tightly from behind, as they both stared at the beautiful hills of Tuscany in the setting sun. Giovanni buried his lips into her neck, and she felt the warmth of his breath. She arched her neck to expose more of it, enjoying the sensation as she lifted her hand and stroked the side of his face.

Eventually, they made their way back to the car. They climbed into the car, with her driving this time since Giovanni thought he had drunk too much Chianti, and started the long drive back to Milan, making arrangements for the next time they could get together.

# 11

# A MAGICAL PLACE

*T*he next day, when Giovanni arrived at the *Casa Verdi*, he was looking forward to beginning his second week of training with Alfredo. He was sure that Alfredo would let him sing this week.

Lydia was seated in her normal location in the lobby. As Giovanni spoke to Lydia, he noticed an old man come shuffling into the foyer from the hallway leading to the residents' rooms. Lydia said to the old man, "Signor Catalanatto, why don't you stay inside today and play bingo."

The old resident looked up at Lydia, then over at Giovanni, and said, "Life is too short to stay inside. Too many things to see. *Ciao.*"

Lydia told Giovanni, "May I introduce you to Signor Salvatore Catalanatto. He is one of the oldest residents here at 95 years young. He sang for many years in the chorus at La Scala."

Giovanni shook the old man's hand. Signor Catalanatto reached into his pocket and pulled out a very worn leather wallet. He showed it to Giovanni and said, "This wallet was given to me by Grace Kelly when I sang with the La Scala chorus at her wedding in Monaco. If only she would have met me before Prince Rainier, things may have been different."

"That's a wonderful gift," Giovanni told him.

With that, the old man shuffled past them and out the front door. Both Lydia and Giovanni smiled as he left. Giovanni told her, "I love this place. The residents are so wonderful."

Lydia said, "It's a great place for them to stay. They are well-fed, have activities, have musical guests every now and then, and are well cared for by the staff. There is no depression here. Every resident here loves to tell you and each other all about their careers."

"That probably keeps them young. Well, I have to go meet Alfredo. Nice seeing you again, Signora Lydia."

Giovanni met Alfredo in the salon. Alfredo said, "Giovanni, today we are going to move away from listening to the three miracles and listen to the great tenors of the past, singers like Gigli, Pertile, de Lucia, Schipa, and Lauri-Volpi, to name a few."

Giovanni said, "Signor Alfredo, with all due respect, I have come to you to learn to sing, not listen to recordings. Am I ever going to sing?"

Alfredo asked, "*Finito*? Ah, my young friend. You grow impatient. No need. You have told me you can sing. I trust you. But you must listen to learn. You will sing, but you will sing with knowledge. That is how it must be done. Many young singers today never listen to the singers that came before them. They don't even know the names of Gigli, Pertile, Masini, Merli, and Bonci. These were the early masters. In order to sing well, you must study them and learn. Now, let us begin."

Giovanni settled back into his chair. Alfredo continued, "To sing opera, you must know the history of opera and the purpose of the art form. Giovanni, do you know where and how opera began?"

Giovanni said, "I know it started in Florence."

Alfredo said, *"Bene.* In the 1560's, a group of Florentine poets and musicians formed a group called the *Camerata Fiorentina.* Their goal was to go back to the spirit of the ancient Greeks in music and theater. They were convinced that the ancient Greeks used music in their theater. They derived this inspiration by studying Greek literary sources, primarily Aristotle. Their research showed that music often accompanied certain passages of the play, with the words probably being sung.

"Vincenzo Galilei, the father of the great astronomer, and one of the founders of this society, believed that the words sung along with the music should have the natural rhythms of speech and that the words must be clearly enunciated. It was essential that the words be understood.

"So the group set about writing music that explored the feelings and emotions of the character singing it. Thus, opera was created. The composer, Claudio Monteverdi, was the first to champion it.

"It soon flourished throughout Italy, with Milan becoming the capital of opera. When one studies Italian music, it becomes obvious that the voice rules Italy's musical heritage.

Singing is as natural to Italy as are its vineyards. And singing allows passion to enter music. Great singers are the ones who can take the music and add passion by the use of the voice and allow an audience member to feel the emotions of the character. That is what you must do."

Giovanni said, "*Si.*"

Alfredo continued, "But even more important are the words. The great operas are the ones where the librettist and the composer worked in tandem to create a masterpiece, such that the text and the music mesh together and are forever joined. These great teams of librettist/composers like Lorenzo da Ponte and Mozart; Felice Romani and Bellini; Salvatore Cammarano and Donizetti; Arrigo Boito and Verdi; and of course, Giuseppe Giacosa and Luigi Illica with Puccini, come to life every time their operas are performed.

"Never forget the importance that composers put on words. After all, the words came before the music. Verdi, when writing an opera, would read the words of the libretto out loud, over and over again, while he walked up and down in his room. He pronounced every word until they became music in his head. Thus, when you sing Verdi, you must enunciate the text, and in so doing, Verdi lives again through you. His music, when sung correctly, becomes perfection, like a great artist sculpting a statue.

"Maria Callas, Giuseppe di Stefano and Tito Gobbi are some of the great word sculptors. They act through the use of their voice and the use of the words. And through the use of their voice and by emphasizing the text, they can achieve '*passione.*' And at the heart of opera is passion, a passion that once it takes hold, you can't shake. I agree with the opera historian, Charles Osborne, who says that Verdi's '*Otello* may be superior to Shakespeare's *Othello*'. The reason is due to Verdi's melodic, passionate music, which enhances the story and allows the audience member to feel the emotion. That is the purpose of opera.

"The composer has written music; it is true. But never forget, the music was written to tell a story. *La storia*. And finding and using the correct technique will aid the singer in telling the story with passion in his voice.

"And being Italian, you must stress the beauty of the Italian language. Italian is such a melodic romance language. By its very nature, it exudes passion.

"Even your Puccini understood this. That is why when Puccini was criticized for writing the opera, *Manon Lescaut*, because the French composer, Jules Massenet, had already written an opera on the same subject, Puccini said, 'Massenet feels it as a Frenchman, with the powder and the minuets. I shall feel it as an Italian, with desperate passion.'"

Giovanni laughed out loud and said, "Ah, Puccini. He was so full of passion."

Alfredo said, "Use the Italian language to your advantage. Di Stefano, Callas and all the greats understood this and used the language to bring out the passion. And when you bring out the passion, the story comes to life. The truly great operas are the ones whose story follows the mandate of Aristotle for great drama: concentration of time, place and action."

Giovanni, his voice bounding with excitement, said, "Puccini understood that mandate. Just look at his opera, *Tosca*. The opera takes place all within twenty-four hours, with a few characters and within actual Roman locations. The 1953 recording of this opera with Callas, di Stefano and Gobbi and the La Scala Orchestra shows that it is a perfect opera and why Puccini was a master. I can't think of one Verdi opera that comes as close to the Aristotelian principle."

Alfredo thought for a moment and said, "I can't either. But that's because Verdi's plots are much more complicated."

"Will you ever admit Puccini was the better composer?"

With a wry smile, Alfredo said very slowly, "Never."

"I'm not surprised, Alfredo."

Alfredo said, "Verdi was a genius. Sometimes in his operas, the strings in the orchestra, particularly the cellos, play in such a way that it is as if you are hearing the very heartbeat of Verdi."

Giovanni responded quickly and said, "*Si*. With Verdi, you hear his heartbeat. But with Puccini, you get a window into his soul."

Alfredo bowed to his young student and then said, "Come, we will begin our training today by listening to Pertile sing 'Parmi veder le lagrime' from *Rigoletto*."

For hours Alfredo and Giovanni listened, dissecting each singer and each aria they listened to. Alfredo's knowledge was unbelievable. Giovanni listened to the recordings and to what Alfredo was telling him very intently.

---

EVERY YEAR, around the 15<sup>th</sup> of March, Angelo closed the restaurant for one week while he went to the spas located near Lake Como. He didn't trust his staff enough to let them run the restaurant without him being there.

So with Angelo's closed for the latter part of Giovanni's second week of training, Giovanni was able to dedicate himself completely to his studies with Alfredo. They listened to more and more of the great singers from the past, as Alfredo also related to Giovanni stories of opera lore. And while away from Alfredo, Giovanni tried to instill in his voice everything that Alfredo had discussed with him. By the end of the week, Alfredo still had not heard one note from the throat of his pupil.

On Sunday, Giovanni met Isabella at the cinema. The classic movie, *Casablanca,* was being shown that day and Giovanni just had to see one of his favorite movies with Isabella.

Their love grew with each moment they spent together. Isabella knew Giovanni's driving passion in life was opera. And yet, he still found time to make her feel as though her feelings, concerns and interests were of importance.

Isabella hated dating behind her father's back, but she loved Giovanni. She hoped one day her father would accept him. She didn't know when or if that day would ever come. For now, she just enjoyed spending time with the person who had quickly captured her heart.

# OPERATIC MEMORIES

*T*o Giovanni's consternation, the training with Alfredo continued exactly the same with the start of the third week. Giovanni continued to work hard with Alfredo, listening to recordings. He also found that the more time he spent at the Casa Verdi, the more fascinated he became by the place itself as well as by its residents. That Tuesday, during his third week of training, was such a day.

As Giovanni was walking the hallway toward the dining room to meet Alfredo, he heard a distant voice, singing. Slowly the sound grew nearer. It was a deep, booming, male voice. Giovanni stopped walking and recognized the song as the Don's Serenade from Mozart's opera, *Don Giovanni*.

Suddenly a door in the hallway leading down to the cellar flew open, and a very tall, elderly gentleman walked out. The man was dressed all in black, with a plumed hat tilted to the left on his head. Sequined, silver stripes ran down on the sides of his pants leg. Giovanni stared in disbelief as he thought he was looking at Don Giovanni himself.

The old man, all the while singing, closed the door from where he came and when he noticed Giovanni, stopped singing and in a deep voice, said, *"Buon giorno, amico.* Have you seen any fair maidens today?"

Giovanni looked up at the old man who towered over him and said, "No."

The man sighed and said, *"Ebbene.* They must be hiding today. I'll have to go find them." The old man walked briskly by Giovanni, again singing the Serenade from *Don Giovanni.*

When Giovanni met Alfredo in the dining room, he related to him the strange occurrence in the hallway. Alfredo chuckled and said, "Ah, Giovanni. You have met our Don Juan here at the Casa Verdi. That gentleman is Enzo Pinzotti."

Giovanni asked excitedly, "The great bass from the '30s?"

"The same. During his career, he owned the role of *Don Giovanni.* I believe over the course of his career, he sang the role over 400 times. When he dies, they will probably lay him out in his costume. The residents at the *Casa Verdi* are allowed to keep their old costumes down in the cellar. A few times a month, Enzo gets all decked out in his costume and pursues the ladies. They love the attention."

"Alfredo, this place is unbelievable."

Alfredo replied, "What do you expect? There is no place in the world like the *Casa Verdi.* Most of the residents spent their life on the stage. Even in retirement, they still are involved in the show. Some of our residents can't remember their own name but play a few notes from an aria, and they can give you the name of the aria, the composer and if they ever sang the role on stage. If you show any interest in talking to a resident about their career, you will end up down in the cellar looking at their old costumes. Verdi knew musicians are unique. That's why he wanted to create a place where they could live together in old age."

"To live with their memories, Alfredo, in peace."

"*Si, Giovanni. Memoria.* Both good and bad. Come, let us go to work."

---

LATER THAT WEEK, on Thursday, when Giovanni left the pharmacy, he had arranged to meet Isabella at a coffee shop located near her high school, *Figlie di Christi*, an all-girls school. Angelo Basta was back from Lake Como, so Angelo's would be opened later that night. But Giovanni didn't have to be at Angelo's until nine, and he would not be seeing Alfredo that day.

The coffee shop offered wonderful views from the windows and open double doors of the famous gardens of nearby *Porta Venezia*. The name of the shop was *Fiori di Toscana* (The Flowers of Tuscany). It was small but meticulously kept by its owners, Signori Riccardo Romano and Federico Montefeltro. Signor Romano and Signor Montefeltro both were on the heavy side. Both had dark wavy hair and heavy beards. Each table in the shop was adorned with fresh flowers from the Tuscany region.

The entire shop smelled of a mixture of freshly brewed espresso and flowers. The walls were lined with photographs of the landscape of Tuscany. The specialty drink served at *Fiori di Toscana* was *Caffe Corretto*, a strong *espresso* laced with *grappa.* If you were having a bad day, this drink surely fit the bill.

Giovanni arrived at the coffee shop at 4:30 p.m. Isabella was not there yet. He found a table located by one of the double doors that were opened out toward the street. He sat at the table and waited for Isabella. Signor Romano came up and asked if he wanted anything.

"No. *Aspetto una bella donna.*"

"*Bene.* We are always waiting for the beautiful women."

Giovanni smiled and told Signor Romano how much he loved the photographs of Tuscany and how he loved the region and the wines.

Signor Romano said, "I'm a novice photographer. I took those pictures of my beloved Tuscany over the years."

"They are great. You are very talented."

"*Grazie.* My partner over there, Signor Federico Montefeltro, and I always have fresh flowers from Tuscany on the tables at the start of a new week. We pick them ourselves. I'm originally from Tuscany. A small town called Viareggio. I moved to Milan to be with Federico."

Giovanni said, "Viareggio was the last home of Puccini after he moved from *Torre del Lago.*"

"*Si.* You must like opera?"

"I am studying to be a tenor."

Signor Romano asked, "Whom are you studying with?"

"Alfredo del Monte, a retired tenor who lives at the Casa Verdi."

Signor Romano replied, "I never heard of him. *Buona fortuna.*"

Just then, Isabella walked into the shop. She made her

way over to Giovanni and gave him a huge hug. Signor Romano whispered to Giovanni, "Well worth the wait."

Isabella said to Signor Romano, as she kissed him. *"Buon giorno. Come va?"*

Signor Romano replied, *"Molto bene.* I have been chatting with your friend here. I never knew he was waiting for you. Signorina Isabella is one of our best customers and a wonderful girl."

"I come here often to study after school. Don't you just love this place?"

"I do love it."

Signor Montefeltro came over to the table and hugged Isabella. Signor Romano told him, "This young man is studying to be a tenor. Federico loves music and plays the organ at our church."

Signor Montefeltro clapped his hands together and told Isabella, "A *tenore.* You must be careful of them. Tenors have a tendency to think that by opening their mouth and singing, it entitles them to open other things, if you catch my drift."

Isabella laughed and looked over at Giovanni, whose face had turned bright red. She said, "Federico, I don't think we have to worry about this one."

Signor Montefeltro came over and hugged Giovanni and said, "Any friend of Isabella's is a friend of ours."

Giovanni said, "Very nice to meet you. I love your coffee shop."

Isabella said, "Just wait till you taste the coffee."

Both men thanked Giovanni, took their orders, and left the two lovebirds alone. Isabella told Giovanni, "I'm so glad I got to see you today. How is your training going?"

"It's going well. But Alfredo has yet to hear me sing. I just don't know if his method of teaching is working."

"He's the one who has had a career. You must trust him, Giovanni."

After Signor Romano dropped off their coffee, Giovanni and Isabella spoke about things that most couples talk about as the seed of love begins to blossom in their hearts.

When they left each other a little later, they made plans for the next time they could meet. Giovanni kissed her goodbye and made his way to Angelo's.

---

GIOVANNI THOUGHT about Isabella the whole time on his way to Angelo's. A large crowd was expected tonight at the restaurant. Puccini's *La Bohème* was the opera at La Scala that night with Ileana Cotrubas and Luciano Pavarotti. The opera had been sold out for months.

Angelo, nicely tanned from spending hours at the tanning salon at the spas in Lake Como, caught Giovanni right as he walked into the restaurant. Angelo said, "I hope you had a lot of rest on your week off. Big crowd expected tonight."

"Angelo, I will sing well so they will stay late and eat and drink a lot."

Giovanni then made his way to the piano, where Mario and Jacopo were setting up. As Giovanni approached, Mario said, "You should have seen the people streaming into La Scala tonight. Angelo's will be packed. Let's go over the aria and song choices."

He told Mario, "Since Angelo's was closed last week and I

haven't sung in a while, let's start with a short aria, something like 'Amor ti vieta'."

"An excellent choice," Jacopo chimed in.

Giovanni sat on the piano bench as they discussed the other choices for the evening. When they finished, Mario asked Giovanni, "Would you like to join our bet? I think Angelo will leave tonight with a blonde. Jacopo believes a redhead. What do you think?"

Giovanni said, "I'm surprised the both of you are only limiting him to one choice. After all, he has been off for a week."

Both Mario and Jacopo cracked up laughing. Mario told his brother, "Maybe you should find a redhead tonight for yourself."

Giovanni told Jacopo, "That's a wonderful idea. Your red hair and her red hair would make quite a show."

Jacopo said to both, "Stop matchmaking. Me and my red hair are happy the way we are." Giovanni slapped Jacopo on the back and went to the back of the restaurant to vocalize.

Soon the opera at La Scala ended, and the restaurant began to fill. The Maenza boys started the evening by playing operatic selections from La Bohème on their instruments. Giovanni was in the back, still warming up his voice. As he did so, he remembered that Alfredo encouraged him to practice at Angelo's what they had discussed the past few weeks. He would do that tonight.

When he made his way back into the main dining area of the restaurant, it was filled with people. The crowd was energized from the spectacular performance at La Scala.

Mario and Jacopo ended the instrumental selections, and Giovanni stepped out into the area in front of the piano. The crowd welcomed him with a warm round of applause. He bowed as he accepted the applause. He then began to sing the aria, 'Amor ti vieta' from Giordano's *Fedora*.

The moment Giovanni began to sing, he noticed that the sound he was producing was different; stronger, rounder and with more control.

When the aria was completed, the patrons cheered. Mario Maenza sat motionless. He finally leaned over to Giovanni and said, "I have never heard you sing like that before. That was magnificent."

Giovanni smiled and bowed to the crowd. His thoughts turned to Alfredo. The old man was right. Just by listening to and talking about singers, he had picked up a little of their technique.

Mario started the next selection, Cilea's 'È la solita storia del pastore' from *L'Arlesiana*. The more Giovanni sang, the better he got. Even Angelo, with his arm around a rather young female patron with fire red hair, came over to Giovanni and told him how well he sounded tonight.

As Angelo walked away, Giovanni told Jacopo, "*Amico,* I think you won the bet."

Jacopo extended his hand to Mario to collect his debt.

Before leaving, the Maenza boys pestered Giovanni over and over again about the reason behind his improvement. He first told them that it was due to his finding "*l'amore*" in his life. Mario Maenza was surprised to discover that Giovanni had been seeing Isabella. He said, "There are some who say the Judge is connected to the mob. *Guardati, Giovanni.*"

Giovanni laughed, and after being pestered more and more, finally told them about his training with Alfredo del Monte at the *Casa Verdi*. They cried when Giovanni mentioned the *Casa Verdi*, and they again had to relate to Giovanni the story about their father playing at the premiere of Verdi's *Falstaff*.

Giovanni couldn't wait to see Alfredo on Saturday and tell him about the improvement in his voice. He was certain that Alfredo would want to hear him sing.

# 13

# THE POSTER

On that Saturday, it was storming as Giovanni began the trip to the *Casa Verdi*. He asked his mother if he could use her car. She said she had no plans and would just be home with Gabriella so he could use it. She asked Giovanni how his training was going. Giovanni smiled broadly and told her about his improvement. He then left for the *Casa Verdi*.

When he entered the *Casa Verdi*, an elderly gentleman was working behind the counter in place of Lydia, who was off on Saturdays. The elderly man informed Giovanni that his *"zio"* was in his room.

After receiving directions, Giovanni walked the halls to Alfredo's room. When he reached Alfredo's room, he saw two names by the door, Alfredo del Monte and Francesco Contadini. He rapped on the door and heard Alfredo's voice telling him to come in.

Alfredo was seated in a chair next to his bed, listening to

an opera tape. The room was quaint yet nice. It consisted of a bed, a desk, an armoire, and a nightstand. The room was separated by a curtain. On the other side, lying in bed sleeping, was Alfredo's roommate. Giovanni remembered the conversation he'd had with Alfredo, when they first met, about Verdi wanting two residents to live together so they could help each other.

"Signor Alfredo, I have come for my lesson," Giovanni said as he entered.

"Ah, it is my pupil. Let me put my tape away so that we can begin another week of training."

"Alfredo, what were you listening to?"

"An old Cetra recording of Verdi's *Nabucco* with Paolo Silveri and Caterina Mancini. She was such a wonderful singer. And the chorus is majestic when they perform 'Va, Pensiero', Verdi's greatest choral piece."

"Do you ever listen to new, stereo recordings of operas? Or do you just listen to the recordings in mono sound?"

"Rarely to the new ones, Giovanni. Sure the new recordings have great sound. But, these old recordings made by Cetra were usually the first recordings made of the opera. They may not have the most famous singers or the best singers for that matter, nor is the quality of the sound that great, but what they do have is something magical. All of these artists knew how to sing Verdi. They sing with a passion and a confidence that you do not get with most of today's newer recordings."

"Alfredo, I wish you could have met my father. He would have loved to have spoken with you about opera and listen to opera recordings with you. Of course, he would have insisted that you play more Puccini."

"Well, Giovanni, if he was anything like you, I know I would have enjoyed it."

As Giovanni waited for Alfredo to put the tape he was listening to away, he looked around the room. The room was very neat. Above Alfredo's bed was a portrait of Verdi as a young man. A small desk was located by the door. On top of the desk, Giovanni noticed an old picture in an elegant, gold frame. Giovanni picked up the picture and stared in disbelief.

He immediately recognized Alfredo in the picture. He must have been no more than 30 years old. He was standing next to the great conductor, Maestro Gennaro Prandelli. Both were standing outside the La Scala Opera House.

Between the two of them was a giant poster from La Scala. It was one of the posters that hung outside of La Scala during the season, announcing the opera and its cast for the coming performance. The poster read:

*Teatro Alla Scala Di Milano Presenta*
*TURANDOT*
*di PUCCINI*

*7 DICEMBRE, 1943*

*Turandot: Gina Cigna*
*Liu: Magda Olivero*
*Calaf: Alfredo del Monte*
*Timur: Afro Poli*
*Direttore d'orchestra: Gennaro Prandelli*

The cast list for the opening night performance in 1943 boasted a stellar cast with Alfredo del Monte singing the lead tenor part. Giovanni knew it was opening night because La Scala's season always begins on December 7<sup>th</sup>, the feast day of St. Ambrose, the patron Saint of Milan.

Next to the picture on the desk was some old parchment paper in a frame with a drawing of a costume for the role of Calaf. The date on the parchment was August 15, 1943. There was writing at the bottom that said, "*Grazie, amico.* I owe you my life," signed Castranzio Castarini.

Giovanni asked, "Signor Alfredo, I'm looking at this picture of you and Maestro Prandelli. You said you never sang at La Scala."

"That is correct. I never sang there."

Giovanni stammered back, "But what about this cast list, this poster and this drawing of a costume. It says you sang in Puccini's *Turandot*."

"Giovanni, life doesn't always turn out the way it should. I was to sing, but the performance was cancelled due to the war. My career ended before I ever got the chance to sing there again. Now let us go to your lesson."

"But why, why didn't you sing there again?" Giovanni asked emphatically.

"I have said why, now I don't wish to speak of it again. Some things are left better in the past. *Andiamo!*" He brushed past Giovanni out of the room and made his way to the music salon.

When they entered the salon, Giovanni noticed that it had a few residents sitting in it today. One of the residents was playing the piano. So Alfredo and Giovanni went to one of the wood-paneled practice rooms.

Once they settled into the practice room, Giovanni told Alfredo about his performance at Angelo's on Thursday and

Friday and about how well he had sung. Alfredo broke out into a huge smile and said, "We still have much listening and analyzing to do. Keep up the hard work. Let us begin."

Giovanni and Alfredo listened to more recordings. Giovanni was aggravated that Alfredo would never let him sing. But his voice had improved when he sang at Angelo's, so he kept his disappointment to himself.

***

FOR THE NEXT TWO WEEKS, Giovanni worked hard with Alfredo. He saw Isabella whenever he could, and he continued to practice at home and at Angelo's everything he had discussed with Alfredo. Nothing else was said about the photo in Alfredo's room.

# 14

## TEMPESTA SINGS

*B*y the end of those two weeks, Giovanni was determined to get Alfredo to hear him. It was a Saturday morning when Giovanni made his way to the *Casa Verdi*.

He found Alfredo seated in a chair in the lobby of the *Casa Verdi*, awaiting his arrival. While they walked to the salon, Giovanni asked, "Alfredo, will you allow me to sing today?"

"No. Not yet. We still have a lot of listening to do."

Giovanni sighed with disgust. He finally blurted out, "What is the matter? Why won't you hear me? We have listened for weeks to recordings and discussed techniques for singing, breathing and vocalizing. Yet, you won't hear me. While away from you, everything we have been discussing, I have tried to instill in my voice. Yet, you still won't hear me. Are you afraid that if I do not have the voice, you will lose my companionship? You won't have me around to listen and discuss operas with you. I beg you, hear me. Let me know if I have the gift."

The old man had his head bowed while Giovanni spoke. When he was finished, Alfredo nodded his head, saying, "*Va bene*. Perhaps it is time. *Vieni*, let us hear that voice."

Giovanni, almost tearing up, replied simply, "*Grazie*." Since that first day Alfredo had taken him under his wing, Giovanni had waited for this day, to sing for him and get his true opinion. Both of them made their way to the salon. The salon was empty today, so there was no need to go to a practice room. Once inside the salon, Alfredo took his position at the piano.

Giovanni asked, "What would you like to hear?"

"When we started our lessons by listening to singers, we played the bel canto operas first. The reason we began with the operas of Bellini and Donizetti is because they teach perfect breath control, have long melodic lines, and allow for ornamentation and passion. They are the perfect learning tool. Therefore, I want you to sing for me 'A te, o cara' from Bellini's *I Puritani*. I will play it on the piano, and I have a copy of the music for you. I know it's a hard piece to sing. But if you sing it well, then there is no question that you are a singer."

Giovanni told Alfredo, "I don't need the music. I know it."

"We will see. Let me hear Giovanni Tempesta, the opera singer."

Alfredo began playing the introduction to the aria. When he got to the beginning of the aria itself, he cued in Giovanni with a thrust of his hand. Giovanni began to sing:

*A te, o cara, amor talora*
*To you, beloved, love led me*

*mi guidó furtivo e in pianto;*
*in secret and in tears;*

As Alfredo played, his face became rigid as he listened to that voice. Giovanni continued singing. Then he reached the hardest part of the aria, a high D.:

*Al brillar di si bell'ora, se rammento...*
*In such a happy moment, when I remember...*

At the word, "rammento", Giovanni hit the high D perfectly and held it for a long time. Alfredo stopped playing the piano and just listened. Giovanni finished the aria without any piano accompaniment, as Alfredo sat dumbfounded.

When Giovanni finished the aria, he was met by applause from about fifteen residents who had heard the singing and came into the salon.

Alfredo sat at the piano in disbelief. This boy, he thought. This boy who came to him saying singing was his destiny. This boy whom he had taken on as a pupil mostly for the companionship he would offer. This was no ordinary voice. This boy possessed a voice of pure molten gold. The voice was perfectly placed. The technique was almost perfect. This voice was, without a doubt, one kissed by God. The voice was tonally beautiful, but what set it apart was an emotional drive, touched with melancholy.

Alfredo finally whispered to Giovanni the only words that came to him at that time, "Who sent you to me, God?" A huge smile broke across Giovanni's face. He knew the words spoken by Alfredo were the same Puccini had spoken when he first heard Caruso sing for him.

The fifteen residents all came up to Giovanni and congratulated him and told him how wonderful he sang. They demanded an encore.

Alfredo said, "I'll let you sing your Puccini. What do you want to sing?"

"His 'Ch'ella mi creda' from *La Fanciulla del West*."

Alfredo began to play the aria, and Giovanni began to sing.

He sang the aria perfectly. By this time the salon had close to 35 residents listening to Giovanni who all cheered him when the aria was completed. Alfredo sat up with a look of pride on his face. A few residents came up to Giovanni and told him how good he was and that if he wasn't being trained, he should get training immediately.

Giovanni told them, "I am being trained. Signor Alfredo is my teacher."

There was silence for a few seconds before the room burst out in laughter. Giovanni grew serious and looked at Alfredo, who had dropped his head down. The residents slowly left the room with some of them advising Giovanni to "get a real teacher, someone who sang at La Scala."

After the residents had departed, Giovanni patted Alfredo on the back and said, "You play the piano very well."

Alfredo picked his head up, grabbed Giovanni's hand, and said, "Signor Giovanni Tempesta, you are an opera singer. Your voice is like velvet dipped in olive oil. Your diction is perfect. You have a natural talent, one handed down by God. Your voice just needs a little work. But you have what cannot be taught; tone, legato and passion. You will be a singer. You can have a career. I understand if you agree with them that you need to find a teacher."

Giovanni grabbed Alfredo's hand tighter and said, "Signor Alfredo, you are my teacher. No one else cared about me. I trust you. In just these few short weeks, you have already improved me."

Alfredo smiled and said, "Today, we will begin our new training. We will still listen to the old singers, but today you will begin to vocalize. You will develop that voice and the technique."

For the rest of the day, Alfredo and Giovanni began the hard work of vocalizing. When the lesson was over for the day, Alfredo told Giovanni to come back on Monday. After hearing him sing, he had to do something tomorrow.

Giovanni began to leave the salon. He walked a few feet, then came back and hugged Signor Alfredo, thanking him for his kindness in teaching him.

As Giovanni walked downstairs, he thought of the reaction of some of the residents when he told them Signor del Monte was his teacher. He wondered if that was why Alfredo was somewhat of a loner at the home; that if you didn't sing at La Scala, you were treated differently by the other residents who did sing there. He remembered that Alfredo had told him the residents at the home were very competitive.

Giovanni thought about the picture in Alfredo's room. Why didn't Alfredo sing at La Scala? He needed to know the answer to that question but didn't know how he could find out.

As he left the *Casa Verdi*, Giovanni was excited. His singing had affected professional singers, and they wanted to hear him. He was on his way.

## A CONCERNING MOMENT

When Giovanni awoke on Sunday, he felt great about his impromptu concert at the *Casa Verdi* the day before, but he was also nervous because that Sunday morning was the day Giovanni ordained as the day his mother would finally meet Isabella. It is the day that most Italian boys dread. Every Italian mother thinks no woman is worthy of dating her son. It's even worse with Sicilian mothers. The mothers look upon the girls as evil beings trying to steal their precious boys away.

Since Giovanni and Isabella's trip to Vicopelago four weeks ago, their love for each other had grown. Giovanni knew this was the woman for him. That is why he wanted his mother to meet her.

Giovanni waited for Isabella in the *Piazza del Duomo*. As Isabella approached, Giovanni couldn't take his eyes off of her. She looked gorgeous in a beautiful blue sundress.

Milan is the capital of opera. Milan is the capital of

finance. But, especially for women, Milan is the fashion capital of the world. If one had the means, one could dress in the newest trends in fashion. Isabella had the means.

She ran up to Giovanni, gave him a hug, and asked, "Is she here yet?"

"No, not yet. I'm a nervous wreck." Giovanni and Isabella sat on a bench in the piazza and waited for Anna and Gabriella.

As Anna approached the Duomo a short time later, she was surprised to see Giovanni sitting on a bench with Isabella. She stared at the two of them. It was the stare of the *malocchio* (evil eye).

Giovanni got up and met his mother's stare. "Mamma, this is Isabella Monterone. I wanted you to meet her. Isabella, this is my mother, Anna, and my sister, Gabriella."

Little Gabriella put her hand out to shake Isabella's hand. Anna quickly pulled Gabriella behind her. Anna stood like the statue in the middle of the piazza. Her breathing was short and erratic. She finally said, "I did not know my son was seeing anyone. I guess the two of you must not be close since he has never mentioned you."

Isabella bit her lip. She understood the game and how it is played with Italian mothers. Gabriella was standing directly behind her mother, but leaning over, waving and smiling at Isabella.

Anna, while trying to get Gabriella to stop, continued, "My son has never had a girlfriend. I hope your purpose in seeing him is not to hurt him. If it's money you are seeking, we are poor. You should look elsewhere." Giovanni wished he could vanish.

Isabella grabbed Giovanni's hand and said, "No, Signora

Tempesta, I am in love with him, and he is in love with me." Giovanni closed his eyes and flinched.

Anna quickly crossed herself and said, "Come, we must all go pray for salvation." Anna pulled Gabriella with her toward the church. Giovanni and Isabella followed close behind. Gabriella kept trying to look behind to wave to the couple, as Anna dragged her to the cathedral.

Giovanni told Isabella he couldn't believe what she had said to his mother. She whispered back, "Don't worry, she respects me now. All is fine."

During Mass, Isabella caught Anna staring at her. Anna kept shaking her head, muttering a prayer as she crossed herself.

After Mass, Giovanni and Isabella told his family goodbye in the piazza. Before Giovanni and Isabella left to go have lunch together, Isabella went up to Anna and tried to give her a hug. It was obvious none was forthcoming. Isabella quickly told Anna how nice it was to meet her.

Anna told her very coldly, "Nice to meet you. If I don't see you again, take care."

Giovanni asked, "Mamma, can Gabriella come with us?"

Gabriella begged with her mother to let her go. Isabella was shocked when Anna agreed to let her go. Anna kissed Gabriella and told her to be good. She then left them, without uttering another word to Isabella.

Giovanni apologized to Isabella about his mother's actions. Isabella laughed and said, "Such is an Italian mother. She will accept me one day. Letting her daughter come with us is a step."

Giovanni, Isabella and Gabriella ate lunch at the *Il Salotto Café* in the *Galleria Vittorio Emanuele II*, which the Milanese said served the finest coffee in all of Milan. Giovanni and Isabella were partial to the coffee at *Fiori di Toscana*. They ate at one of the tables under the glass ceiling dome covering the *Galleria*. Giovanni talked at lunch about how Giuseppe Mengoni, the architect of the *Galleria*, had fallen to his death from the roof just a few days before it was opened. Gabriella said she couldn't finish her lunch since someone had died right where she was sitting.

Giovanni also related to Isabella that whenever he sat in the *Galleria*, he hoped he would have the same luck as the tenor, Giuseppe Borgatti.

The opera composer, Umberto Giordano, and his librettist, Luigi Illica, were finished working on the opera, *Andrea Chénier*. The debut of the opera was less than a month away, and the scheduled tenor had fallen ill. While walking through the *Galleria*, the favorite haunt of artists, Giordano and Illica came upon the tenor Giuseppe Borgatti, who was having lunch. They offered the role to him. Borgatti did what any tenor would do when offered an opera with four arias, two duets and a sword fight; he accepted on the spot. Borgatti, only twenty-five at the time, had a huge success in the opera at La Scala. He had his first success at the very same age as Giovanni.

Giovanni also told Isabella about his studies with Alfredo and how well they were going as well as his belief of how the home treated Alfredo differently because he never sang at La Scala.

After lunch, they took Isabella's car over to the *Castello Sforzesco* in downtown Milan. The *Castello*, a Renaissance palace, has a forbidding exterior of brick but with a delightful interior. A series of courtyards is interspersed within its walls.

It once housed the Dukes who ruled Milan. Now, contained within the palace, was the *Civiche Raccolte d'Arte Antica* with its fine collection of art, including Michelangelo's unfinished sculpture known as the *Rondanini Pieta,* on which he was working the week he died.

Milan is a city of beautiful art. However, non-Milanese charge that Milan purchased more art than it produced. If that is true, Milan spent its money well.

After the tour of the palace, the three of them continued their day as tourists in their own city by visiting the church complex of *Santa Maria delle Grazie,* close to where Isabella lived, to see Leonardo da Vinci's painting of the Last Supper. There was only a short line to get in. Once inside, they viewed the magnificent painting, which captures the moment Christ tells his disciples that one of them will betray him. Leonardo didn't finish the Christ figure because he did not consider himself worthy to complete it. This was the first time Gabriella had ever seen the piece of work. She was mesmerized by it.

Giovanni knelt down by Gabriella and pointed out more things in the painting. As he was doing so, Isabella thought to herself how wonderful the interaction was between Gabriella and Giovanni. There was no doubt he came from a loving family. Isabella never believed at anytime that she would ever go against her father's wishes. But that was before she met someone like Giovanni.

As she watched Giovanni and Gabriella, she was proud of how she had stood on her own and dated who she wanted to date. As her love grew, it gave her more confidence. So much so, she even could speak to Giovanni's mother the way she did earlier that day. Isabella had never been happier in her life.

Suddenly, a voice from behind them was heard. "Isabella?"

As they turned, Giovanni noticed a middle-aged gentleman who came up and gave Isabella a hug. Giovanni saw Isabella's face go ashen white.

The man continued, "How are you? Are your parents well? I'll be seeing your father later this month at a meeting."

Isabella told him, "They are fine, Signor Carmelito."

Signor Carmelito extended his hand to Giovanni. "Ah, you must be a friend of Signorina Isabella. I am a close friend of Isabella's family. My name is Antonio Carmelito."

Giovanni shook his hand without providing his name in return. Signor Carmelito also shook hands with Gabriella.

The man continued, "Isabella, I'm so happy you are doing well. I will make sure to tell your father that I ran into you. I really must go. I have to go find my wife."

After he left, Isabella was very quiet. She finally spoke and said, "If my father finds out I am seeing you, I dare not even think what he would do."

The more they spoke, the more depressed and afraid Isabella became. It was obvious to Giovanni that she feared her father. As they departed, he promised to meet her after school on Monday by the coffee shop near her school. It would be a short visit since he had to see Alfredo that day.

## AN INVITATION

*T*he next day, Monday, Giovanni left the pharmacy early and went to meet Isabella at *Fiori di Toscana*. As usual, the start of a week meant new flowers from Tuscany on the tables, picked personally by Signori Romano and Montefeltro.

Isabella was still very upset about the occurrence yesterday. Giovanni tried to reassure her that all would be fine and that Signor Carmelito probably forgot about it already. It was all to no avail. Isabella was convinced that her father would find out. After about an hour, Giovanni kissed her goodbye and started his trip to the *Casa Verdi*.

Alfredo was sitting in the salon awaiting his arrival. Giovanni walked into the salon and immediately apologized for being so late, but blamed it on getting caught up on something at work.

Alfredo bit his lip as Giovanni spoke. After a moment, the old man said two simple words, *"Una donna."*

Giovanni asked quizzically, "A woman. How did you know?"

"I am blind, which gives me a great sense of smell. Never lie to me again. Who is she?"

Giovanni sat down next to his mentor and said, *"Isabella Monterone, la piú bella creatura che conosco."* (The most beautiful creature I know.) I am in love with her, but her father thinks I am poor scum."

Alfredo laughed and said, *"Ah l'amore!* It will make you crazy. But it does add passion to the voice. However, you must promise me that your tardiness was a one-time occurrence. *Prometti!"*

Giovanni responded with a faint, *"Si."*

Alfredo spoke louder, "Starting today, you must dedicate yourself completely to becoming a singer. *Tutto.* Everything else must take second place, including *'la bella donna'.* After listening to you sing on Saturday, I said I had something to do. Well, I have done it. As you know, Giuseppe di Stefano and I are from the same town and were taught by the same teacher. I called di Stefano on Sunday and went to see him at his apartment near La Scala."

Giovanni sat rigidly in place.

Alfredo continued, "I told him about you and how I believe you have one of those voices which God gives to this world very rarely. I told di Stefano that you were 25 with no training and that you desperately needed a break. Di Stefano sponsors a voice competition here in Milan every June. I asked him to do me the favor and to let you enter the competition. Only the best-trained voices from Italy are allowed in this competition. All of the singers come from the great music schools in Milan, Parma, Turin, Florence, and

Rome. Di Stefano has done me the favor of allowing my student to enter this competition, waiving the rule that you must come from a music school."

Giovanni didn't know what to say. He finally slipped out the words, "Signor Alfredo, I can't believe you did that for me. *Tutto per me*. Do you think I am ready?"

"For the first time, Signor Tempesta is showing signs of fear. You ask if you are ready. You have a natural talent. Your voice is great. It just needs refinement. We must work to get you ready. If you work hard, you will be ready, and you will win. And by winning, I mean, you will get a contract to sing in an opera house and begin your career."

"Does the winner get a contract?"

Alfredo said, "Yes. The winner gets a contract to sing at the San Carlo Opera House in Naples."

"What shall I sing for the competition?"

Alfredo responded, "You must choose five arias. One from a French opera, one from a Verdi opera, one from a Puccini opera, one from a verismo opera, and one from a 20th century composer. The judges at the competition will pick the aria they wish for you to sing. So you must have all of these arias prepared. The competition will be held on June 5th at the *Teatro Lirico* in Milan. Here at the *Casa Verdi* is a reading room. The residents have placed music scores from most of the major operas there. We will go look around and see which arias you want to sing. You will then study the music, and I will help you learn to sing them."

Giovanni muttered, "Signor Alfredo, I can't read music. I sing by memorization."

"You sing like that, and you can't read music. That is strange. But, it shows we have something in common and why I am a good teacher for you. I no longer can read music since I became blind. I play and sing by ear now. Thus, I can help you since I must learn music the same way as you."

Giovanni replied, "I know all of the arias from years of listening and singing with my father."

"Then we have a lot of listening to do. We can use the scores for the words, recordings to teach you, and with God's help, you will perfect that voice. We have a lot of work."

Giovanni thought to himself how lucky he was to have Alfredo as his teacher. Alfredo had really tried to help him and had succeeded in getting him into a voice competition. He knew he owed him a lot. Without Alfredo, he never would have had the chance. And he knew this was his last chance. He would work hard for his teacher and make him proud at the competition.

Alfredo sat at the piano and played the scales while Giovanni vocalized. Through vocalization, Alfredo was developing Giovanni's technique. A technique that, according to Alfredo, Giovanni already possessed, but just needed to be cultivated. In Giovanni's mind, Alfredo was now treating him as a real pupil, not just someone with whom he enjoyed listening to operas, but a pupil with vocal talent.

GIOVANNI SPENT the next few days with Alfredo making the choices of the arias he would sing. After much debate, Giovanni told Alfredo, "I have thought about it a lot. The French aria will be 'Ah, fuyez' from *Manon*; the Verdi aria will be 'La donna é mobile' from *Rigoletto*; the Puccini aria will be

'E lucevan le stelle' from *Tosca*; the verismo aria will be 'Addio alla madre' from *Cavalleria Rusticana* by Mascagni; and finally the 20th century aria will be from Korngold's *Die Tote Stadt*."

Alfredo said, "Those are all excellent choices. But I think a better choice for the verismo opera would be 'Vesti la giubba' from *Pagliacci* by Leoncavallo.

Giovanni said, "Ah, yes. Caruso's favorite aria from the opera your that own teacher sang with him. I think you are correct. I will sing that one."

Alfredo said, "Soon, we will practice each one until you can sing them without thinking. When you are not here practicing, sing them at home, sing them at Angelo's, sing them in your sleep. With training, you will be ready. Now, it is late. Practice hard while you are away. *Buona notte, Giovanni*."

---

FOR THE NEXT TWO WEEKS, Giovanni worked diligently with Alfredo. During this time, he saw Isabella off and on, but most of his time was taken up with study and vocalizing.

Alfredo worked long hours with his young pupil, teaching him how to breath properly and project the voice. The natural talent that Giovanni possessed impressed Alfredo. Alfredo came to believe that the reason behind this extraordinary voice was due to Giovanni's years of singing with his father and then later, singing at Angelo's with the Maenza boys.

Giovanni begged Alfredo that if he ever met the Maenza boys, to never tell them that he felt they deserved credit for his voice because the patrons at Angelo's would never hear the end of it.

The more time Giovanni spent with Alfredo, the more fascinated he became by his mentor's knowledge of singing as well as Alfredo's still beautiful tenor voice. Yet the question as to why Alfredo never sang at La Scala still remained unanswered.

# A SECRET FROM THE PAST

On Thursday night, April 26th, Giovanni arrived at Angelo's before Mario and Jacopo Maenza. The restaurant had a few patrons enjoying a good meal before the crowd from La Scala arrived.

When Giovanni walked into the restaurant, he noticed Signora Lydia from the *Casa Verdi*, sitting at a table with three other people. Giovanni approached the table.

Lydia saw Giovanni immediately and said, "Signor Tempesta. We have come to have our dinner and catch the beginning of your singing. I would like you to meet my husband, Tito Trepidoro. Tito, this is Giovanni Tempesta."

Tito was an older gentleman but very good-looking. He rose up and shook hands with Giovanni and told him, "So, you are the Caruso of Angelo's. You have a splendid voice."

"*Grazie, Signore,*" Giovanni responded.

Tito continued, "Let me introduce you to our good friends, Vincenzo and Floria Asaro. Wait till you hear him sing. He should be singing next door at La Scala. He is that good."

Giovanni asked, "Signor Trepidoro, can I borrow your wife for a second? I need to discuss something with her."

"Sure, we are just having some drinks before dinner. No rush."

Lydia rose up and followed Giovanni out of the restaurant. Once outside, as they walked to the piazza in front of La Scala, Lydia grabbed Giovanni's hand and said, "Some of the residents are still talking about your incredible voice."

The moon hung directly over the roof of La Scala. It was a beautiful night. Giovanni sat on a bench and told her, "I know you are close to Signor del Monte. I am too. I get the feeling he's treated like an outcast around the home. I wonder if that's because he never sang at La Scala?"

"You observe very well," Lydia replied.

Giovanni continued, "One day when I was in his room, I noticed a picture of Alfredo with Maestro Prandelli in front of a poster for *Turandot* at La Scala in 1943 with him listed as the lead tenor and also a drawing of a costume for the performance signed by a Signor Castranzio Castarini. Why didn't Alfredo sing at that performance? What happened?"

"If Alfredo never told you, it's probably not my place to say."

"Signora Lydia, I must know. Please tell me."

She looked kindly at Giovanni and said, "You are close to him and deserve to know. You must promise to never tell him I told you."

"I promise," he replied.

Lydia continued, "To understand the story, we must go

back in time to Milan in 1943. I was a young girl back then, and my father was the costume designer for La Scala. His name was Castranzio Castarini. He was around 50 years of age at that time."

Giovanni asked, "The same person who signed the costume drawing in Alfredo's room?"

"The same," said Lydia. "Milan in 1943 was a different place. It was the time of Hitler and Mussolini. It was a time of war. Italy had joined the Germans in the war. It was a huge mistake. Slowly, the Allied forces were making their way up the peninsula. Fascism was collapsing as the Allies took over new towns.

"Mussolini ordered that the performances at La Scala would continue. Puccini's *Turandot* was the opera that was chosen to open the 1943 season on December 7th.

"On August 15, 1943, my father went to work as usual at La Scala. He was going in to meet with the conductor, Maestro Gennaro Prandelli, and a new young tenor to discuss costumes for the upcoming opera. Around 6 p.m., Maestro Prandelli called my father into the *Sala Gialla*, which is the rehearsal hall at La Scala." Lydia pointed to the right second-floor corner of La Scala and showed Giovanni where it was located.

She continued, "The *Sala Gialla* is a windowless room with a massive table located in the center of the room. At the far end of the room is a grand piano, which is used during the rehearsals. Above the piano is a terrifying portrait of Toscanini. For a singer, the room is very intimidating.

"When my father entered the room, he was met by Maestro Prandelli, who was sitting by the piano. Standing next to him was a young, wide-eyed tenor, with gorgeous green eyes, very good looking, and with a Sicilian accent. His name was Alfredo del Monte."

―――――――

MAESTRO PRANDELLI ROSE UP from the piano and said, "Signor Castranzio, let me introduce you to Signor Alfredo del Monte. He will be making his debut here at La Scala in our *Turandot*. I am rehearsing the music with our young tenor."

Castranzio extended his hand to Alfredo and told him how nice it was to meet him.

Maestro Prandelli continued, "I have asked you here so that you may discuss with Signor Alfredo ideas for his costume. This production will be stupendous. That is why Signor Alfredo is here working on the music four months before the opening. The actual rehearsal will begin in mid-November, but Signor del Monte was free this week so I asked him to get an early start."

Castranzio nodded his head in agreement.

Maestro Prandelli continued, "Therefore, we will finish the musical rehearsal, and then you will come back and sit with Alfredo and devise a costume. Alfredo, this man is a genius when it comes to costumes. Give him your ideas and watch the master at work."

Castranzio extended his hand and congratulated the young tenor on his debut. He then turned and left the *Sala Gialla*. As he left, he heard Maestro Prandelli tell Alfredo, "All right then, we will take it again from 'Nessun dorma'."

The rehearsal lasted until the late evening. Finally, Maestro Prandelli called Castranzio back to the *Sala Gialla*.

"You can work with Signor del Monte. I'm going home. Show me the sketch tomorrow." The Maestro left the room.

Castranzio sat down at the huge table with a sketchpad in his hands. He asked Alfredo, "Are you nervous about making your La Scala debut?"

"*Si, tanto*," Alfredo responded.

Castranzio continued, "That is understandable. The audience here is the toughest in the opera world, especially on opening night of a new season. The catcalls cascading down from the *loggione* have ended many a career. The great opera composer, Ponchielli, always referred to the *loggione* as 'that monster that could eat you up within two hours'. Although it is a baptism of fire, if you want to be considered a great singer, you must sing here." Alfredo nodded his head in agreement.

Castranzio asked him, "What brought you here to La Scala? Where are you from?"

Alfredo replied, "I'm from Catania, Sicily."

"The hometown of Vincenzo Bellini. I heard it's beautiful, but I've never been to Sicily."

Alfredo said, "Sicily is celebrated as the Garden of Persephone, the playground of the Arab princes and the prize of the Norman Kings. The Greeks established Catania. It has the unlucky privilege of being destroyed so many times, its citizens have lost count. It sits right at the base of Mount Etna. Bellini is its most cherished son. It's a magical place.

"At a very young age, it was recognized that I could sing. My parents put me in the church choir. After a few weeks, the local priest asked me not to sing because my voice was too big. He finally sent me to a local voice teacher to 'tame that beast'.

"Soon, I landed in the hands of Luigi Montesanto. My career started slowly, but one day, I received a call to sing *La Forza del Destino* at the outdoor Arena in Verona in place of the great Gigli who was ill. My career picked up after that event. I have sung at Parma, Rome, Turin, and Naples, as well as Vienna, Paris and London. Now I anxiously await my La Scala debut. My voice has led me many places. It has also saved me from having to join the army and go to war. A war I don't want to fight in, at least on the side of those bastards, the Germans. I mean, does Italy really want the world to be taken over by Wagner lovers? We don't need Wagner. We have Verdi. Anyway, I know I owe my voice a lot for keeping me out of the war."

Castranzio asked, "Are you married?"

Alfredo's face broke out into a huge smile, and he said, "I am engaged to a wonderful girl from my hometown, Signorina Pasqualina Cippilioni. She and my parents will all be at my debut here at La Scala."

Castranzio pressed Alfredo with more questions, "Who is the greatest composer?"

"Verdi," yelled Alfredo.

Castranzio said, "I'm partial to Donizetti. But, today, Puccini is the Maestro. Let us discuss his *Turandot* and come up with ideas for a costume for the unknown prince, Calaf."

For about an hour, Castranzio and Alfredo discussed at length the opera. They spoke about the sets, the plot and the music. Alfredo listened intently to Castranzio's ideas. Alfredo was surprised to find out that Castranzio had started as an apprentice in 1926 at La Scala. The first opera he worked on was the premiere of Puccini's *Turandot*, an opera Puccini did not finish due to his death.

Toscanini, who was to conduct the opera, recommended to Ricordi, the publisher, that Franco Alfano be hired to complete the opera based on the sketches left by Puccini. But, at the premiere, when the opera reached the part where Puccini had died, Toscanini laid his baton down, turned to the crowd, and said, "The Maestro died here." He then walked off the podium, and the curtain came slowly down.

Alfredo asked many questions about that night and the way the crowd reacted to it all. After the lengthy discussion, Castranzio opened his sketchpad and started drawing the idea for the costume the both of them had arrived at. Alfredo was amazed at the ability and knowledge of Castranzio. With just a few short strokes, the costume was taking shape.

While the sketch was being drawn, neither Alfredo nor Castranzio heard the faint hum coming from outside. Being a rehearsal room and windowless, the *Sala Gialla* was well insulated from sound. The hum grew louder and louder and closer. Finally, Alfredo asked, "Do you hear something? What is that?"

Before Castranzio could even get a word out, the first Allied B-17 bomber dropped its load. The first bomb landed about 30 feet from the front door of La Scala. Castranzio yelled, "Get out of here. The Americans are bombing the city." Alfredo darted for the door and out of the *Sala Gialla* but looked back and noticed that Castranzio had tripped trying to get out.

At the same time, a second bomb made a direct hit on the right side of La Scala, right near the *Sala Gialla*, causing heavy damage. Alfredo ran back into the room, lunged for Castranzio, who had finally just gotten to his feet, knocking him off his feet again, and saving his life, just as a huge piece of the ceiling came crashing in where Castranzio had been standing. A large piece of metal struck Alfredo right in his face. Both men landed with a thud on the ground with Alfredo lying on top of Castranzio. The fire and heat were unbearable for both men. The bombs continued to rain down on La Scala and all of Milan. Alfredo rolled Castranzio under the massive table and lay on top of him, protecting him from the falling debris.

After what seemed like an eternity, the bombing stopped. Castranzio was lying flat on his back, with a gaping head wound. Alfredo was still lying on top of him. Castranzio grabbed Alfredo tightly and said, "My young tenor, I owe you my life. Are you all right?"

Alfredo's face was covered with blood. He put his head down on Castranzio's shoulder and muttered, "I can't see. I think I'm blind."

---

LYDIA GRABBED Giovanni's hand tightly and said, "Signor del Monte saved my father's life that day. Instead of running for his life, he saved my father. To his grave, many years later, my father never forgot the bravery of Alfredo and the unselfish act he performed. He gave Alfredo the sketch of his costume he was working on and signed it as a token of thanks."

Giovanni sat in disbelief and said, "I knew La Scala had been bombed. My father told me stories about how badly it was torn apart. I had no idea that is how Alfredo lost his eyesight. What happened after the bombing?"

Lydia continued, "After losing his eyesight, his singing

career was over. Alfredo's fiancée left him. He sunk into a terrible depression. He was so close to achieving his dream. Slowly, Alfredo picked up the pieces of his battered life and moved on as best he could.

"Years later, I got a job working at the *Casa Verdi* through the connections my father had at La Scala. I'll never forget the day Alfredo came to stay there. I had met him a couple of times before that with my father. Alfredo was very pleased when he learned that I worked where he would be living. I have always thought it appropriate after what he did for my father.

"Alfredo is somewhat of a loner around the home. I think he feels that by not singing at La Scala, the other residents do not consider him a singer. You have brought him such joy. Through you, he lives again. He has a career again. That is the story of Alfredo del Monte."

Giovanni noticed a few people starting to leave the performance at La Scala. It was coming to an end. He knew he had to get back to Angelo's to sing.

As Lydia and Giovanni walked back to Angelo's, Giovanni realized how much he had come to love Alfredo, not only as a teacher and a friend, but also almost as a father. Right before going into the restaurant, Giovanni leaned over and gave Lydia a kiss on her cheek and thanked her for telling him the story of Alfredo. They entered Angelo's, and Giovanni went to prepare for that night's performance as the Maenza boys began to play some instrumental selections.

## A SIMPLE MOMENT TOGETHER

*T*hree days later, on Sunday morning, Isabella met Giovanni for Mass at the Duomo. After Mass, hand in hand, they walked past La Scala and up the Via Verdi, passing Angelo's. The *Via Verdi* turned into the *Via Brera*.

The Brera district in Milan was a sprawling shopping district located near the Brera Museum, known as the *Pinacoteca di Brera*, which housed very appealing artwork. This district has often been compared to New York's Greenwich Village because of its cafes, shops, antique stores, and art students.

Off of the *Via Brera*, Giovanni and Isabella walked along the pedestrian-only *Via Fiori Chiari*. The street was lined with shops and packed with tourists and locals. Vendors pushed carts along the street, selling trinkets. A few of the carts were laden with fresh cut flowers of every color of the spectrum. The entire street was alive with excitement. Giovanni remarked to Isabella how the entire street made him think of the second act set of Puccini's *La Bohème*.

They stopped in the small shops located along the street. Isabella purchased a nice pair of leather gloves from a store. Giovanni noticed that Isabella didn't even look at the price tag.

While they walked and looked into the different shops, Giovanni told Isabella about his conversation with Lydia on Thursday night and the story he learned about Alfredo del Monte. Isabella commented on how awful it must have been for Alfredo to be so close to achieving his goal to only lose out at the last moment.

A short distance from the *Via Fiori Chiari*, Giovanni and Isabella walked to *Via Solferino*, one of the truly great shopping streets in the district. The stores were much bigger and more expensive. One could spend the day merely walking the street, looking at the window displays, which were gorgeous, as they are throughout all of Milan. Giovanni and Isabella shopped at several stores. It did not come as a surprise to Giovanni that most of the salesladies seemed to know Isabella.

The stores sold leather goods from Florence, glass from Venice, lace from both Florence and Venice, and ceramics from Faenza in Emilia-Romagna and Assisi. And of course, being in Milan, the street had stores of the great designers, such as Pucci, Valentino, Armani, Missoni, Gucci, Versace, and Ferré.

At a small jewelry boutique, Giovanni bought Isabella a not too expensive, but beautiful all the same, gold bracelet. It was simple yet very elegant.

After shopping, the two of them found a quiet café, with

outside tables, to get a bite to eat. While they awaited the arrival of their food, tortellini for both, they reminisced about how far their relationship had come.

"Giovanni, you have made me so happy. Never in my wildest dreams did I ever think I would find someone like you."

Giovanni looked into her huge brown eyes and said, "I hope you have been happy. I don't know what type of life I can offer you, but I know you are the one for me."

Isabella broke out into a huge grin, and she said, "Giovanni, I know what type of life you can offer me, one filled with love and happiness."

Giovanni said, "I know. But you are rich, I am poor. Hopefully, one day, if we do marry, I will be able to provide for you. But I will never be able to give you the life you live now."

Isabella grabbed his hand across the table and said, "I don't want the life I lead now. My father and stepmother do not have a financial worry in the world. Yet, they are two of the most depressed, unloving people I know.

"When I met you, I knew for certain happiness is not about how much money you have or what kind of things you possess. Happiness is being with the person you love. You say that you are concerned about being able to provide for me. My mother would have given up all of her possessions if she could have achieved happiness in her marriage. You can provide for me by always loving me and being there for me. This gold bracelet you just bought for me is better than receiving some outrageously priced diamond necklace because it is from you. *Ti amo.*"

"*O gran Dio. Ti amo, Isabella. Ti amo tanto,*" Giovanni said as he leaned across the table and kissed her.

As they spoke, Giovanni realized that with the passage of time, it seemed as if Isabella was no longer concerned about her run-in with Signor Carmelito. She no longer seemed worried that her father would find out about Giovanni seeing her. He was glad that chapter was over. Giovanni and Isabella spent the rest of the early afternoon together until Giovanni left her to go meet Alfredo at the *Casa Verdi*.

## JUDGE MONTERONE

*G*iovanni awoke Monday morning and, before rising, lay in bed reflecting on his life. Within a matter of a few months, his entire world had changed. Not only was he in love with a beautiful girl, but he also would be singing in a vocal competition in only 37 days. Giovanni was still trying to wrap his mind around the thought that his life's dream was potentially reachable. It scared him how fast everything was moving.

He knew he needed to work even harder with Alfredo to get ready for the competition. He also knew that every waking moment he was away from Alfredo should be spent practicing for and thinking about the competition. But, for the first time in his life, Giovanni began to find it difficult to focus on his task at hand, and he began to seriously question how he could concentrate entirely on the competition. For there was something else distracting his mind away from the competition, and that something was Isabella. His every thought was filled with Isabella. Her eyes, her mouth, her hair, the way she moved, the way she smelled, and the way she smiled.

His unwavering belief that without Isabella, he never would have been in the position he was, so close to attaining his dream, gave him great comfort and made him realize that the two now most important things in his life, Isabella and his dream to become a singer, went hand and hand. Lying in bed, Giovanni became convinced that with Isabella's full support, he would find a way to not only prepare for the competition but also win it.

He glanced at the clock on his nightstand and quickly realized that his delay in getting out of bed this morning would now make him late for work. He rushed to get dressed.

As he drove his motor scooter to work, he hummed the aria from *Manon*. He looked down at his watch and noticed that the pharmacy had opened five minutes ago. He wouldn't be too late.

He finally reached the pharmacy. As he went to open the door, it was swiftly opened from the inside. It startled Giovanni. He was about to say '*mi scusi*', but the words never left his mouth. From the store, out stepped Isabella's father, Judge Pietro Monterone. He towered over Giovanni.

The presence of Giovanni seemed to startle the Judge as well. However, the Judge quickly composed himself and snarled. He said not a word but just stared at Giovanni. Finally, he brushed passed Giovanni with a laugh. Under his breath, Giovanni thought he heard him say, "Singer, ha." Giovanni went inside, wondering what on earth the Judge was doing here. Roberto Casa was standing behind the counter. He looked troubled.

Roberto said, "Giovanni, I just got finished speaking with Judge Monterone. I owe it to you to tell you that he advised me to fire you, or I will have problems."

Giovanni's face showed confusion, and he asked, "Why?"

Roberto continued, "The Judge was going on and on about his daughter and you sneaking around after he demanded that you not see her anymore."

Giovanni asked, "Are you going to listen to him and fire me?"

Roberto couldn't look at Giovanni's eyes. He responded with just a shake of the head. He finally said, "I don't know what else I can do. He is a very powerful man."

Giovanni looked at Roberto in disbelief and said, "Say no more. I can't believe you won't stand up for me. I have done nothing wrong. Thank you for letting me work here these past few years. You do not have to fire me. I quit. *Addio.*"

As Giovanni turned and left the store, Roberto called out, "Giovanni! Giovanni!" But Giovanni was gone. Roberto covered his face with his hands.

Once outside, a rush of emotions seized Giovanni. All at once, he felt confused, hurt, angry, and disgusted.

As he walked a little bit further, the full weight of what had happened dawned on him, and it raised many questions in his mind. These questions fluctuated between: What would the actions of Judge Monterone mean to his relationship with Isabella, and what would he do now without the money from his job? He also turned his gaze inward and asked himself many more personal questions such as: Why was life so hard?

Why wasn't life easy for him? Why was everything a struggle?

He had no answers other than the absolute belief that if he didn't win the competition, then his dream would be finished and any chance with Isabella would be ended.

The morning, which had started with such hope and happiness with him thinking of Isabella, had now turned to despair. Just when it seemed like everything was fine with Isabella and that he was on his way with his career, everything came crashing down, all because of her father.

Didn't her father understand true love? Didn't he understand the feelings Isabella and he had for each other?

Giovanni only got more upset as he drove to the Casa Verdi.

---

GIOVANNI WAS ASTONISHED by the reaction of Alfredo when he related to him what had happened that morning. Alfredo was thrilled to hear the news about his "firing" from the pharmacy, and he told Giovanni that more training was needed and that by no longer working at the pharmacy, they could work longer hours training for the competition.

Fighting back tears, Giovanni said, "Alfredo, with the loss of my job, the competition is my last chance. If I don't win and get a contract, I know that I can no longer pursue my dream anymore."

Alfredo remained silent.

Giovanni, unable to hold back the tears any longer, said, "I guess, deep down though, with or without my job, I knew that was the case anyway. Everything comes down to this competition. That is the only way I can ever become a singer."

Alfredo reached out his hand for Giovanni to grab, which he did. Alfredo squeezed Giovanni's hand tight and asked, "Giovanni, these tears are not just for the loss of your job, are they?"

"No, Alfredo."

"Nor for your fear of never becoming a singer?"

"No, Alfredo."

"These are the tears touched by a woman. These are the tears of a broken heart, of which only true love can produce. I myself have cried these same tears. Have faith, my friend. Some women will surprise you what they will do for love. You just need to be receptive to their actions."

"Alfredo, I am completely in love with her. How in God's name could her father have produced such a wonderful creature is beyond me."

Alfredo asked, "Her father is quite the bastard, eh?"

"Yes, and a very imposing figure when he stands over you."

"Are you upset with Signor Roberto?"

"I was, but not anymore. He was scared. I could see it in his eyes. He does not have the courage to stand up to the Judge."

Alfredo said, "My father, Antonio del Monte, would look at people and would trust only those whom he could put into one category; that category he called '*un uomo di trincea*'." (A foxhole man)

"What is that?"

"Would that person stay in a foxhole with you in the

middle of a battle, or would he run for cover. Signor Roberto would run. You, *amico*, are a foxhole man."

Giovanni looked surprised and asked, "What do you mean?"

"A few weeks ago, when you sang for me for the first time, and the residents laughed when you told them I was training you, you stood by me. You stood up to their ridicule. I will never forget that."

Giovanni felt a sense of pride run through him. Both men made their way to one of the practice rooms to begin vocalizing for the day.

They trained until three o'clock that afternoon. Alfredo told Giovanni to take a break and return at 6:30 later that night. Giovanni immediately left the *Casa Verdi* and hurried to see Isabella at her school. His heart was racing. He wanted to hold her. He needed to tell her what had happened. He wanted to share everything with her. Deep down, he wanted to make certain that all was well between the two of them.

He waited for her outside the fence by her school. She noticed him the moment she came out the building. As she approached, she spoke very fast. "Oh Giovanni, my father found out about us. He spoke with Signor Carmelito. My father knew it was you. He screamed all night long. I don't know what he is going to do."

As the two of them made the short walk to the *Porta Venezia* and the enticing gardens located there, Giovanni tried to make Isabella believe that he wasn't upset. He smiled and said, "Somehow, he found out where I work. Your father tried to have me fired from the pharmacy. I quit before Roberto had to do it."

Isabella put her hand over her mouth as she held back

tears. She repeated over and over again, how sorry she was for her father's actions. "He had no right," she told Giovanni.

Giovanni smiled reassuringly at Isabella and replied, "Don't worry. It will all work out. Alfredo is thrilled since it means I have more time to get ready for the competition."

Isabella looked down toward the ground and, through her tears, asked, "How can we continue to date? Your seeing me will only bring you misery."

Giovanni grabbed her chin and lifted her face toward his and said, "That's not true. You have brought me nothing but joy. *Sei tutta la mia vita.*" (I live for you)

Suddenly a look of fear came across her face. "If my father did that with the pharmacy, he will probably do it with Angelo's."

Giovanni grinned and said, "Don't worry. Angelo knows how much money I make for him. He won't let me go. He is not afraid of your father."

But Isabella was still upset. "What's the point? Our relationship can go nowhere. I've never wanted anyone as much as you, yet I know I can never have you. To be with you, I must hide. To continue our relationship, I know that I must give up my family. I love you, but I feel that I am lost."

"You are not lost. I love you. You love me. We have each other. Your family will respect me once I win this competition. Once respected, they will welcome me."

Isabella sat down on one of the benches alongside the *Porta Venezia*, and told Giovanni, "It won't matter to my father. He hates you and will never welcome you. To have you, I must give up my family. But I don't know if I can do that."

Giovanni tried to reassure her again, "I'm not asking you

to do that. Let's just keep going how it has been and see what happens. And hopefully, we never run into any of your father's friends again."

A faint smile broke out across her face. Giovanni rubbed the back of his hand across her cheek and smiled at her. With determination, he said, "It will work out because we are in love."

The smile went away from Isabella's face, and she said, "Sometimes love is not enough, Giovanni."

Giovanni shook his head in disagreement and said, "Sometimes, all that is left is love, and that is enough." He then quoted to Isabella the lines from an aria from the opera, *Andrea Chènier.*

*O giovinetta bella,*
*Oh beautiful young girl,*

*d'un poeta non disprezzate il detto.*
*do not scorn the words of a poet.*

*Udite! Non conoscete amor,*
*Listen! You do not know love,*

*amor, divino dono, non lo schernir,*
*love is a divine gift, don't scorn it,*

*del mondo anima e vita è l'amor!*
*the soul and life of the world is love!*

When he finished, Isabella said not a word. Giovanni

broke the silence and said, "I love you. I don't care what your father thinks. Just give us a chance."

Deep down she knew she had to end their relationship. It would never work because of her father. But she couldn't bring herself to do it. She loved Giovanni too much. Isabella cried as she put her head on Giovanni's shoulder, while they both sat on the bench in the *Porta Venezia*.

She then turned toward him and they kissed deeply.

## THE GHOSTS OF LA SCALA

*T*he last few weeks before the competition was the hardest Giovanni had worked his entire life. He didn't mind the hard work as it relieved him from continually thinking about his relationship with Isabella.

Their relationship had slowly returned to the status quo, yet Giovanni was certainly aware that Isabella was still very much conflicted between her perceived choice between Giovanni and her family. Giovanni knew Isabella would have to eventually make that decision, and there was nothing he could do to help her with it. So, Giovanni threw himself completely into his preparation for the competition. He saw Isabella off and on, but most of Giovanni's time was taken with study and practice.

Giovanni was with Alfredo, on average, 12 hours a day. Alfredo pounded into Giovanni's young head different ways to phrase a sentence or inflect a word to make it exude passion. Giovanni's voice had become like a well-oiled machine. Over time, it had become even more warm and graceful, a true *tenore lirico* with a wide range of colors in it. But, what set his voice apart from most was a touch of *spinto*, which added heft to his vocal production, which enabled his voice to have a strong, emotional drive behind it, particularly at climaxes.

Alfredo felt very confident about Giovanni's chances. Giovanni echoed Alfredo's feelings, and he too felt very confident, but his thoughts continually turned to Isabella.

On Monday, June 4th, Giovanni went to the *Casa Verdi*. Alfredo met him in the foyer and said, "My dear Giovanni, so we come to the day before the competition. I believe you are ready. Your voice is perfect. Just remember to sing with passion."

"I will," Giovanni assured him. "What are we going to practice today?"

"*Nulla*. You are ready. Today we will take a field trip."

Giovanni asked, "A field trip? Where?"

"Come, we must take the bus to La Scala," Alfredo said.

Soon the two were on the bus traveling to La Scala. Alfredo did not leave the home very often, except for doctor visits, so he enjoyed the air and sun on his face.

They finally arrived at their destination and departed the bus. Alfredo told Giovanni to take him to the left corner of La Scala and enter there.

As Giovanni approached the door, he read the sign on the door, *Museo di La Scala*. Giovanni had been to the museum often as a young child with his father. He hadn't been back since Franco's death.

As they entered the museum and paid the attendant, Alfredo told Giovanni, "I wanted you to come here today before the competition and see the faces and costumes of all the people we have listened to these past few months. You need to see why you have worked so hard."

Giovanni and Alfredo roamed the museum for hours. Alfredo related different stories about a particular singer, composer or opera. Of course, the majority of the museum was devoted to exhibits of Verdi, who was like a god to La Scala. But the museum did have exhibits from every major composer, singer and conductor. Alfredo's knowledge was unbelievable. He told Giovanni, "Opera is so full of stories, they are countless in number. And to truly fall in love with and be touched by opera, you must know these stories." He related to Giovanni, as they stood in front of a picture of Leoncavallo with the first cast of *Pagliacci*, how the composer based the story on a real-life murder trial that he had witnessed as a young child, which his father presided over as judge.

He also told Giovanni how Leoncavallo and Puccini had been great friends and how one day, Leoncavallo came across Puccini having an espresso in the *Galleria* in Milan. "Puccini asked Leoncavallo what he was working on. Leoncavallo told Puccini that he was working on an opera based on Mürger's *La Bohème*. At which point, Puccini said he was working on the same subject. Needless to say, the two composers were at war, both claiming that the other one stole the idea. Who was right is still debated today. However, Puccini summed up the battle lines this way, 'Let him compose. I will compose. The public will judge.'"

"As you know, Puccini won," Giovanni said. Alfredo laughed heartily.

During their visit, Giovanni felt better, but he continued to think of Isabella and wished she were there to share in the stories and his love of opera.

Eventually, they came before the bust of Umberto Giordano. Giovanni said, "We are in front of the composer of *Andrea Chènier*, an opera that I adore."

Alfredo broke out into a smile and said that Giordano should be his inspiration. "He had women problems just like you."

Giovanni asked, "What do you mean?"

Alfredo, still smiling, said, "It's a good story. The opera composer, Alberto Franchetti, was given a sketch of an opera, *Andrea Chènier,* by the great opera librettist, Luigi Illica. Franchetti passed the sketch on to Giordano. This would not be the only libretto Franchetti would pass on. Later, he would give up or had it taken away, depending on whom you ask, the rights to Illica's *Tosca,* which was turned over to Puccini."

Giovanni laughed out loud.

Alfredo continued, "I digress. Giordano was a very young, inexperienced, unsuccessful composer. Giordano moved to Milan to be close to Illica while he worked on *Chènier*. Giordano could only afford to live in a depressing, ground-floor storage room in a funeral parlor, filled with gravestones, candles and mortuary statutes. It was there, working in this romantic gloom, that the creative flame kindled in his heart, and the opera took shape."

Giovanni asked, "Alfredo, how does this story help me?"

Alfredo continued, "It was about this time that Giordano met and fell in love with Olga Spatz, whose very wealthy father owned the Grand Hotel in Milan. Her father would not hear of his daughter seeing such a commoner. However, after unsuccessfully trying to prevent his daughter from seeing

Giordano, he did what any nervous father would do. It so happened that Verdi was staying at the Grand Hotel. So, Signor Spatz took the completed score of *Andrea Chènier* to Verdi. Verdi went into another room where he played the entire score on the piano. Upon completion, Verdi left the room and came out to meet Signor Spatz, where he advised him to allow his daughter to marry Giordano. After the successful premiere of the opera, Giordano and Olga Spatz were married."

Giovanni was smiling by this time as well. He said, "That is what I have been trying to tell Isabella. Her father will accept me once I have a career, like Giordano. Thank you for that story."

Alfredo said, "It's a good story."

As they continued their tour of the museum, a sense of peace and resolve came upon Giovanni. Alfredo's story of Giordano confirmed what Giovanni always knew, and that was that he had to win the competition. And in so doing, his voice would be the key to winning the heart of Isabella.

Finally, Alfredo and Giovanni found themselves on the third floor of the museum. A red curtain was in one corner. Alfredo and Giovanni made their way to the curtain.

As Giovanni pushed through the curtain, he found himself in an opera box, staring into the empty La Scala opera house. Alfredo was standing right next to him.

The interior was just as Giovanni had remembered it. It had that typical theater smell, a wonderful smell. With the auditorium being empty, the theater had a spooky feel to it. There was a single lamplight on the stage, an old theater trick to scare the ghosts away. The problem at La Scala is that the ghosts are old singers who, during their life, were always in front of the footlights; thus, they were not afraid of the light. The deep red velvet draperies in the boxes were exactly how Giovanni remembered them.

Alfredo spoke almost in a whisper. "*Udite. Ascolta.* Listen. Pertile, Lauri-Volpi, Caruso, Gigli, de Lucia, del Monaco, Bjorling. Their voices still resound off the walls. They still reside here. Every breeze that blows through this old building carries them on. My young friend, I have done my best. Your voice is magnificent. All the singers I mentioned, at one point in their career, had to stand up and sing formally for the first time. Tomorrow is your day. Have no fear. Let your voice do your work for you. Thank you for giving me the opportunity to teach you."

Giovanni grabbed Alfredo by the shoulder and said, "I should thank you. Without you, I would never have this chance. You have given me confidence. I will admit that at first, I thought your teaching style was a little unorthodox - by just listening to singers - but now I understand what you were trying to do. To sing and sing well, you must learn from those who came before you since they were the closest to the composer. Unlike most other types of music, we opera singers perform the works of composers who are long gone. Therefore, we must rely on history to teach."

Alfredo smiled broadly and said, "You have learned well, my young friend. Listening and learning from the singers of the past is a lost art. I had no idea the treasure you held inside your throat until you sang for me. I should have let you sing earlier. But, I just had no idea. Come, it's been a long day. You should just relax the rest of the day and try not to think about tomorrow."

As they turned to leave the box through the curtain,

Giovanni turned one more time to the interior of the old house and said two simple words to himself, to his father and to the ghosts. But these words summed up for him his entire life's dream. "*Un giorno.*" (One day.)

———

WHEN GIOVANNI LEFT Alfredo later that same day, he went to see Isabella. Giovanni met her at their coffee shop. As he entered, she was sitting at a table, studying. "*Buona sera,* Isabella," he said as he approached her table.

Tears immediately poured from her eyes.

"What's wrong, Isabella?"

"I've thought about it and thought about it. I don't know what to do. I love you so much, but I don't know if I can keep seeing you although you are all I think about. I wish my mother were still alive. I would speak to her."

"What are you saying, Isabella? Your thoughts are all over the place."

"Forgive me, Giovanni. I can't do it anymore. I can't see you. I won't see you."

"Isabella!"

"I think my father still knows I am seeing you. Not that he said anything in particular. I can just tell. I am so afraid that he will try to do something to you. He will never understand our feelings for each other."

Giovanni responded with great emotion and said, "We know how we feel. He cannot take that away from us, Isabella. You have given me a reason to dream – to hope - to know that my future holds a great possibility. Your love was all that I needed. It has lifted me."

She looked down at the table and said, "But what future do we have?"

"We will have each other. That is all that matters. Your father can either agree or not agree, but it is not his decision to make," he said.

"I do agree, Giovanni, that it is not his decision. It is mine. And I know what my decision should be, but it breaks my heart."

Giovanni reached into his pocket and pulled out a ticket. He said, "This is a ticket to the competition at the *Teatro Lirico.* I want you to come. I need you to come."

Isabella said, "I cannot. It's over."

Giovanni forced open her hand and put the ticket in her hand, "*Vieni, amore, vieni.* I will look up in the box tomorrow and look for Alfredo. If you are sitting next to him, then I'll know you want to be with me. If you're not there, I will know what decision you have made. But remember, I am committed to you."

Isabella closed her hand around the ticket.

As he kissed her, he told her again, "*Vieni, amore.*"

She buried her head in her hands and cried even harder. Giovanni placed his hand on the back of her head and gently stroked her hair. All the while, he fought back his own tears, trying to show her that in his own mind, he had no doubt that she would be at the competition tomorrow when in reality he had no idea.

She picked her head up from the table, and with her eyes extremely red from crying, told Giovanni she had to leave. She then rose from the table, and Giovanni walked Isabella to her car. As she got in, she looked deep into his eyes and said,

"I am so sorry for doing all of this to you, particularly before you sing tomorrow. I do wish you good luck tomorrow."

"No. Never wish a singer luck. Say '*In bocca al lupo*' (In the mouth of the wolf)."

Isabella asked, "Why '*In bocca al lupo*'?"

"If you plan on a disaster, perhaps good fortune will result."

She smiled through her tears and told him, "*In bocca al lupo.*"

He responded, "*Crepi il lupo.*" (Kill the wolf.) He then leaned into the car and just said, "Please come."

She didn't say a word and drove away.

As she did so, Giovanni could not restrain his feelings anymore, and tears burst forth. He mumbled to himself, "*Ti amo*, Isabella."

He hoped, with all of his heart, that she would be there tomorrow.

# 21

# THE COMPETITION

*T*uesday, June 5$^{th}$, finally arrived. Giovanni hadn't slept a wink the night before the competition because he was a bundle of nerves. He spent the morning reviewing the arias he had selected to sing. Alfredo had instructed him not to sing the arias in the hope of saving his voice for the competition.

At noon, he went to Babeto's to pick up his outfit for the competition. His mother had picked out the best of cheaper, rentable tails to give to her son to wear for the competition. However, when Giovanni arrived at the store, Giorgio Babeto, still very handsome at sixty-five, inquired what he was doing there. After Giovanni told him, Giorgio produced a beautiful set of tails that had been designed personally by him. Giorgio said, "*Il piccolo Tempesta*, your mamma sewed these very tails last year. It would be an honor for me if you would wear them to the competition. I remember how much your father loved opera."

Giovanni thanked his mother's boss. Giorgio waived the rental fee, for which Giovanni was very pleased. Before Giovanni left, Anna made Giovanni try on his tails, and she did some quick hemming. As she sewed, she told Giovanni, "I wish I could be there tonight. But you know Giorgio's fashion show is in two days. We are so far behind."

"Mamma, I understand. I will tell you all about the competition when I get home. Thank you for the tails. They are special."

He hugged Anna tightly and then left for home, where he waited until it was time to leave for the theater.

Meanwhile, Alfredo had a female friend, who was visiting from out of town, pick him up from the Casa Verdi, and bring him to the theater. When Giovanni arrived, he found Alfredo standing alone by the entrance to the *Teatro Lirico* at 5:30 p.m., a full hour and a half before the start of the competition.

Giovanni walked up and said, "Alfredo, I am here."

"Right on time. I would expect nothing less. Let's go check-in."

Giovanni grabbed Alfredo's arm and led him into the theater by way of the stage door. They were soon backstage. Giovanni walked up to a table set up in the back and checked in with a young woman who looked over the list and found Giovanni's name. Giovanni then led Alfredo away from the table. Alfredo asked him, "Are you nervous?"

"*Si. Tanto*," was Giovanni's curt response.

"Lead me to the stage, Giovanni."

Giovanni led him to the now empty stage. As they walked onto the stage, Giovanni was taken aback at the view. It was stunning. The theater was very old and beautiful. It looked like a provincial Italian theater, which are so numerous across

Italy. Box seats were located on the sides of the theater overlooking the stage. There was hardly anyone seated yet.

Alfredo said, "Get comfortable out here. This is where you will be judged. Do you see a lady sitting in a box seat by herself?"

Giovanni scanned the theater and then said, "Yes, I see her, Alfredo."

"That is the lady, a close friend of mine, who brought me here tonight. I will be sitting with her during the competition. I will introduce her to you later. Stand out here and just get a feel for the atmosphere."

Alfredo took a few steps backward, allowing Giovanni to stand by himself, taking in the view of the theater from the stage.

Looking around made him quickly realize how large the theater was. At the same time, a feeling of fear washed over him. He immediately began to think that he had only sung in public at Angelo's. He had never sung on a stage in front of a packed theater. How could he sing in such a large place?

As he looked around, Giovanni saw, in the box seat where Alfredo would be sitting, the lady Alfredo had mentioned. She was an elderly lady with a bright orange hat on her head. She would be easy to spot. Alfredo would be seated to her right, and to Alfredo's right would be Isabella, that is if she came. He hoped she would.

Alfredo interrupted Giovanni's thoughts when he called out, "Giovanni."

"I'm here," he responded as he walked back toward the place Alfredo was standing.

"I know you are nervous. I know you doubt yourself, as you look out across this theater. There is no denying the fact that the seats will be filled. The auditorium will be alight with excitement as each new singer takes the stage. But, when it is your time to sing, sing as if you are just singing to one individual, me. Pretend you are back at the *Casa Verdi*. Let your voice go. It is a beautiful instrument that does not matter where it is released. It is a voice meant for the stage. Now, let's go get ready."

More people were now milling around the backstage of the theater. As Giovanni walked with Alfredo, he heard some of the competitors warming up. They sounded very good. Backstage was quickly becoming filled with singers, coaches and friends.

Alfredo said, "Giovanni, don't be intimidated by the other competitors. Some may seem like they are not nervous. That's because a majority of them have spent their entire careers singing in these competitions. Year after year they try but never win. Today is your first time in a competition. It's expected that you are nervous. Just do your best."

Each competitor was given a small room where they could vocalize. Alfredo and Giovanni made their way to the small room assigned them. As they turned a corner, they ran right into the great tenor, Giuseppe di Stefano. Giovanni was spellbound as he stood in front of his favorite tenor.

Di Stefano had had a major singing career. He was the frequent partner of Maria Callas and the darling of La Scala. His voice was probably the most naturally beautiful of all the tenors, but his career ended early due to respiratory problems that he fought his entire career. Rudolph Bing, during his observation year before becoming General Manager of the Met, always said that the most glorious sound he ever heard in his life from the throat of a singer was di Stefano's high C in the *Faust* aria. All in one breath, di Stefano swelled the note and then diminished it to a sweet whisper.

Di Stefano was now 58 years old and retired, but looked great in his all-white suit. For many years he sponsored this competition. Di Stefano had a huge smile on his face as he hugged his old friend, Alfredo. They spoke a few brief seconds. Di Stefano then turned to Giovanni and thanked him for coming to sing at his competition and said he looked forward to hearing him sing. Giovanni had met one of his childhood idols. His father would be so proud.

Giovanni made his way to his small room, and for the next thirty minutes, he vocalized. His voice sounded great, and he was content with the sound he was producing. At 6:45 p.m., a whistle sounded, which signaled that all teachers must leave the area and the competition would begin.

Giovanni walked out of the small room with Alfredo and found someone who worked at the theater to help Alfredo to his seat. Alfredo grabbed Giovanni by the hand and said, "I'm so proud of you. You are ready. Sing as I know you can. Don't be nervous. *In bocca al lupo*."

"*Crepi il lupo*," Giovanni responded. It was after Alfredo left him that Giovanni really felt the nerves build up in his stomach. He tried to calm himself.

Suddenly, the person in charge called all the singers into the area directly off stage. Giovanni could hear the voices of a large crowd gathering out in the auditorium. All the singers circled around the man speaking.

The man told them, "My name is Antonio Fiorelli. I am Giuseppe di Stefano's personal secretary. I am in charge here. We have 25 contestants. In five minutes, the judges will call for the first singer. The judges will choose the order of the contestants and will also choose the aria for you to sing. The pianist will give you one minute to compose yourself before starting the aria. Once completed, bow and leave the stage unless the judges want to ask you a question or make a comment."

Giovanni looked at the other contestants. It was a mix of women and men. Most were younger than he was. Once again, a feeling of doubt came into his mind.

Signor Fiorelli wished everyone luck, and then he left for the stage. The footlights came on, and Giovanni rushed to get a view of the auditorium from the wings. He had a perfect view of the stage and the seats in the theater, which were packed. Giuseppe di Stefano was sitting in the front row. Signor Fiorelli walked to the front of the stage and said, "Ladies and gentlemen, thank you very much for attending the Giuseppe di Stefano Voice Competition. First, let me introduce you to the great tenor, Giuseppe di Stefano." The crowd rose in a thunderous applause. Signor Fiorelli continued, "We have 25 contestants tonight. Each contestant will come out, and the judges will pick which aria they want to hear. It is now time to meet our distinguished judges.

"First, direct from La Scala, we have its musical director, Maestro Massimo Torcelli." Giovanni strained his neck to see him. Giovanni knew of Maestro Torcelli. He recollected that Maestro Torcelli's nickname was *"no do"* since he opposed interpolated high C's when he conducted and demanded a strict following of the composer's score.

Signor Fiorelli continued, "Next, we have the great Italian soprano, Christiana Flagello." The crowd roared when her name was mentioned. She was around 70 years of age and was now retired after a remarkable career.

"And lastly, we have that great conductor and teacher, Maestro Federico Toscano."

Giovanni felt his heart sink. He recognized the white hair immediately and remembered how Toscano told him he could never be a singer. He watched Signor Toscano make his way to his seat. Maybe he wouldn't remember Giovanni. As Toscano sat down, Giovanni lost all hope. Signor Toscano sat down in front of Judge Pietro Monterone, who Giovanni would later learn was one of the sponsors of the competition. Giovanni hurriedly looked around the auditorium to find Alfredo and to see if Isabella was there. Neither was in their seats yet, only the woman in the orange hat.

Signor Fiorelli returned to the backstage area and yelled for all the singers to return to their practice rooms until their name was called. As Giovanni walked back to his room, he heard a voice blaze out from the auditorium, *"Soprano, Luisa Tettra, vieni."*

As Giovanni sat in his practice room, he thought to himself that all was lost. He had no hope in winning the competition with Judge Monterone and Maestro Toscano involved. He could hear the soprano singing 'Mi chiamano Mimi' from Puccini's *La Bohème*. When she finished, Giovanni heard polite applause. Then he heard Signora Flagello ask, "Signorina Tettra, do you pay the person who is training you?"

Giovanni closed his door. He was a nervous wreck. He did hear the poor girl come running pass his door in tears when she left the stage.

After about 6 more contestants, Giovanni heard a knock on the door next to his and the words, *"Baritono, Riccardo Zanito, vieni."*

Giovanni sat and sat in his room, as contestant after contestant was called to sing. He felt ill. Finally, after more than two hours, what seemed like an eternity to Giovanni, the 25th and final contestant was called, *"Tenore, Giovanni Tempesta, vieni."*

Giovanni knelt in his practice room and said a quick prayer to his father, saying he would do his best. As he left the room, he could feel that his tails were soaking wet with nervous perspiration.

When he walked on stage, he saw the piano with a young, very attractive woman sitting behind it. He nodded to her and then turned to the audience. He realized at once why Alfredo had made him come to the theater early and go on the stage. The theater was filled with people. The atmosphere was charged like a soccer game. Italians love these voice competitions. Giovanni tried to picture himself on the stage when the house was empty to help calm his nerves. Out of the corner of his eye, he finally noticed Alfredo, sitting on the edge of his seat in his box. To Alfredo's left was the very attractive elderly lady with the orange hat. The seat to Alfredo's right was empty. Isabella had not come. She had made her decision. Their relationship was over.

He looked at the judges and noticed Judge Monterone leaning over, whispering to Toscano. Maestro Torcelli bellowed out, "Signor Tempesta, sing 'Vesti la giubba' from *Pagliacci* by Leoncavallo."

This was the very aria that Alfredo had picked out for him to sing. *Pagliacci* is an opera about a traveling group of clowns. The lead player's wife is having an affair. The aria Giovanni was asked to sing takes place in the opera right before the clown, Canio, goes on stage to perform the play, even though he has just discovered his wife was unfaithful. He sings about having to perform even though his heart is broken over his lost love. Giovanni knew how Canio felt.

Giovanni walked back toward the piano. The young lady sitting at the piano scrambled through some music books, and then told Giovanni she was ready. He picked his head up and stared at Alfredo. He thought about Isabella. His heart was broken. And on top of that, he was a nervous wreck. His train of thought was broken by the young lady who whispered, "Time, *andiamo*."

Giovanni gave a shake of his head, and the music began. Giovanni was a beat late in starting. But, he quickly found the timing.

*Recitar! Mentre preso dal delirio,*
*To act! While I am delirious,*

*non so più quel che dico e quel che faccio!*
*I don't know what I'm saying or doing!*

*Eppure é d'uopo sforzati!*
*Still, I have to try!*

*Bah, sei tu forse un uom?*
*Bah, are you a man?*

*Tu sé Pagliaccio!*
*You're a clown!*

Giovanni got through the first part of the aria in a strong voice. As he waited for the aria proper to start, he glanced at

Alfredo and again noticed the empty seat. Tears welled up in his eyes.

*Vesti la giubba*
*Put on your costume*

*e la faccia in farina.*
*and whiten your face.*

*La gente paga, e rider vuole qua.*
*The public has paid, and wants to laugh.*

*E se Arlecchin t'invola Colombina,*
*And when Harlequin steals Columbine,*

*ridi, Pagliaccio, e ognun applaudirá!*
*laugh, clown, and everyone will applaud!*

*Tramuta in lazzi lo spasmo ed il pianto;*
*I must change my tears and sorrow into jokes;*

*in una smorfia il singhiozzo il dolor! Ah!!!*
*change my crying into a laugh! Ah!!!*

Giovanni held the note on the word "Ah" for a long time, then brought it upward, with high emotion, just as the tenor Giovanni Martinelli had done on the old Met recording that Giovanni had studied with Alfredo. He stepped forward toward the front of the stage, outstretched his hands to the empty seat next to Alfredo, and with tears streaming down his face, finished the most famous part of the aria:

*Ridi, Pagliaccio, sul tuo amore infranto.*
*Laugh, clown, laugh at the despair.*

*ridi del duol, che t'avvelena il cor!*
*Laugh at the grief, that is poisoning your heart!*

As Giovanni sang the last word, he buried his head into his hands. He thought about Isabella. He loved her, but she had made her decision.

There was complete silence for a few seconds. Then the entire crowd cheered in what was without a doubt the greatest ovation of the night. Some of the crowd in the upper tiers rose to their feet. Slowly, Giovanni removed his hands from his face. His eyes were red with tears. He looked toward Alfredo and noticed both Alfredo and the woman with the orange hat, standing, cheering him. Giovanni bowed toward the crowd. He then motioned to the pianist to accept the applause. Tears were in her eyes. To Giovanni, she mouthed the words, "You won."

The crowd was still cheering so loud that Giovanni didn't hear the question from Signor Toscano. When the crowd finally settled down, Signor Toscano asked again, "Signor Tempesta, how old are you?"

Giovanni tried to compose himself and put Isabella out of his mind. He stepped forward and said, "I'm 25."

"Whom do you study with?"

Giovanni said, "I study with the retired tenor, Alfredo del Monte."

"Who?" was Toscano's reply.

Giovanni repeated himself.

Signor Toscano pressed further, "Have you ever studied in a music school?"

"No," Giovanni responded.

"Have you ever sung on stage before?"

"No."

With that, Toscano waved his hand as if to shoo Giovanni off of the stage. As he turned to leave the stage, a few members of the audience cheered him off. Giovanni saw Toscano lean backward and speak to Judge Monterone.

Once backstage, all the singers from the competition were circled around Signor Fiorelli, who told them that the judges would now make their decision and that they would be back shortly. Giovanni patted one singer on his back and told him how well he thought he had sung. He got no response.

Giovanni sat backstage alone. Not one competitor said a word to him. Giovanni thought he had sung well. Based on his listening to the other contestants, he thought he had a good chance of winning, even with Toscano as a judge. He had to win, he told himself. As he awaited the decision, he kept thinking that if he lost, his dream would be finished.

Finally, the judges were back. All twenty-five contestants went on stage. The crowd greeted them with applause. The first to speak was di Stefano, who graciously stated that all the singers were winners tonight. He then produced a card that was handed to him by the judges. The card had the name of one contestant - the one person whom the judges hailed as the best of the night. Di Stefano opened the card and read the name to himself first. He then announced the winner. "The winner of the Giuseppe di Stefano voice competition for 1979 is tenor . . ." Giovanni felt his chest tighten. Alfredo gripped the bar in front of his chair . . . "Alessandro Bachi."

Alfredo fell back into his seat. Giovanni's shoulders slumped as he stared aimlessly out into the crowd. He caught the eye of Judge Pietro Monterone, who looked right at him and mouthed the words, "Café singer."

The rage inside of Giovanni was about to burst. As Signor Bachi went to get his trophy, a few members of the audience were booing and saying the name Tempesta over and over again. Giovanni realized what they were saying as he left the stage. All Giovanni wanted to do was leave and go home. The night, which had begun with such promise, now ended with his dream finished and his relationship over. As he made his way backstage, families and friends of the singers had made their way to the stage door. As Giovanni made his way through the crowd and the other singers who were being congratulated by friends and family, a few people patted Giovanni on the back and told him how wonderful he sounded.

Giovanni finally got through the crowd by the stage door and found Alfredo speaking with the woman in the orange hat. Alfredo told Giovanni how proud he was and how great he sounded. Alfredo could tell Giovanni was very upset. Alfredo said, "You won tonight, *amico*. Trust me. Giovanni, I want you to meet a good friend of mine, Signora Renata Prandelli."

The elderly woman in the orange hat extended her hand and congratulated Giovanni. He was too upset to even have a conversation with her. He quickly said *addio*, patted Alfredo on the back, excused himself and left, broken-hearted, both over the ending of his dream and his love. Alfredo tried to stop him but couldn't.

As Giovanni left quickly from the theater, he ran into

Maestro Massimo Torcelli, the director of La Scala and one of the judges of the competition. Torcelli said, "Young man, you got my vote. Keep working. Your voice is one of a kind. The other judges put too much credence in their belief that without having been trained in school or with a prominent teacher, you will not succeed. They were wrong. With a voice like yours, you could be successful. Keep working at it."

Giovanni thanked Signor Torcelli, turned, and left for home, shaking his head as he left. That comment was now too late, he thought. It was all over now. Tempesta's dream was finished.

# 22

## RENATA PRANDELLI

*G*iovanni went straight to his house after the competition. All of his hard work resulted in nothing. What was the point of pursuing a singing career any further? As he entered his house, his mother was sitting in the front room. The moment he walked in, Anna stood up and said, "I just got home from work. Did you make papa proud tonight?" Before she finished her thought, she noticed the tears in her son's eyes. He came over to her and fell into her arms.

"I lost," he cried. "I thought I should have won. But I didn't. I will never be a singer. I let papa and you down."

"Don't talk like that, Giovanni. We are all so proud of you, including your papa." She held him tight, but there was no consoling him.

Eventually, he made his way to his room. He opened the door and looked at all of the opera posters on the walls. He could do nothing more than shake his head. He got undressed, throwing his tails in a lump on the floor and went to sleep without even putting an opera recording on. His thoughts turned to Isabella as he drifted off to sleep. If she had been there, his losing would have been easier to take.

Giovanni must have been very tired, because very soon after he had gone to sleep, he didn't hear the commotion going on in the front room of his home. However, he did wake up when his mother opened the door to his room and said that he had to come down to the living room because some people were there to see him. That was all she would say. He dragged himself out of bed, put a robe on, and went downstairs to the living room. As he made his way to the front room, he remembered that the last time there was a commotion like that in the middle of the night, he was told that his father had died.

When he walked into the living room, he saw, sitting on the sofa, Alfredo del Monte and Isabella Monterone. Isabella sprang up from the sofa and ran to the arms of Giovanni. "*Ti amo, Giovanni. Vedi*! I came," she said as she enveloped him in an embrace. Anna shook her head while the two were hugging.

Giovanni was thoroughly confused. He was about to say something but kept quiet because Alfredo had risen from the sofa and was about to speak. Isabella stayed in his arms. Anna was standing right next to Alfredo; she too looked very confused. Alfredo spoke very firmly and said, "Giovanni Tempesta, you are a tenor. You have won."

Giovanni said, "You were there. You know that's not true."

Alfredo continued, "You were in such a hurry to leave after the competition, you didn't even speak with me. If you had, then you would understand. So, I wanted to come see you and thought you would be home. My companion tonight, Signora Prandelli, was going to bring me here, but a very attractive woman found me as I was getting into the car and introduced herself as Isabella. She guessed correctly that the old blind man at the competition was the one who had trained her love."

Giovanni smiled at Isabella.

Alfredo said, "She told me that her father had caught her entering the theater and sent her home. But she did not go home. She listened to the competition from the back of the house, standing behind a throng of people."

Isabella said, "You sang like a god. Everyone around me said you were the best."

Giovanni whispered excitedly back to her, "You did come. You did."

She smiled back at him.

Alfredo continued and said, "After the competition, she couldn't find you and was afraid to see you because of her father. I told her you ran off before I could speak with you. So, she brought me here."

Giovanni said, "Signor Alfredo, I know you mean well when you say I won, but what counts is the actual winner of the competition, and that was not me."

Alfredo chuckled and asked, "When I said you would win, what did I say I meant by that?"

Giovanni said, "The winner of the competition would get a contract to sing in Naples."

"Wrong," Alfredo said emphatically. "I said you would get a contract to sing opera. I didn't say you would sing in Naples. You are correct that the winner of the competition got a contract to sing in Naples. You, my young friend, you are a winner because you have a contract."

Giovanni looked bewildered and asked Alfredo, "What do you mean?"

"If you would have stayed and talked with me, you would have found out for yourself. The lady I was with . . ."

Giovanni jumped in and asked, "The lady in the orange hat?"

"The same," Alfredo said. "As I told you, her name is Renata Prandelli. She is the wife of the late, great conductor, Gennaro Prandelli."

Giovanni again jumped in and said, "He was the conductor for *Turandot* at La Scala when it was bombed, injuring you." Giovanni spoke so fast that he didn't realize what he said until it was too late.

Alfredo thought for a second and said, "Lydia told you. That girl. Well, yes, he was. Maestro Prandelli moved to America in the '60s and conducted all over the United States, including at the Met. He became General Director of the New Orleans Opera and a music teacher at a local university, Loyola, in New Orleans.

After he passed away, his wife became head of the board of directors of the New Orleans Opera. This July, the New Orleans Opera has a special performance of Puccini's *La Bohème*. Renata and I have remained very close friends all these years. I knew Renata was in town and was also looking for a young tenor to sing the lead since the tenor under contract had pulled out. I invited her to the competition and told her all about you. After she heard you sing, and received a rave review from di Stefano with regard to your voice, she gave me this."

Alfredo reached into his pocket and pulled out some papers. He handed them to Giovanni. Giovanni looked at the top of the first page. It read:

### New Orleans Opera Association
### Contract For Professional Services

The contract ran for about five pages with all sorts of legal language. Giovanni was speechless. He had a contract to sing opera.

Alfredo said, "The contract calls for a week of rehearsal in New Orleans and two performances of the opera, on July 11th and 14th. The pay is $3,000 per performance. All travel expenses paid by the opera. Signor Giovanni Tempesta will be making his operatic debut."

Giovanni's eyes grew wide. Isabella kissed him. Tears were streaming down Anna's face. Alfredo continued, "And since I am your teacher, I will take the voice teacher's prerogative, which is, I will offer you some financial support while you train for your debut."

Giovanni said he couldn't accept it.

But Alfredo said, "Giovanni, voice teachers sometimes offer support for their most cherished and talented pupils. You fit that category. I will not take no for an answer. That way, your quitting the pharmacy will be an easier burden for you to bear as you prepare."

Isabella leaned over to Giovanni and said, "Take it."

Giovanni went up to Alfredo and hugged him. Anna was crying.

Alfredo continued, "We don't have much time to prepare. You will be ready to sing."

Anna came over and hugged Alfredo too, and thanked him for all he had done for her son. She then went into the kitchen and returned with wine glasses and a bottle of Chianti Ruffino. The Tempesta home only had wine, never champagne. That was Franco's rule when he was alive. When the wine was poured, Alfredo led the room in a toast to Giovanni Tempesta, Tenor.

Little Gabriella was awakened by the loud clapping from the front room, and upon entering the room, climbed into her mother's lap. She asked what all the commotion was about.

"Your brother is going to sing in the opera," Anna told her.

Gabriella looked at Giovanni with her sleepy eyes and said, "I sure hope that means you won't have to sing around the house anymore." The room erupted in laughter.

The group sat in the front room and just relished in the good fortune for Giovanni. Alfredo looked like a proud father on the day his son has a huge success. Anna cried intermittently, so happy for her son. But she was certain that Isabella was not the girl for him.

After the wine was drained, Giovanni and Isabella took Alfredo back to the *Casa Verdi*. After dropping off Alfredo, Isabella and Giovanni spent a little while together. Giovanni was so happy that she had come to the competition, which meant that she had decided that she wanted to have a life with Giovanni.

Giovanni dared not tell her how her father had been speaking to Signor Toscano, which no doubt caused Giovanni to lose the competition. That didn't matter now. He had his contract.

As he drifted off to sleep later that night, the image and

words of Signor Torcelli rang in his head, "Your voice is one of a kind." And that comment was made by the head of La Scala. The dream was alive and well.

---

LITTLE DID Giovanni know the entire truth of what had transpired that night. It was true that Isabella hid in the back of the theater during the competition. After the performance, she tried to see Giovanni but was afraid of running into her father.

As she left, she noticed a blind man being led to a car by a lady in an orange hat. She approached the blind man and asked, "Signor Alfredo del Monte?"

The blind man stopped, slowly turned around, and said, "*La donna*. I am Alfredo, Signorina Isabella Monterone."

His use of her name surprised Isabella. She asked, "How did you know who I am?"

Alfredo chuckled and said, "Just a guess. And the perfume you have on, Giovanni often smells of it."

They both laughed at that comment. She asked Alfredo if he had seen Giovanni.

Alfredo told her, "I believe he went home. He was very upset about losing." As she turned to leave, Alfredo said, "If you are going to him, I would like to come. I need to speak to him."

Isabella said, "*Si*. You can come with me."

After telling Signora Prandelli that he would be going with Isabella, he was led to her car and started the trip to the Tempesta home.

While they drove, Alfredo told Isabella about the news he

had concerning New Orleans and Giovanni's debut. Isabella was very excited to hear that, and she said, "Alfredo, he will be thrilled to hear he has a contract. His voice is wonderful."

Alfredo said, "I can't wait to see his reaction. After all, he sang so well tonight."

Isabella related to Alfredo how she had stood in the back of the theater to watch the competition and how everyone around her had loved Giovanni's voice.

Alfredo said, "Giovanni possesses a voice that God demands he uses in such a way that when people hear it, they know God does indeed exist. It is a voice of pure beauty. But, he still needs to perfect it. Giovanni needs to train this whole month to get ready for his debut."

"I know my father was the reason he lost his job at the pharmacy. When my mother died, she left me some money to help me later in life. I want Giovanni to have it. But, you know as well as I, he will not accept it from me. If you offer it to him as a teacher, he may take it."

Alfredo said, "You are everything he described to me. I wish I could support him, but I'm a poor, retired, handicapped, singer. If you really want me to do this, I will do what you ask."

She smiled and said, "Giovanni means everything to me. I do want you to do this, but you must promise me that you will never let him know the money was from me."

Alfredo replied, "*Si,*" as they pulled in front of the Tempesta home at *Via Umiltá 9*.

# 23

# THE PREPARATION

When Giovanni awoke the next day, he had a hop to his step. He was now a singer who would be making his operatic debut. As he dressed, he was so happy that the opera he would be making his debut in was Puccini's *La Bohème*. He knew virtually the whole opera by heart since it was one of his favorites.

He arrived at the *Casa Verdi* and was greeted by Lydia, who offered her warmest congratulations. Alfredo had told her about Giovanni's good fortune first thing that morning.

Alfredo was in one of the practice rooms awaiting his arrival. He greeted Giovanni warmly and told him how proud he was of his performance yesterday. Alfredo said, "Your voice was perfect. Now we must prepare for your debut. I have something here for you."

He reached into a bag and pulled out three items. The first was the libretto for *La Bohème*. "Use this libretto to study and memorize the words."

The second item was the 1946 recording of *La Bohème* with Licia Albanese and Jan Peerce conducted by Toscanini. Alfredo said, "Listen to this recording whenever you are not with me. Toscanini, in 1896, conducted the premiere of *La Bohème* in Turin. Thus, his knowledge of the opera is invaluable. He studied the opera closely with Puccini. Toscanini loved this opera, and it's his voice you hear humming along in the first and fourth act of the recording."

Lastly, Alfredo pulled out an old, tattered book, which he handed over to Giovanni. Giovanni read the title, *Scenes de la vie de Bohème* by Henry Mürger. This was the episodic novel upon which Puccini and his librettists, Luigi Illica and Giuseppe Giacosa, based the opera. Alfredo said, "To fully understand the character you will be portraying, it is essential to read the inspiration for the opera. This book was given to me by Antonino Votto, who was the conductor the first time I sang *La Bohème*. He had received this book from Toscanini. I now want you to have it."

Giovanni didn't know what to say. He could never repay Alfredo for all that he had done. Alfredo told him, "Come, let's listen to Toscanini conduct the aria 'Che gelida manina' from the first act. We will discuss the opera. Then, you will sing it for me."

Also called the "narration aria", the aria is sung by the character Rodolfo to his new love, Mimi. Rodolfo has just met Mimi in his apartment garret in Paris, which he shares with three other friends. In the aria, he introduces himself to Mimi and tells her his hopes and dreams. Giovanni and Alfredo listened as Peerce's voice soared.

After listening to the recording, Alfredo told Giovanni, "When singing *La Bohème*, one must never forget the genesis of the opera. It is true Puccini based the opera on the novel by Mürger. However, he also based it on his own Bohemian life when he lived in Milan as a poor student with a fellow composer, Pietro Mascagni.

"Through the use of your voice, the singer must emphasize all of the emotions of the character. Rodolfo is young, attractive, poor, happy and yet also melancholy at the same time. He completely falls for Mimi. The joy of falling in love must be expressed in the aria. Not to mention that the final high C is probably one of the most famous in opera. Miss it, and the public will never forgive you. That is why most tenors transpose the aria down a key. But to sing the aria as Puccini wrote it, and to hit and hold the final note, creates a sensation when done well.

"The tenor must establish the wonderment of love upon it first entering the heart of Rodolfo. Think of when you first met Isabella when you sing it. Bring your own feelings into the role. You must sing it with emotion so that at the end of the opera, when Mimi returns to die in your arms, the audience will feel Rodolfo's agony and despair. Now, you will sing it for me. Never forget, although I know I don't have to tell you this, melody was the master of Puccini. The man peed melody."

Giovanni laughed out loud as he said, "Alfredo, you don't have to tell me that. On top of the melody, you have the passionate music, the romance, the tragedy, all in a simple love story. Unlike Wagner, Puccini didn't strive to achieve this great huge piece of musical truth. He wrote for the story. He wrote for romance, passion and tears."

Giovanni spoke very excitedly as he related to Alfredo the story of what happened when Puccini finished writing *La*

*Bohème.* "Puccini worked on *La Bohème* for three years. At midnight on December 10, 1895, Puccini finished the opera at his house in his beloved *Torre del Lago*. The moment he completed it, Puccini stood up from the piano and burst into tears. The death of Mimi in the opera was like experiencing the death of his own child."

Alfredo said, "You do know your Puccini, Giovanni. Now sing." Alfredo turned and started playing the aria on the piano.

"Remarkable," was all Alfredo could say when Giovanni finished. He turned around on the piano stool and told Giovanni, "New Orleans will hear a first-class tenor. Your voice is getting better and better. But we still have a lot of practice."

---

GIOVANNI THOUGHT he had worked hard, getting prepared for the competition. It was nothing compared to how hard Alfredo worked him the weeks prior to his debut. For weeks, Giovanni practiced the opera over and over again, all the while perfecting his technique.

Alfredo even had a female resident at the *Casa Verdi*, Giuditta Cantu, a retired soprano who was 78 years old, sing some of the duets from the opera with Giovanni. Signora Cantu was one of the few residents close to Alfredo. Giovanni got to know her very well. She called Giovanni, "*Il piccolo tenore*". Giovanni would laugh at the stories she told of singers she sang with and other opera related stories. She was an expert on what singer slept with what singer, composer or conductor. Added to the way these stories were told was the fact that Signora Giuditta had a touch of dementia. Thus, the comments sometimes had Giovanni and Alfredo in stitches.

Giovanni was surprised at how well Giuditta still sang. Of course, her dementia meant that sometimes she would sing the wrong words in the duet, but it didn't matter. It gave Giovanni the opportunity to practice singing duets. It helped him to get his timing down.

Signora Cantu was a minor singer in the '40s, although she did sing some performances at some of the major opera houses, but not La Scala. She specialized in the Bellini roles. She would tell Giovanni, "I know you are a tenor. But I'm old. So, I can't sleep with you. I know from first-hand knowledge how you tenors are with the ladies." Giovanni would laugh and tell her he would try to restrain himself.

As the weeks of practice progressed, Giovanni still found time for Isabella. Since the night of the competition, their love had blossomed. When Isabella graduated from high school, the only gift she wanted from Giovanni for graduation was a return trip back to their secret garden at Vicopelago. Giovanni willingly obliged, and, in mid-June they made the trip.

The old abandoned convent looked different on that trip. With the arrival of summer, flowers, irises mostly, had sprung up all around the courtyard. Isabella was still enchanted by the spot. Giovanni and Isabella enjoyed a nice early dinner and enjoyed the company of each other. The view as the sunset was spectacular.

That evening, as the moon hung over the Tuscan hills in the distance, Isabella and Giovanni laid in a quiet embrace in the middle of the courtyard under a blanket of stars.

That trip to Vicopelago could not have come at a better time for Isabella. She was in a constant battle with her father about where she should go to school and what she should study. Her father wanted her to go to Bologna to study pre-law. She wanted to stay in Milan and study education. Giovanni and Isabella did not speak about what would happen once he left for America and what would happen if she went to Bologna. They just enjoyed their time together.

As the end of the month drew near, Giovanni prepared for his trip to America. He got his passport, got his clothes in order and told Angelo that he would be quitting his job at the restaurant at the end of June. He wasn't sure, but he thought a tear came to one of Angelo's eyes. When he told the Maenza boys that he would be quitting, both cried like babies. They were so proud of him and believed that they were responsible for that voice.

Also, during this time, Alfredo secretly called a number of different directors of the smaller opera houses throughout Italy to see if they would be interested in allowing Giovanni to audition for them. But with Giovanni having no school training and not having been taught by a prominent teacher, every director rejected the offer.

Alfredo wondered if Isabella's father had put the word out against his young singer. Alfredo also began to question whether he should send Giovanni to a more prominent teacher. He was sure that once the teacher heard that voice, the teacher himself would support Giovanni. Alfredo decided that decision could be made after America. Signora Prandelli was where Giovanni's hope now laid. A success in America could pique the interest of the opera directors in Italy. And if Isabella's father had put the word out against Giovanni, then a successful appearance in America could be just the ticket to counteract it.

Exactly a week before Giovanni was due to leave, Alfredo sat Giovanni down and told him, "You will be leaving for America to sing. I have spoken to Signora Prandelli. She has a tremendous amount of connections throughout America. When you leave Milan and go to America, you must forget about us for a while. I asked her to take you under her wing and further your career. That is where your hope lies. Make your success in America and Italy will open its doors to you. After New Orleans, she is in negotiations for you to sing at another locale within a month of your debut. She will not tell me that place until it is finalized. If you have a success in New Orleans, you will probably have another contract to sing at the other locale within a month. Rehearsals will begin right away. So you won't be home after New Orleans. That is why I wanted to speak with you. You are leaving, and I'm not sure how long you will be gone. Signora Prandelli has given you permission and agreed to cover your costs to stay at the dorm at the University where her husband taught, in case there is any lag time between your performances and when you are due at the next location. I will still provide some funds to you while you are in America."

"I will repay you one day," he said to Alfredo.

"New Orleans is a perfect opportunity for you to begin your career."

"My father wanted me to be a singer. I will do what I have to do. After all, you did for me, a few weeks in America is the least I can do for you. I will go but will never forget all that you have done for me. Alfredo, *ti amo.*"

Choked with emotion, Alfredo hugged Giovanni and said, "*Bene.* Let's continue our practice and get ready for your debut."

# 24

# A VISIT TO PUCCINI'S TORRE DEL LAGO

*A* few days before Giovanni was to leave for New Orleans, Alfredo had a surprise for his pupil. He told Giovanni to bring Isabella with him to the *Casa Verdi*. Giovanni did just that. Alfredo and Giovanni climbed into Isabella's car and took a road trip. When they had left the city, Alfredo told them of their destination, *Torre del Lago,* and the home of Giacomo Puccini. Giovanni sang the entire part of Rodolfo during the car trip.

*Torre del Lago* is situated between the town of Lucca and the seaside resort town of Viareggio, very close to the convent in Vicopelago. After they reached Lucca, they made the short 10-mile drive to *Torre del Lago.* They found themselves on a long avenue, the *Viale Puccini,* which ran toward *Lago Massaciuccoli.* The streets off the avenue had such names as the *Via Tosca, Via Turandot, Via Gianni Schicchi,* and so forth. Giovanni read each street name to Alfredo as they drove along.

Torre itself is located in a flat plain separating the Apuan Alps from the Mediterranean. It offers wonderful views over *Lago Massaciuccoli* to the opposite shore and the villages in the distance. *Torre del Lago* got its name from a tower, which once stood right by the lake. Puccini built his villa close to where the tower once stood.

For Puccini, *Torre del Lago* was paradise. It was somewhat secluded, which afforded Puccini the peace and quiet to compose. It also allowed him to have a place to go to get away from the constant pressure from opera managers and librettists. But most importantly, it provided to Puccini ample opportunity to delve into his passion for hunting, which he did daily, shooting the birds which lived in the reeds along *Lago Massaciuccoli*.

Isabella parked the car close to the *Villa Puccini*. By the entrance to his villa stood a statue of the composer and a huge, magnificent palm tree. A crushed stone path that was bordered by flowers in clay pots led to the front door. The home looked much the same way Puccini had left it in 1924 when he died. The trio entered the home.

Most of the ground floor of the villa was taken up by the study, a bright room with a large fireplace. Opposite the fireplace stood a desk and a piano. On the desk laid Puccini's spectacles. The chair to the desk was turned to the Forster upright piano.

Alfredo said, "Before you leave for the States, I thought it would be nice to come here and see the home of your Maestro. Although Verdi is a greater composer."

Giovanni was all smiles. He walked over to the piano and looked upon it with awe. It was on this very piano that Puccini had played the very first notes of his operas. At Torre,

Puccini composed all of his operas from *La Bohème* onwards, except for *Turandot*.

Giovanni pointed out to Alfredo and Isabella the special damper on the piano.

Isabella asked, "Why is there a damper on the piano?"

Giovanni responded, "Puccini would hunt early in the morning. In the afternoon, he would hang out with his friends at a place they called *Club La Bohème*. In the evenings, they would all come back to the Villa Puccini, where the friends would play cards and converse while Puccini worked. He did most of his composing at night, thus the damper on the piano."

Alfredo interjected, "Puccini loved working with people in his study. The one rule was no one could hum a tune while he was working."

Giovanni, mesmerized by it all, replied, "I can just picture him sitting at this piano. He would sit here, always with his hat on and a cigarette dangling from his mouth. It all happened right here. This is where he made his masterpieces."

Pictures of composers and singers, like Caruso, Jeritza, and Mahler, lined the room. Giovanni pointed out the picture of Rosina Storchio on the piano. She was the first Butterfly. *Madama Butterfly* was a disaster on opening night. The audience at La Scala that night, both in the *loggione* and throughout the theater, booed so loud that the last act could not be heard. Across her portrait, Storchio had written remarks to Puccini, soothing his hurt feelings, quoting from the opera, "Renounced, yet happy."

The caretaker of the *Villa Puccini* was impressed by how

much Giovanni knew and jokingly offered him a job on the spot as a tour guide.

Off of the study was Puccini's gunroom. It was filled with stuffed birds and Puccini's gun collection. Puccini loved hunting. He always said, next to the piano, the gun was his favorite instrument.

Giovanni, Alfredo and Isabella also walked into the area between the study and the gunroom, where Puccini, his wife, Elvira, and their son, Tonio, were laid to rest. Fittingly, his tomb is arranged so that it is just on the other side of the wall from the upright piano at which he composed so much of his music. Alfredo and Isabella left Giovanni alone by the tomb for a few moments.

As Giovanni left the interior of the Villa toward the gardens, a plaque attached to one of the outside walls caught his attention. It read:

*Il popolo di Torre del Lago,*
*The people of Torre del Lago,*

*pose questa pietra a termine di devozione nella*
*out of their devotion, have placed this plaque on*

*casa ove ebbero nascimen le innumeravoli*
*to the house where were born the innumerable*

*creature di sogno che GIACOMO PUCCINI*
*creatures of dream that GIACOMO PUCCINI*

*trasse dal suo spirito immortale e*
*created with his immortal spirit and*

*rese vive col magistro dell'arteto*
*which he brought to life with such masterful art*

*perché dicessero all'universa ITALIA.*
*that they speak to all of ITALY.*

Giovanni called to Alfredo and Isabella, who were standing at the water's edge. Giovanni read the plaque to them, and upon completion, said, "Creatures of dream. That is what my destiny is; to become Puccini's characters. Through me, Puccini's music will spread, and the stories I love can be told to others."

Alfredo patted his pupil on his back and said, "Giovanni, you are ready to sing."

Giovanni looked out toward the lake and tried to imagine Puccini out on the lake in the morning fog, shooting his ducks, while humming different tunes in his head for an opera he was working on at the time. This place was Puccini's inspiration, and without a doubt, the atmosphere could be heard throughout his operas. The villa and its grounds had such a feel to it that it seemed that at any moment, Puccini, dressed in his hunting attire, would come out of the bushes, carrying his ducks from that day's shoot. Giovanni thanked Alfredo for taking him to Torre del Lago, "The king of composers," Giovanni said.

Alfredo shook his head in disagreement and said, "One day, when you sing a Verdi opera, you will understand."

Before leaving, they walked to Butterfly's, a restaurant situated very close to the Puccini home. It goes without saying what music was played at the restaurant. Close by was the outdoor theater at the foot of the lake. Forzano, the librettist for *Suor Angelica*, and Mascagni, the composer and conductor, came up with the idea for the theater.

When Forzano visited the dying composer at *Torre*, Puccini said how he loved to come out to the lake and shoot snipe, but he would really love to come out by the lake and see one of his operas. After his death, Forzano and Mascagni made his dream a reality. Since 1930, when Mascagni conducted *La Bohème*, every July and August, the Festival Puccini is held at the theater. Giovanni would have to come back with Isabella to see an opera here one day.

Giovanni enjoyed spending time with Alfredo and Isabella. In only a few more days, he had to leave for New Orleans and his opera debut.

# 25

# A FAREWELL PERFORMANCE

Friday, June 29th, the night before Giovanni's departure, came fast. He felt like he was prepared. He knew the opera perfectly. Yet, he had sung in a theater only one time, and that was only with a piano and not with a full orchestra.

Giovanni arrived at Angelo's for what would be his last night of work at the old restaurant, which held so many memories for him. The regulars all had heard of his good fortune and had turned out in force to wish him good luck and goodbye. The restaurant was packed. The Maenza boys were beaming. They considered that Giovanni's voice was a direct result of his working with them. "After all, our father had played the oboe at the premiere of Verdi's *Falstaff*," they told the customers.

Anna, Alfredo and Isabella all were there, sitting at the table closest to the piano. So were Lydia and her husband. Signori Romano and Montefeltro were both there. Even

Roberto from the pharmacy was there. Against the far wall, sitting with two other gentlemen, was Maestro Torcelli from La Scala. Giovanni gulped hard. He had never seen Torcelli before at the restaurant.

As the patrons settled into their seats, the Maenza boys started with some instrumental music. Angelo was busy checking out the ladies in the restaurant as well as counting his money from the overflow crowd. He would miss Giovanni.

When the time came for Giovanni to sing, he stood by the piano and thanked everyone for coming. He also thanked Angelo for allowing him the opportunity to sing at his place for all these years. Angelo came out to take a bow; more so, to get a better view of the ladies in the crowd. Giovanni also thanked the Maenza boys for playing for him all these years. Lastly, Giovanni said, "I owe my entire reason for leaving you, to my mentor, that great tenor, Alfredo del Monte." There was a cheer from the crowd.

A few of the opera nuts in the crowd knew the story of del Monte and how he lost his eyesight. They cheered him out of respect. The ones who didn't know the story, cheered him because he was the teacher of the "Caruso of Angelo's".

Giovanni continued, "Thus, I would like to dedicate my first selection to him. I will sing Verdi's 'De' miei bollenti spiriti' from *La Traviata*." The crowd cheered. The Maenza boys were shocked it wouldn't be Puccini. But to Giovanni, this was the perfect aria to dedicate to his mentor. This was the very aria Alfredo was singing when Giovanni was standing outside the Casa Verdi the first day he met him. The Maenza boys started the aria, and Giovanni began to sing. He sang with great emotion and feeling.

*De' miei bollenti spiriti il giovanile ardore*
*My rebellious spirit and the ardor of youth*

*ella tempro col placido sorriso dell'amor!*
*is tempered with her calm smile of love!*

*Dal dí che disse:*
*From the day she said to me:*

*"Vivere io voglio a te fedel!"*
*"I want to live, faithful to you alone!"*

*dell'universo immemore,*
*I have forgotten everything,*

*io vivo quasi in ciel.*
*and I live like one in heaven.*

When he finished, the crowd erupted in applause. Giovanni bowed and as he straightened up, he looked at Alfredo who was standing and clapping. Giovanni also noticed that Maestro Torcelli was standing, clapping for him.

Giovanni sang aria after aria, with hardly any break. He sang arias from Bellini, Donizetti, Leoncavallo, Mascagni, Cilea, Rossini, Verdi and of course Puccini. After a few hours, he grew tired. As encores, he sang some Neapolitan love songs. By then, the vino had taken full effect with the patrons, and they were singing along, which meant Giovanni could save his voice. Giovanni finally reached the final selection of the night. Again he thanked everyone for being there. It meant so much to him, and he would never forget this night.

Before he sang the last song, Angelo came forward and asked everyone to give Giovanni one last round of applause. Angelo, with his arms lifted, shaking his hands to get the crowd to be quiet, told the audience, "New Orleans will hear the best Italian tenor in all of Milan. Giovanni has been very good to me. As a token of thanks, I, along with the Maenza boys, want to give him a little something to remind him of us when he sings in America."

Angelo reached into his pocket and pulled out a jewelry box and handed it to Giovanni. Giovanni opened it and took out a chain. On the end of the chain was a golden oboe, which was inscribed on the back with the words, "The Caruso of Angelo's". As Giovanni put the chain around his neck, he was laughing and said, "Whenever I look at this golden oboe around my neck, I will always remember my days singing at Angelo's with the Maenza boys, whose father" . . . at which point almost the entire restaurant finished the sentence with Giovanni . . . "played the oboe at the premiere of Verdi's *Falstaff*." The regulars roared with laughter. The Maenza boys were so proud of their gift.

Giovanni walked over to the piano, and before singing his last selection, he looked around the room one last time. It struck him that for all these years, this was his stage. It really had prepared him. Singing in front of an unknown audience in New Orleans would be easy compared with singing in front of his hometown crowd. He took in one last smell of the aroma of the Sicilian food mixed with the open wine bottles. Giovanni said, "Thanks again for coming. My last selection is reserved for the person dearest to me. Although I am going, my heart will remain with her. Isabella, *ti amo*."

Anna, who thought he was speaking about her, frowned.

The Maenza boys started the song. Giovanni stared at Isabella as he had done that first night he saw her at Angelo's. He sang *Non ti scordar di me* by de Curtis.

> *Non ti scordar di me;*
> *Do not forget me;*

> *la vita mia legata é a te.*
> *my life is tied to yours.*

> *Io t'amo sempre piú,*
> *I love you more every day,*

> *Nel sogno mio rimani tu.*
> *you are always in my dreams.*

> *Non ti scordar di me;*
> *Do not forget me;*

> *la vita mia legata é a te.*
> *my life is tied to yours.*

> *C'é sempre un nido nel mio cor per te.*
> *There will always be a nest in* my *heart for you.*

> *Non ti scordar di me.*
> *Do not forget me.*

When Giovanni finished the song, he walked over to Isabella and gently kissed her hand. Tears were in her eyes. The crowd loudly applauded. Everyone came up at once to congratulate Giovanni. A few people gave him money, telling him to spend it on Bourbon Street in New Orleans, the most famous party street in the world. Roberto, the pharmacist, came up, and before he could say a word, Giovanni told him how much he missed his old boss and gave him a hug. Roberto cried, knowing that all was forgiven.

Out of the corner of his eye, Giovanni saw Maestro Torcelli coming toward him. Torcelli said, "*In bocca al lupo.*"

"*Crepi il lupo.*"

Maestro Torcelli replied, "You will do very well over there." He patted Giovanni on the back and left.

By this time, Alfredo and Anna had come up to Giovanni. Anna said, "Papa would be proud." Giovanni agreed. After the restaurant started to clear out, Giovanni sat at a table with Isabella, Alfredo, Anna, the Maenza boys, Signori Romano and Montefeltro, Lydia and her husband, and Angelo. The chef brought out a bowl of minestrone and a huge portion of Giovanni's favorite dish, veal parmigiano covered with red gravy with a nice glass of Ruffino Chianti Classico.

The whole group sat around and laughed and just had a good time. Giovanni wished they all could come to New Orleans and see him. Angelo said that they would all be at his debut at La Scala. Giovanni just smiled. After an hour and a half, the party broke up, and Giovanni left with Isabella. Anna would take Alfredo back to the Casa Verdi.

Giovanni exited Angelo's holding hands with Isabella. He made his way to the bench across from La Scala, the same bench where Lydia had told him the story of Alfredo. It was a beautiful night in Milan. Giovanni looked at the moon hanging above La Scala and told Isabella, "*La bella luna.* The next time I see the moon, I will be in New Orleans. Yet all of my thoughts will be of you. When you see the moon, think of me."

"I will," she said. "But I will be thinking of you the whole time you are there. *Ti amo*."

"*Ti amo*, Isabella. I am so glad we are together. I will miss you while I am gone."

Giovanni and Isabella kissed. He then pulled the chain from around his neck and asked her, "How do you like my gift?"

She laughed and said she loved it. They kissed for a long time under the moon in front of La Scala. He would be leaving tomorrow. He didn't know when he would be back. He had no idea after New Orleans where he would be going. He got home very late and went to sleep for a couple of hours before he had to get to the airport.

# 26

# THE DEPARTURE

*G*iovanni arrived at the *Aeroporto Malpensa* around 10:00 a.m., Saturday morning. His flight was leaving Milan at noon. Anna, Gabriella, and Alfredo all came to the airport to see him off. Isabella had to do something with her father that morning, but she was on her way.

While Giovanni was waiting in the concourse, Alfredo pulled him aside and said, "These past few months have been remarkable. You have brought such joy to my life. Your career is underway. Never forget, sing for the audience who is listening to you. I know I have told you opera stories upon opera stories, so the day you leave, I must give you one more. The tenor Giacomo Lauri-Volpi was singing Verdi's *Aida* with Toscanini conducting. Toscanini, like Maestro Torcelli today, hated singers who changed anything with the music. In the Nile scene of the third act, the tenor is arrested for treason. The tenor gets the last line in the act."

Giovanni spoke up, "Sure. I know the line. He sings 'Io resto a te'."

"That's right," said Alfredo. "Verdi composed the music such that on the word 'te' the singer sings a B flat. Lauri-Volpi, in this performance, interpolated a high D on the word. The crowd went crazy. Toscanini took his baton and threw it at the tenor and stormed out of the pit ending the performance."

Giovanni laughed. He would miss the stories from Alfredo.

Alfredo continued, "But Lauri-Volpi was singing for the audience. Do the same. Bring joy to people. Make the performance exciting for them. Don't be afraid to make a sensation."

"I will try," Giovanni responded.

Alfredo continued, "And being Italian and having the kiss of God on your voice, it is your duty to spread Italian passion when you sing. When they hear you sing, in their mind will run pictures of sun-splattered piazzas and grape and olive covered fields and hills. You will promote Italy. The great tenor Beniamino Gigli knew this, and that is why carved on his tomb are the words from his favorite opera, *Andrea Chénier*:

*Con la mia voce ho cantato la patria!*
*I have raised my voice to hymn my motherland!*

"Non-Italian singers can be great. Italian singers can be perfect. There is something embedded in the soul of an Italian singer. You have your own style of singing. Never lose it. Great singers have that one song that becomes their trademark. For example, Caruso had 'Vesti la giubba'. Over time, you will find your own."

Just then, Isabella showed up at the Airport. While she spent a few moments alone with Giovanni off in a corner, Anna came up to Alfredo and thanked him for all he had done for her son.

"You have a special boy there. It has been my pleasure."

Anna said, "He owes everything to you. Your financial support has allowed Giovanni to continue his studies with you. I don't know how we can ever repay you."

Alfredo was quiet for a moment and then told her, "Signora Anna, I can't let you believe that. I am an old retired singer with a handicap. I'm lucky to be able to support myself. That wonderful girl over there speaking to your son was the person who supported Giovanni financially. She was adamant that he must never know. He does not know, and I ask you not to tell him. But I wanted you to know."

Anna turned to look at Giovanni and Isabella. Maybe she had been too hard on the young girl. Her son was so happy with her. Perhaps she was wrong in not accepting Isabella.

Soon Giovanni and Isabella returned to his mother, sister and Alfredo. The group chatted the rest of the time. Finally, the time came to board the plane. He hugged his mother and his sister. Anna told him, "Giovanni, when you come back, perhaps Isabella can come over for dinner, and I will cook my *scaloppine alla Milanese*."

Giovanni's mother made that dish only for people she liked. Isabella was accepted. He turned from his mother and gave Isabella a huge hug and a kiss. He whispered into her ear, "You're accepted."

Lastly, he turned to Alfredo, who was standing nearby. "*In bocca al lupo,*" the old man said. "You have made me very proud."

Giovanni hugged him and said, "*Crepi il lupo. Ti amo,* Alfredo. He then turned to the rest of them and said, "*Ti amo* to all of you." With that, he walked down the long hallway to board the flight to America, where Giovanni Tempesta would be making his operatic debut and fulfilling his dream.

# PART III

NEW ORLEANS, LOUISIANA
JULY, 1979

# 27

# THE CRESCENT CITY

*G*iovanni arrived in New Orleans around 8:00 a.m. He was less than two weeks away from making his operatic debut. He couldn't believe how fast everything was moving.

As he walked down the jetway and out into the concourse, he noticed a black, middle-aged gentleman dressed all in black holding a sign with Giovanni's name on it. Giovanni went up to the man and introduced himself in Italian. The man grabbed Giovanni by the hand and, in an accent that Giovanni found very strange, said, "Nice to meet ya. I don't know any other language than English, so speak it, if you know it."

"*Si*. I mean, I do," Giovanni responded in his broken English.

"Great. My name is Hermann Bienvenu. I'll be driving you to your hotel. Welcome to N'awlins." With that,

Hermann put a collection of Mardi Gras beads around Giovanni's neck.

Hermann led Giovanni to the luggage pick up spot, and once Giovanni's luggage was collected, the duo made their way to the parking garage. Hermann pointed to a black limo and said, "This will be your car while you are here. I'll be your driver for all of your driving needs. Climb on in, and we will be off."

"Off?" asked Giovanni.

"Leaving."

"Good," replied Giovanni.

Giovanni had never seen a vehicle that size. As he climbed in, he felt like a king. The vehicle surged toward the interstate.

Soon Giovanni and Hermann were on the interstate en route to the hotel. Hermann asked how his flight went. "Well, I have never flown before. It was fine, except very long."

Hermann stretched his neck to look into the rearview mirror at Giovanni and said, "You sure do talk kinda funny. Where do you come from?"

"Milano. In Italy, as you say," he told Hermann.

Hermann smiled and said, "Italy. I sure do love your pizza. I was told you are a tenor. You're not fat like most of those opera people I drive. I like opera and always get this gig to drive singers like you around when they come to town. Are you any good?"

Giovanni chuckled out loud and said, "Non male. Oops, I mean not too bad. Have you drive long."

"You mean, have I driven long? For about 15 years. Before becoming a driver, I used to be a streetcar conductor on the St. Charles Avenue line."

"Oh really," Giovanni responded, having no idea what Hermann was referring to.

"Yep, but now I just drive big wigs like you around." Hermann reached into his pocket and said, "That reminds me, I'm supposed to give this to you."

Hermann handed an envelope to him. Giovanni opened it and pulled out a letter, thankfully written in Italian. It was from Signora Renata Prandelli welcoming him to New Orleans and providing him with an itinerary for his stay. For the remainder of the drive to the hotel, Giovanni reviewed the itinerary. Every now and then, Hermann would interrupt to point out something while driving into the city. As they drove, Giovanni became aware of the flatness of the city. Not a mountain or even a hill was in sight.

As Giovanni read the itinerary, he was happy to see that he was free all of today. He could rest up from his flight. The only itinerary item for tonight was dinner with Signora Prandelli. His first rehearsal with full orchestra would be tomorrow morning.

Hermann interrupted Giovanni's thoughts when he said, "Here we are. This is your hotel. The beautiful Monteleone Hotel right in the heart of the French Quarter. Those opera people sure do treat you well."

Giovanni laughed and said, "Yes, it would seem."

Hermann took out his luggage and handed it over to the bell captain. He then came back to where Giovanni was standing, shook his hand, and said, "Here is my card with all my phone numbers on it. If you ever need me to bring you anywhere, just call me. I will see you at 8:45 a.m. tomorrow morning to bring you to your rehearsal. Have a wonderful day today. Don't drink too much on Bourbon Street."

"*Grazie*," Giovanni told Hermann.

Hermann got back into the vehicle and drove off. Giovanni walked into the hotel to check-in and to settle into his new home.

---

AFTER GIOVANNI CHECKED in and had put his luggage in his room, he took the advice Alfredo had given him when he departed Milan. "When you get to New Orleans, don't go to sleep until nighttime. That is how you counteract jet lag." Giovanni thought there was no better way to stay awake than to take a tour of the city. He made his way to the lobby and out the front door of his hotel and found himself standing on Royal Street, which was lined with antique shops and galleries. Each building on the street was adorned with balconies, having delicate wrought iron railings, a symbol of New Orleans.

Giovanni took out a little map he had picked up in the hotel and started walking down Royal Street. Within seconds, Giovanni felt the impact of the New Orleans heat. As he walked down Royal Street, he entered some of the shops and looked around at the beautiful artwork and antique furniture. The entire street gave Giovanni the feeling that he had never left Europe.

On one of the corners, a jazz band was playing in the middle of the street. Giovanni sat on a curb and just listened to them play. He thought how much his mother would love this place. After all, New Orleans was the birthplace of jazz, and Louis Prima was born here.

Giovanni soon found himself walking through Jackson

Square. The pigeons in the square and the cathedral overlooking it reminded Giovanni of home. His thoughts turned to Isabella. He made his way to the St. Louis Cathedral, went inside, and said a quick prayer.

After walking all over the Quarter, Giovanni grew hungry. He passed an old building with a cupola on top. The name of the place was the Napoleon House. He went inside and found a table. The walls were stained with tobacco. Pictures of Emperor Napoleon Bonaparte covered the walls. The doors were opened to the street outside, which made Giovanni think of *Fiori di Toscano* back in Milan. Over the stereo, Puccini's *Madama Butterfly* was being played. Giovanni heard two notes and knew immediately that it was the recording with Victoria de los Angeles, Giuseppe di Stefano and Tito Gobbi. And to think, di Stefano liked his voice.

The waiter came up and gave Giovanni a menu. Giovanni ordered a glass of Italian red wine, a Chianti Ruffino of course, and looked over the menu. The house specialty was a muffuletta. Giovanni asked his waiter what was a muffuletta. The gentleman explained that New Orleans had a huge immigration of Sicilians in the late 1800's and early 1900's. The muffuletta was invented by them. It was a sandwich on special bread with ham, pastrami, Genoa salami, Swiss cheese, provolone cheese, and olive salad. Giovanni just had to try it.

As he waited for his lunch, he read a pamphlet about this place. The house was once the home of the mayor of New Orleans. However, when Napoleon Bonaparte was imprisoned on the island of St. Helena, a plot was hatched in this house to rescue Napoleon and bring him to New Orleans to live out his days, here in this very home. The pirate, Jean

Lafitte, took part in the forming of the plot. But Napoleon died in exile before the plot could be hatched. Since then, the Napoleon House became a restaurant and a bar, run by a family of Italians. Giovanni looked around the room and thought that the building probably hadn't changed much since the days of Napoleon and expected to see the pirate, Lafitte, seated at one of the tables.

Giovanni's muffuletta arrived, and he started to eat. It was delicious. The sandwich had been heated, which melted the cheese. It was probably one of the best sandwiches he had ever eaten. He would have to tell his mother about it and see if she ever heard of it. After lunch, he ordered a cappuccino and a cassata for dessert and just sat at his table enjoying the music.

As Butterfly sang about 'Un bel di' (One fine day), Giovanni thought that here he was in New Orleans, in America, getting prepared for his operatic debut. Giovanni took a sip of his cappuccino and thought to himself that if he awoke from this dream right now, he would be very upset.

When he left the Napoleon House, he walked around a little more and took a stroll along the great Mississippi River, looking at the paddle wheels along it.

Finally, he made his way back to his hotel to relax, look over the libretto of *La Bohème,* and to shower for his dinner tonight with Signora Prandelli.

## REHEARSAL

Giovanni went down to the lobby at 7:15 p.m. to meet Signora Prandelli. The lobby of the hotel was beautiful. He found a plaque on the wall that explained how the hotel was established by Antonio Monteleone, a cobbler from a small Italian town, who immigrated to New Orleans and opened this hotel. That would explain all the marble around the lobby, Giovanni thought.

Giovanni found a seat at the Carousel Bar located directly off the lobby. The bar rotated around. He ordered a glass of wine and waited. Signora Prandelli walked into the hotel. She was an elderly lady with white hair, very stately and attractive. She had her characteristic orange hat on, the same she had worn to the competition back in Milan. She walked up to Giovanni in the bar and said, "You probably don't remember meeting me that night back in Milan, but I remember you. I hope your trip to New Orleans was fine."

"*Si*. And I have already fallen in love with your city."

"That happens to all of our visitors. Just wait till you have the food. *Andiamo*. Let us go eat. And please call me Renata."

Giovanni and Signora Prandelli walked the two blocks to Arnaud's Restaurant, one of the old-line restaurants in the city.

The maitre d' came up and kissed Signora Prandelli on the hand who, in turn, introduced Giovanni Tempesta, an Italian singer making his debut at the opera.

The maitre d' led them to their table in the gorgeous dining room. The room reminded Giovanni of the salon at the *Casa Verdi*. Potted ferns were scattered all over the room. The room was dominated by large frosted glass windows. Ceiling fans revolved slowly, evoking the feeling and atmosphere of old New Orleans.

They sat at the table, and the waiter came to take a drink order. The wine was picked out by Signora Prandelli, a French wine, *Chateauneuf du Pape*. Giovanni would have gone with the Chianti.

As they looked over the menu, Signora Prandelli explained that the food at Arnaud's was some of the best in the city. They specialized in French Creole cooking.

Once their order was placed, they relaxed and began to speak about Giovanni's day and his impromptu tour of the city. She asked Giovanni would he rather speak in Italian, which he said he would.

She said, "A muffuletta. Don't you just love those sandwiches?"

"Perhaps the best I ever had. How long have you lived here?"

Signora Prandelli took a sip of wine and said, "A long

time now. My late husband, Gennaro Prandelli, moved here to teach and conduct."

Giovanni said, "I know all about your late husband. I know what happened with Alfredo as well."

Signora Prandelli sighed and said, "A tragedy. Alfredo had a beautiful voice and was such a nice man. Unlike many singers, he did not have an egotistical bone in his body. When he was injured, he was devastated. To be so close to achieving your goal and have that happen, I can't even imagine what he had to go through.

"He would have given anything to be able to have one chance to stand on the stage of La Scala and sing an aria to an audience and hear them cheer him in return. Then and only then would he feel complete as a singer. But it was not to be. My husband tried to help Alfredo out of his depression, but Alfredo just sank deeper and deeper into it.

"Slowly, over time, Alfredo pulled himself together. However, it wasn't until he met you that I can say that he is truly happy once again. You have brought him so much joy. All he does is talk about you. You have given his life a purpose. I have noticed a complete change in my good friend."

The waiter interrupted the conversation as he brought out the appetizers, Shrimp Arnaud for Giovanni and soufflé potatoes for Signora Prandelli. Once the waiter left them, Signora Prandelli asked, "How is your food, so far?"

"*O gran Dio. Molto buono.*"

Signora Prandelli continued, "It is a tradition of the New Orleans Opera that a singer who is making his debut at the opera dines at Arnaud's the first night he is in town. You are the only debutante we have singing in *La Bohème*. Everyone else has sung here numerous times. As a matter of fact, the singer for Mimi, Pamela Monsard, is a native of New Orleans, returning home after a few years hiatus up in New York and other American cities. She is the sole reason for this special performance, scheduled outside the opera season. This was the only time she was available."

"Oh great," Giovanni said out loud and sarcastically. "People will really be interested in hearing me."

Signora Prandelli laughed. She asked Giovanni, "Do you know anything about the history of opera in New Orleans?"

"Not really. My father was a great fan of Caruso. He loved the movie, *The Great Caruso*, which came out in the '50s with Mario Lanza. He always told me that Lanza could have sung in the opera and not just in the movies and that he only did so once, in two performances of *Madama Butterfly*, here in New Orleans."

Signora Prandelli smiled and said, "That is true. As a matter of fact, it was at this very restaurant, the night before that performance, that Lanza's wife told him that she was pregnant with their first child."

Giovanni smiled and helped the waiter clean away his plates.

Signora Prandelli continued, "At one time, New Orleans was one of the leading cities in the world of opera. Thanks to its strong French influence, many French operas had their American premieres here. New Orleans also saw the American premieres of a few Italian ones as well, like Lucia di Lammermoor and Norma. In 1920, Caruso gave a recital here, which packed the auditorium."

Giovanni listened in awe.

"In the '50s and '60s, all the great singers came here.

Milanov, Kirsten, Albanese, de Los Angeles, Warren, Tucker, Bjorling, del Monaco, and di Stefano."

"Di Stefano sang here. In what?"

"In *La Bohème*, with Licia Albanese in 1959. Exactly 20 years ago. The same opera you are singing. He also sang in *Werther* and *Rigoletto*."

"I love that voice. It is filled with so much passion."

"The feeling is mutual. He loves your voice, as do I."

Giovanni bowed his head and said, "*Grazie*."

"*Prego*. You just need a break. Your coming to America reminds me of a young American singer I met in Milan many years ago. His name was Sydney Rayner."

"I have heard of him. I believe he sang with Bidu Sayāo at her Metropolitan debut in *Manon* in the '30s."

"*Bene*. You are correct. Rayner was born and raised in New Orleans. His friends, aware of his talent, raised enough money to send him to Milan to study with my good friend, Maestro Raqusa. Rayner's success in Italy forced America to open its doors to him. I hope the reverse happens for you."

Giovanni said, "Me too."

"I believe you have nothing to worry about, Signor Tempesta. Sydney Rayner was a lovely singer, but with a muscular sound. What he lacked is what I call, '*poesia di voce*'. (Poetry of the voice.) The moment I heard you sing in Milan, I knew you had it. When one listens to your voice, there is poetry. It is not just a loud voice, ringing out in the theater, but a voice that is warm and tender."

Giovanni had such a sense of pride he could barely speak. He finally asked, "How do you like being the General Director of the New Orleans Opera?"

"It's hard work, but I love it. My husband loved this city

when we moved here, and he put his heart and soul into the opera. Since his death, I am continuing his work. Although the New Orleans Opera is no longer one of the rated opera houses, it is full of history and intrigue."

Giovanni asked, "Intrigue? What do you mean?"

"New Orleans is a very unique city. Things happen here that just don't happen at other places. Way before my time, in the early 1900's, the Spanish tenor, Florencio Constantino was singing *Il Barbiere di Siviglia* by Rossini. Signor Constantino got in a heated argument with the baritone, Giovanni Gravina, during rehearsals.

"During the actual performance, Signor Constantino 'accidentally' stabbed Signor Gravina in the eye, blinding him. Gravina later died from a heart attack, perhaps as a result of his eye injury. A huge lawsuit followed.

"That is what I mean by intrigue. It continues today, although not with anyone getting stabbed. Just two years ago, the soprano, Carol Neblett, was signed to sing the title role in Massenet's *Thaïs*. She and the director came to me and said that in the first act, they wanted Miss Neblett to appear on the stage naked. As part of the story, it made perfect sense. So I agreed.

"I don't think the New Orleans Opera has had so many stagehands standing in the wings as it did that night.

"When Miss Neblett walked off the stage in the nude at the performance, the New Orleans Opera made its way back into the spotlight. You see, the strippers on Bourbon Street complained that it was against the law for them to get totally nude, yet the opera people were allowed. Every major newspaper carried the story. I don't think opera was ever more popular in New Orleans.

Giovanni laughed and said, "Don't worry. I'll keep my clothes on."

Just then, the waiter brought out their dinner. Trout meuniere for Giovanni and crab cakes for Signora Prandelli. Giovanni's speckled trout was covered with lump crabmeat and smothered in meuniere sauce. It was served with a side order of steamed asparagus simmering in Castelvetrano olive oil. Giovanni melted with every bite he took of both dishes.

As what happens with most restaurants located in New Orleans, the conversation died down between the two once the delicious food arrived. Signora Prandelli did tell Giovanni that after dinner, she would show him something that she knew he would love to see. They ate the rest of their meal with barely a word being spoken between them.

For dessert, Signora Prandelli had an Arnaud's specialty, crème brulée. She insisted that Giovanni have bananas foster, the making of which was equivalent to watching a grand opera. The waiter brought over the cooking cart, and in front of both Giovanni and Signora Prandelli, began making the concoction. The waiter first split a banana. He then created syrup using sugar, butter and cinnamon. Once the syrup had been cooked down, he poured brandy over it and lit the syrup on fire, which had been poured on top of the bananas. It cooked for a few minutes, then the entire pan was poured on top of ice cream and served. Giovanni was in heaven.

After dessert, Renata and Giovanni walked out of the restaurant to Bourbon Street and took a nice leisurely stroll to walk off all they had eaten. The street was teeming with tourists. Neon lights beckoned all to come inside and have a drink at the different bars. Barkers stood out in front of the strip clubs, trying to entice men to come inside. Giovanni was mesmerized by it all.

When they came upon the corner of Bourbon and Toulouse, the street suddenly widened out on the left side for about a half-a-block in front of a hotel. Renata grabbed Giovanni by the hand, pointed down to the street and said, "My young tenor friend, do you see where the street widens out. That is the horse and buggy lane for the old French Opera House, which once stood at this spot. The opera house burned down in 1919 and was never rebuilt. But, at one time, this was the artistic life of this city. Imagine Vincenzo Bellini or Gaetano Donizetti, back in Italy, waiting to receive word on the first reception that their operas had received in front of an American audience. It all happened here. You will be making your debut in New Orleans. Sure, New Orleans has lost its operatic place in the current world, but it will never lose its place in history. This is a good place for the career of Giovanni Tempesta to begin."

They walked down Bourbon for a little while, and then returned to the hotel to let Giovanni get his rest for his first rehearsal. Giovanni thanked Signora Prandelli as she left him by the hotel.

Before going into the lobby, Giovanni looked up at the sky and saw the moon. His thoughts turned to Isabella. He thought of her balcony and hoped that when she looked at the moon, she thought of him as well.

He slowly entered the hotel to get some rest.

# 29

## LA BOHÈME

*H*ermann picked Giovanni up at 8:45 a.m. that next morning to bring him to his first rehearsal. Giovanni felt terrible. He was tired, and he knew he ate way too much the night before. He remembered his long discussions with Alfredo about the impact a career in opera would have on you both emotionally and physically.

Alfredo had told him a career in opera was hard, as your entire life was sacrificed for the voice. All that mattered was the performance schedule. All Giovanni thought and wondered about was whether or not his voice would respond today.

Hermann dropped Giovanni off at the stage door of the New Orleans Theater of the Performing Arts, where Giovanni Tempesta would be making his debut. Signora Prandelli came over to meet Giovanni once he got backstage.

"*Buon Giorno*, Giovanni. I had a very nice time last night."

As he kissed her on both cheeks, he said, "I did too. I hope I didn't overdo it. But it was very good. *Grazie tanto.*"

"*Prego.*" She grabbed his hand and said, "*Andiamo,* let me introduce you to our conductor."

Signora Prandelli took Giovanni around the back of the stage. There were people milling all about, and some chorus members were warming up their voices. Giovanni came upon a row of dressing room doors. The very first door had his name on it. It gave Giovanni quite a feeling to see it. He was officially a singer.

The fifth door down was the conductor's room. Signora Prandelli knocked gently and quickly received a reply to enter. Giovanni and Signora Prandelli entered the room and were met by an imposing, six foot, seven inch, giant of a man. Signora Prandelli said, "Giovanni Tempesta, please meet Pierre Gustave Lamere, your conductor for your debut in an opera."

Giovanni extended his hand and shook hands with his conductor. Monsieur Lamere was born in France and moved to the United States at the age of 35. He was now close to 50 and was a successful conductor, having conducted at most of the smaller opera houses in America. He was an excellent singer's conductor. Signora Prandelli had told Giovanni that Monsieur Lamere would be the perfect conductor to have for his debut.

Monsieur Lamere said, "It's very nice to meet you. Signora Prandelli has told me a lot about you. I look forward to hearing you sing. We will have a rehearsal with full orchestra in one hour. Go to your room and warm-up. Be on stage at 10:45 a.m. I will introduce you to the rest of the cast members and our director, Augusto Sardino. I know you are making your debut and are nervous. Don't be. Nerves will not allow you to sing well. Until then, *adieu.*"

With that, Giovanni walked back to his dressing room. Don't be nervous. That's easy for him to say, Giovanni thought.

For the next hour, Giovanni warmed up in his dressing room. When he started warming up, his voice was dry, with a rough edge. He started getting very nervous until finally, the voice woke up and responded. He was relieved, but he told himself that going forward, he would always pay attention to the voice and what his lifestyle would do to it. As he waited to go to the stage, his thoughts turned to Isabella and Alfredo. Oh, how he wished they both were here.

At the appointed time, Giovanni went to the stage. Monsieur Lamere was sitting in a chair on the stage. Numerous people were all around. As Giovanni stepped onto the stage, Monsieur Lamere said, "Well, it is my honor to introduce to all of you our Rodolfo, tenor Giovanni Tempesta, from Milan, Italy. He will be making his operatic debut here with us."

A tall, good looking, blonde, blue-eyed man, 32 years of age came up and shook hands with Giovanni and said, "Hey. My name is Sean Patrick Dooley from Chicago. I'll be singing Marcello." Giovanni shook his hand. Sean continued, "I bet you're a nervous wreck." Giovanni nodded in the affirmative.

The rest of the cast came up to introduce themselves. All of them had performed with the New Orleans Opera on numerous other occasions but always enjoyed coming to sing here, especially because of the restaurants they would get to enjoy while here. All of the singers were from America. Musetta was being sung by Rosemary Gill, a native of

232 | TEMPESTA'S DREAM

Mississippi, Colline by Jonathan Cousins from Pennsylvania, and Schaunard by Matthew Hemel, a native of Boston.

Last but not least was the role of Mimi. Pamela Monsard, the prima donna assoluta of New Orleans, had returned home for this out of season performance. She had started her career here. She became very successful, moved to New York, and sang at some of the larger opera houses in America, including the Met. Signora Prandelli got a feather in her cap for convincing Mrs. Monsard to return back home to sing in *La Bohème*. Mrs. Monsard almost cancelled when the tenor pulled out, but Signora Prandelli told her that they would spare no expense in finding a replacement. She was not happy that the person they found had no experience and would be making his debut in opera. But Signora Prandelli convinced her to stay and sing. After all, finding a tenor during the summer with so many festivals going on was very difficult.

Mrs. Monsard was 39. She had married a high up executive producer in television, Gregory Monsard, which gave her the connections she needed in New York. She had a beautiful face, black curly hair, dark eyes, and a full figure. Not only did she have the looks, but she also had the voice too. She had been taught by a teacher who had been trained by the great Italian soprano, Renata Tebaldi, who often sang the role of Mimi at the Met. Thus, Mrs. Monsard considered this her best role.

Mrs. Monsard walked over to Giovanni and extended her hand, saying, "I sure hope these people know what they are doing. People are coming to see this opera just to see me. I don't want it ruined by some upstart."

As she walked away, Sean Patrick Dooley came over, put

his arm around Giovanni, and said, "I heard that. Don't you worry about her. That girl just needs to get laid."

Giovanni never chuckled so loud as he did at that comment.

Monsieur Lamere called everyone to order. He said, "We will begin this rehearsal. The chorus can go practice backstage. I just want the soloists. Mimi, we will take your first act aria first."

Monsieur Lamere made his way to the orchestra pit and took his position on the conductor's podium.

Giovanni breathed deeply, relieved that he did not have to go first. Sean pulled him by the shirt toward a chair, and they both sat down. Giovanni looked out into the auditorium and saw Signora Prandelli sitting next to the director, Augusto Sardino. The chorus had already begun warming up backstage.

Mrs. Monsard walked to the front of the stage. Monsieur Lamere said, "From the top. I will set the tempo I want. Ready. Sing the entire aria."

Mrs. Monsard nodded, and the orchestra began to play. The chorus was still singing backstage. But over the noise, Giovanni was awed by the beauty of her voice.

In the aria, Mimi tells Rodolfo all about herself. Mrs. Monsard's voice was warm and full. Giovanni was impressed at how well she sang the Italian language, even though she was not Italian. But Giovanni did notice that her hands never moved from her side. He thought about his training with Alfredo, who had taught him to sing with the whole body, especially the hands. "Let your hands show the emotion that your voice is creating. Let your Italian passion course through your body," Alfredo had told him.

When Mrs. Monsard finished, everyone standing around clapped. Monsieur Lamere complimented her. She then went over to the conductor to speak to him about some different ideas on the aria.

Monsieur Lamere said, "Tempesta, when I'm done with Mrs. Monsard, you will sing the narration aria. Get ready."

Giovanni felt his heart pounding. A few moments later, Monsieur Lamere called for him. As he stood up, Sean patted him on the back and said, "Go get'em, Caruso."

Giovanni half heartily looked back toward Sean, then walked to the front of the stage. He cleared his throat and took a deep breath and waited. He wondered if his voice would project. Would the director and Signora Prandelli, sitting out in the seats, hear him over the orchestra.

Mrs. Monsard made her way to a chair while Monsieur Lamere rummaged through the music. Mrs. Monsard sat down and leaned over to Ms. Gill and said, "Gee, I can't wait to hear this find."

Monsieur Lamere asked someone to hand the sheet music to Giovanni, and he said, "I want you to start by just singing the note breaks in the musical score. I want to get a feel for your voice before you sing the entire aria."

Giovanni started sweating profusely. In his broken English accent, he said, "*Scusi*, Monsieur Lamere, I no read music. I sing by listening."

Mrs. Monsard moaned in her chair and then sneered out loud. Monsieur Lamere looked out into the auditorium where Signora Prandelli was sitting and shrugged his shoulders. He then turned to Giovanni and said, "Very well. Sing the aria for me."

The narration aria is sung by the tenor, Rodolfo, right

before Mimi sings her aria. In the aria, Rodolfo sings about his life and the impact meeting Mimi moments before has had on him. Rodolfo has been struck by the lightning bolt. The aria takes place when Mimi loses her key. They search for it in the dark, and their hands meet on the floor.

Giovanni was very nervous. He told himself over and over again, "You can do this. You have sung this aria countless times. Alfredo believes in you." He reached for his chest and felt the golden oboe necklace through his shirt. Doing so made him relax for a moment. He thought of Isabella. He knew how Rodolfo felt upon finding "that woman ". Giovanni knelt down on one knee and began to search the floor.

Mrs. Monsard laughed out loud and said, "Just like an Italian, overly dramatic." Monsieur Lamere brought his baton down, and the orchestra swelled into action. With one hand extended, Giovanni pretended he had just touched Mimi's hand. He began to sing. *"Che gelida manina, se la lasci riscaldar."* (*What a cold little hand, let me warm it for you.*)

His voice was very lyrical, and he sang the opening lines with a lot of emotion.

As Giovanni completed the initial section, the house became quiet. The chorus slowly, one by one, stopped singing backstage to listen to that voice. Mrs. Monsard leaned forward in her chair. Monsieur Lamere took his eyes off of the music and looked at Giovanni. The orchestra members who were not playing at that moment turned in their seats towards the stage and listened intently to Giovanni. Signora Prandelli had a huge smile on her face. Signor Augusto Sardino sat rigid in his seat.

*Chi son? Sono un poeta.*
*Who am I? I am a poet.*

*Che cosa faccio? Scrivo.*
*What do I do? I write.*

*E come vivo? Vivo.*
*How do I live? I live.*

*In povertà mia lieta*
*In my happy poverty*

*scialo da gran signore*
*I am as generous as a lord*

*rime ed inni d'amore.*
*with poems and songs of love.*

While Giovanni sang, he thought how alike he and the character Rodolfo from the opera were; both were poor yet lived with many dreams. Like Rodolfo, Giovanni's dreams were brought to reality when Isabella came into his life.

*Per sogni e per chimere*
*With my dreams and fantasies*

*e per castelli in aria, l'anima ho millionaria.*
*and castles in the air, I have the soul of a millionaire.*

*Talor dal mio forziere*
*But my treasure chest has been*

*ruban tutti i gioielli due ladri:*
*robbed of all its jewels by two thieves:*

*gli occhi belli.*
*a pair of beautiful eyes.*

*V'entrar con voi pur ora,*
*They came in with you,*

*ed i miei sogni usati,*
*and my beautiful dreams,*

*e i bei sogni miei, tosto si dileguar!*
*both past and present, were stolen!*

*Ma il furto non m'accora, poichè*
*But the theft does not upset me because they*

*poichè, v'ha preso stanza la speranza!*
*have been replaced by hope!*

Giovanni hit the high C on the word "speranza" and held it a long time.

There was complete silence when he finished the aria. Then the entire house, including the orchestra and the chorus who had stopped to listen, broke out in applause. The first person to reach Giovanni was Mrs. Monsard. She leaped from her chair, grabbed Giovanni by the hand, and said, "It will be an honor to sing with you. Your voice is beautiful."

Monsieur Lamere looked out to Signora Prandelli, smiled broadly, and gave a thumbs up to her. Giovanni felt relieved as he received more and more congratulations. Sean Patrick Dooley patted him on the back, and said, "You are Caruso." Giovanni knew he had won them over. Even the chorus members from behind the stage came out to congratulate him.

Shortly thereafter, the house became quiet again, and Monsieur Lamere continued with the rehearsal, which lasted late into the night. When the rehearsal was over, Hermann picked Giovanni up and brought him to his hotel. Giovanni was exhausted but very relieved. The voice had remained strong throughout the day. By the end of the rehearsal, he was straining a bit, but it was better than he thought. He was thrilled when he heard that tomorrow's practice would be easy. No singing, just stage blocking and movements. He could rest his voice. Before going to sleep, he called Alfredo to tell him about today as well as to give him his phone number so that Isabella could call him tomorrow night when he got back to his hotel. She would be calling Alfredo for the phone number. Alfredo was beside himself with excitement when Giovanni told him about his first rehearsal with an orchestra and the reaction to it. He wanted all the details from the moment he walked into the auditorium.

After Giovanni told him about his early voice struggles when warming up, Alfredo reminded him about the rigors of an opera life, and how it curtails the social activities of the singer.

After he finished speaking with Alfredo, Giovanni called his mother. They spoke briefly with Giovanni relating all of the day's events. After he hung up, he went to sleep, content with how everything had gone, and excited about talking with Isabella tomorrow night.

# 30

# CITY PARK

*R*ehearsals went well all that week. They lasted late into the night almost all week. Giovanni felt very at ease with the part since he knew the opera so well. He had been measured for his costume and looked forward to trying it on and taking a picture in it to send to Alfredo. When Giovanni got back to his hotel at night, he would await his phone call from his beloved. Although apart, their love continued to grow.

Giovanni did not have a chance to see much more of the city since rehearsals were lasting all day and night. However, he did go on a haunted tour one night with Sean, which took them throughout the French Quarter. Giovanni had drinks with funny names which he had never had before. When he went to sleep later that night, his entire hotel room seemed to be spinning.

On Saturday, a picnic was planned for the singers to meet and greet a few patrons of the arts in New Orleans. Giovanni was glad to have Saturday off. He was only four days away from making his debut. Hermann picked him up on Saturday around 11:00 a.m. to bring him to City Park for the picnic, a park filled with magnificent stately oak trees. Upon his arrival, Giovanni saw huge tents in a grassy area near the Museum located in the Park. It was a very warm day. Numerous people were milling all around. Hermann parked his car and got out with Giovanni. He would be attending the picnic as well. Hermann was in a very loud colored shirt-purple, green and gold.

The smell of boiled seafood permeated the entire area as Giovanni walked up to the tents. Signora Prandelli was the first to greet him. She was in her trademark orange hat. A jazz band was playing on a makeshift stage under the tent. Giovanni noticed the other singers from the opera. They were talking with different people.

Signora Prandelli took Giovanni around and introduced him to some of the people at the picnic. Everyone, with their southern hospitality, was very cordial toward the young Italian tenor.

A few of the women in the crowd talked among themselves about how good looking the tenor was and did all they could to meet him. Giovanni soon got a pat on his back, turned, and saw Sean Patrick Dooley. Sean said, "Having fun yet? There are some enchanting ladies around today. Caruso should do some mingling."

Giovanni laughed and asked, "What are they cooking in those pots."

"Those my young Italian friend are boiled crabs, very delicious fresh-water blue crabs from Lake Pontchartrain, and also boiled shrimp. Come on, let's have some."

A few of the patrons at the picnic came over to show Giovanni how to open the shells and crack the claws and to peel the shrimp. They laughed at the faces he made while he struggled to extract the crabmeat. "Sure is a lot of work to get a little food," Giovanni told Sean at one point.

After filling up on crabmeat and shrimp, Giovanni had to meet more and more people, such as the Board of Directors of the opera, the Mayor of the City of New Orleans, the beautiful society page columnist, Shannon Rossner, as well as the music critic for the newspaper in New Orleans, Mr. Robert Maestri. Giovanni grew tired of shaking hands and smiling, so he quietly sneaked away from the crowds momentarily and took a stroll over to a group of trees by a lagoon. It was a beautiful spot. He didn't know why, but all of a sudden, he felt very homesick and missed Isabella something awful. On an old oak tree, laden with moss, was a sign that read "dueling oaks". Giovanni was startled by a voice that came from behind him.

"It was in this very spot that the young aristocratic men of New Orleans would come to have their duels in the 1800's," said the young man as he walked up. He extended his hand to Giovanni and said, "My name is Salvatore Dantoni. My father was born in Italy and would love to meet you. We both love opera."

Giovanni shook his hand and asked, "Where is your father from in Italy?"

"He was actually born in Cefalù, Sicily," Salvatore told Giovanni.

"Cefalù. That is where my mother is from. Is your father here?"

"Yes; come, I will bring you to him."

As they walked, Salvatore told Giovanni that his father had come to New Orleans at 15, went to college, then to law school, and started his own law practice. Salvatore joined him in practice following his graduation from law school. They specialized in successions and contracts.

When they got back to the tent, Salvatore introduced Giovanni to his father, Baretti Dantoni. Giovanni told the gentleman, "My mother was from Cefalù. She was Anna Tumminello."

"Tumminello? I knew Piero Tumminello when I was growing up."

Giovanni was stunned. "He's my mother's brother."

Mr. Baretti hugged Giovanni and welcomed him. All three went to sit at one of the tables set up under the tent and spoke for a long time, about Cefalù and about opera.

Mr. Baretti asked Giovanni, "What is Piero doing now? I haven't seen him in years."

"He now lives in Parma. He comes to visit my mother in Milan every so often. He runs a successful export business of parmigiano cheese."

"He was a wonderful guy when we were growing up. We were close as youngsters. Please tell him hello when you see him."

Just then, the Dantonis' wives came up to where they were sitting. Giovanni was introduced to both of their wives as well. Both women were beautiful. It made Giovanni miss Isabella even more.

The picnic lasted for a few hours. Signora Prandelli got up to speak toward the end. She stood on the makeshift stage as the people gathered around. She said, "Ladies and gentlemen. Thank all of you for coming today. So many people have come up to me today and asked about our new tenor for *La Bohème*. I know everyone was nervous when they heard our tenor under contract had cancelled. I had the privilege of hearing Signor Tempesta sing in his native Milan. He is wonderful. I haven't spoken to him yet, but I'm sure he won't mind if I asked him to come on up here and sing one song for us."

The crowd broke into applause. Giovanni reluctantly made his way to the stage. Once he got on the stage, Signora Prandelli said, "Here is our new tenor, Giovanni Tempesta."

Giovanni waved to the crowd. Signora Prandelli called Baretti Dantoni to the stage and asked him to play the piano for Giovanni. Mr. Dantoni loved opera and was an accomplished piano player. He came up to Giovanni and asked what he would like to sing. To this day, Giovanni doesn't know why, but an old, Italian aria came to mind. He asked Mr. Dantoni if he knew "Io conosco un giardino" by Pietri from *Maristella.*

Mr. Dantoni said he knew it and sat at the piano, which had been used for the jazz band that was playing earlier. The opera *Maristella* is never heard today. A few of the tenors in the '30s and '40s would sing this aria in their concerts. Giovanni used to listen to a Gigli recording of it with his father. He didn't know why he thought of this aria today. It had to be because he missed Isabella. Attending a picnic made him think of their secret garden at Vicopelago and the picnics they had there together. Mr. Dantoni began to play, and Giovanni sang.

> *Io conosco un giardino a tutti sconosciuto,*
> *I know a garden unknown to all,*

*un nido di velluto sotto il cielo turchino.*
*a nest of velvet under the blue sky.*

*L'estate, il verno, in fior vi odorano i giaggioli,*
*In both summer and winter irises are blooming,*

*vi cantan gli usignoli la notte in amor.*
*and the nightingale sings of love at night.*

*Deh, vieni vien qui sul mio cuor,*
*So come, come near my heart,*

*io ti porto a quel nido e t'offro un bel cuscino*
*I will take you to that nest and offer you a pillow*

*di piumarelle d'oro e di baci t'infioro la bocca*
*of golden feathers, and I'll cover your lips with kisses*

*e t'offro un gran forzier di sogni iridescenti,*
*and offer you a treasure chest of many colored dreams,*

*di stelle giú cadenti dalle supreme sfere.*
*of falling stars from high above.*

*Mia tenerezza vien deh, vien! deh, vien!*
*My sweet, come, oh come! Oh come!*

Giovanni sang with such passion that his hand was shaking when he finished. Everyone at the picnic erupted in applause. Some people surged toward the stage, cheering.

Sean Patrick Dooley was yelling *"bravo"* at the top of his lungs.

Giovanni shook hands with the people at the foot of the stage. Mr. Dantoni, who was crying, came up behind him and said he had never heard that sung more beautifully. "It is as if that aria was written just for you."

Giovanni remembered Alfredo telling him to find a signature song. Perhaps he had found one. It was appropriate since the song reminded him of Isabella and the spot where they had fallen in love.

Robert Maestri, the music critic, came up to Giovanni and told him how much he was looking forward to hearing him on Wednesday.

After a while, the crowd finally started to disperse. Signora Prandelli told Hermann that she would bring Giovanni back to his hotel because she had something to discuss with him. Giovanni made sure to tell Salvatore and Baretti Dantoni goodbye. Mr. Baretti still had tears in his eyes.

Signora Prandelli and Giovanni made their way to her car. As they did, she told Giovanni, "Your voice is splendid. Everyone who hears you falls in love with it. You are ready for a career."

Giovanni nodded to her as they both got into her car and took off down the street. Signora Prandelli continued and said, "Alfredo told you I would help you. I have been in contact with the Santa Fe Opera in New Mexico who wants you to sing *Carmen* in August. They are sending a scout to hear you Wednesday and, if all goes well, will sign you to a contract after the performance. You will leave here immediately after Saturday to report to Santa Fe for rehearsals."

Giovanni was thrilled. He now officially had a career, not just a one-shot deal. Signora Prandelli continued to speak about further deals, which may be made in the future. "After Santa Fe, I may have another performance lined up. You will come back to New Orleans and stay at Loyola University. While there, I have a teacher I want you to work with until it is time for you to go to your next performance."

Giovanni was enjoying the thought of his calendar filling up and his checkbook getting out of the red. Finally, he was about to achieve his dream.

Neither he nor Signora Prandelli saw the truck that had just run the red light. It came careening into their car, pushing their vehicle some 30 feet, straight into an oak tree. The last sound Giovanni remembered was the sound of screeching tires.

# 31

## A REVIEW

*G*iovanni awoke four days later in the Intensive Care Unit at Mercy Hospital in New Orleans. When he opened his eyes, the first person he saw was his mother. He was very confused and asked his mother; what happened? Where was he? Why was she here?

She grabbed his hand firmly and said in Italian, *"Zitto.* Don't talk too much. I'm so glad you are awake." Tears were rolling down her face. She continued, "You have been in and out of consciousness since Saturday. You were involved in a car accident."

Giovanni tried to sit up but didn't have the strength. He stammered back to his mother, "Four days! The performance is tonight. I have to get ready."

Anna shook her head. She got out of the way of a nurse who had just entered the room and who was very pleased to see Giovanni awake. The nurse left to call the doctor. Once the nurse had left, Anna told Giovanni, "A truck ran a red light and broadsided the vehicle, pushing you into a tree. In the accident, you had a serious concussion. You will need a lot of rest and time to recover. You can't sing in the opera."

He asked, "How is Signora Prandelli?"

Anna was quiet before she said, "*E morta*. She died."

Giovanni started to cry. Anna held him tight until the doctor arrived in his ICU room. The doctor explained to Giovanni what had occurred and what his recovery program entailed, which required a lot of rest. The doctor assured him that he would make a complete recovery. The doctor checked him all over and said everything looked great.

After the doctor left the room, Anna said, "You asked how I came here. Saturday night, I received a phone call from Signor Baretti Dantoni. He informed me of the accident. I thought of your poor father when I got that phone call. You scared me to death. Signor Baretti, out of the kindness of his heart, paid for my airplane ticket here. I can't believe he knows your Uncle. We have to call Piero in Parma and tell him. I've been staying at your hotel room at the Monteleone. The opera people have been very nice. They even allowed me to use your driver, Hermann. He is a very nice man. I've spent most of my time here at the hospital. But, Salvatore Dantoni insisted that I get some rest at night, so he would come sit with you. They are wonderful people."

Giovanni agreed. He asked his mother to go get him a glass of water. When she left the room, Giovanni had a moment to reflect on everything that he had just been told. Poor Signora Prandelli was dead. At least she was now with her husband. As for his career, all hope seemed dim. He would not be singing in New Orleans, which also meant he would not be singing in Santa Fe. Signora Prandelli was the person with the connections, but she could not help him anymore. His dream had died just when he was about to attain it. Giovanni's thoughts turned to Alfredo. He now knew how Alfredo felt when his dream was lost. He wondered if Alfredo knew what happened to him. He also wondered if Isabella knew.

When Anna came back into the room with his water, Giovanni asked her about Alfredo and Isabella. Anna said, "Before I left Milan, I called Alfredo and told him. He was very upset. He called Isabella and spoke to her. Alfredo calls me every night at the hotel to check on you. Isabella also called me. I know they are both going to be so pleased to hear from you. Once you get into your regular room, you can call them."

Giovanni looked forward to that. He grew tired and slowly drifted off to sleep while his mother held tightly to his hand, muttering prayers of thanks for his waking up.

THE NEXT DAY, Giovanni was moved to his private hospital room. Once he got settled into his room, the first person he called was Alfredo, who was very excited to be speaking to Giovanni. Alfredo said, "I thought we almost lost you. I couldn't believe the news about Signora Prandelli. She was a wonderful woman."

Giovanni agreed and said, "Alfredo, I have no chance of ever having a career."

"Nonsense. You will get a break. Just keep working at it. I believe in you. Isabella believes in you. She has called me every day to check on your condition. I know she can't wait to hear from you. When she calls me today, I will tell her to come by tonight. You can call her here with me."

"I will do that," Giovanni assured him. "The doctor says, if everything goes well, I can fly home in a couple of days. I have to find a job."

"Giovanni, we will discuss that when you return home. Get well, *amico.*"

Giovanni hung up the phone with Alfredo and sat in the room very quietly. He didn't know what to do once he went home and recovered from his injuries. Isabella's father would never agree to him seeing his daughter. If he thought he was a nobody before, he was probably even at a lower rung now.

Suddenly the door to his room was opened and in walked Sean Patrick Dooley. As he entered, Sean said, "How are you feeling, Caruso. You took quite a wallop, I heard. You look great. We sure missed you at the performance Wednesday."

Giovanni shook hands with the young American. He asked Sean, "How was the performance?"

Sean smiled broadly and said, "I was fantastic, of course." Giovanni laughed. Sean continued, "Everyone sang well except the croaker who replaced you. He was fat, balding and sang off-key the entire night. Poor Mrs. Monsard was so upset because he kept screwing her timing up. She is adamant that a new tenor must be hired for Saturday's performance."

Giovanni thanked Sean for coming to see him. Sean came closer and said, "I came to bring you something. Do you remember meeting Mr. Robert Maestri, the music critic?"

"I think so. He was at the picnic."

"That's right. He is the music critic for the local paper. He wrote his review. I wanted you to read it." Sean pulled out an article from his pocket and handed it to Giovanni. The title to the article was, "*La Bohème* goes forward after devastating loss to the New Orleans Opera". The article went on to explain how Signora Prandelli was killed in a car accident the weekend before the performance and reflected on all that she had done for the opera association throughout the years. The article did mention that a "promising young tenor was injured in the accident".

Giovanni looked up from reading the article, shrugged his shoulders and said, "Well, although not mentioned by name, he did at least say a promising tenor."

"Read on, Caruso."

The article continued with its critique of the performance. Mr. Maestri raved about Mrs. Monsard's voice but stated that she had "little support from her tenor counterpart". Further in the article, it read, "As for the baritone, Sean Patrick Dooley is quickly evolving into a top-notch performer." Sean had a smile on his face. The article then came to the tenor.

---

*I am sure it was very difficult for the New Orleans Opera to recover from the loss of Signora Prandelli and the injury to the tenor scheduled to sing the role of Rodolfo. However, one would hope that in the future, there is a better contingency plan.*

*In my 35 years of opera-going, never have I heard a worse performance from a "professional" singer. Manuelo Diaz is from Mexico City. He has had a long career. He should quit immediately. This reviewer will not delve into all of the problems with his performance. Instead, I will tell you of a missed opportunity to perhaps hear greatness.*

*As you are aware, Signora Prandelli was killed in a car accident after leaving a picnic put on by the New Orleans Opera. Before she left that picnic, she introduced everyone there to a tenor who would be making his operatic debut here in La Bohème.*

*Giovanni Tempesta, from Milan, made his way to the stage. He is a tall, good-looking man with strong Italian features, except with uncanny blue eyes. Mr. Tempesta proceeded to sing an almost forgotten aria, 'Io conosco un giardino' by Pietri. This reviewer, as a young man, heard this aria sung live in concert by Gigli, Schipa and di Stefano. The voice I heard singing at City Park that day is in the same class. It is a driven, spinto tenor voice, but with a lyrical quality and passion that sets it apart.*

*I was stunned and looked forward with great anticipation to hearing that voice sing from our stage. Such was not to be. Mr. Tempesta is recuperating at a local hospital from his injury. Before he returns to Milan, the New Orleans Opera should sign him to a contract to return here to sing before his career and his price makes it impossible to sign him.*

---

Giovanni put the article down. He was in shock. Sean said, "You didn't even sing, yet you get more press than all of us. Mrs. Monsard is ranting and raving about how unfair it all is." Giovanni laughed out loud. He thanked Sean for bringing the article.

Later, when Sean had left him, Giovanni thought that perhaps he still had a chance to become a singer. It was in the hands of the New Orleans Opera to sign him to a contract.

# A DREAM EXTINGUISHED

*W*hen Giovanni awoke from a nap, Salvatore Dantoni was sitting next to his bed. He had relieved his mother, who had gone back to the hotel to get some needed rest.

Giovanni said, "Salvatore, thank you and your father for all that you have done. You didn't even know me, yet you went through all this trouble."

Salvatore said, "Your mother is wonderful. She invited us to come to Milan one day to visit where she will fix us her *scaloppine alla Milanese*."

Giovanni smiled and asked Salvatore, "In a few days, I will be returning to Italy. I need to speak with someone with the New Orleans Opera about getting a contract. Can you help me?"

"A replacement has already been named for Signora Prandelli. A woman originally from Bavaria, Heather Voelker, has taken over. I don't know her at all. She has only lived in

New Orleans for a couple of years, but that is the lady you must speak to. I also wanted to ask you if you want me to help you with your claim?"

Giovanni looked confused. "Claim? For what?"

"For your auto accident. The person who hit you worked for a large company here in New Orleans, which means nice insurance. I will put a claim in for you and see if they want to settle."

Giovanni agreed, although confused about how legal matters worked. He grew anxious to call Isabella. But first, he wanted to speak to Mrs. Voelker at the New Orleans Opera. He was not going to wait to see if they would call him. He would take the step and get them to sign him for next year. With a signed contract, perhaps other opera houses would open their doors to him in the meantime.

Giovanni called the opera office and was transferred to Mrs. Voelker. Mrs. Voelker spoke with a very heavy German accent. "This is Voelker."

Giovanni explained who he was and asked Mrs. Voelker if the opera was interested in his returning.

Voelker cut Giovanni off before he finished his last sentence, saying, "I am now in charge. Signora Prandelli and I differed in our approach to opera. The opera is interested in changing direction from the past."

Giovanni slumped back in his bed. He was about to hang up but was stunned with what Voelker was saying.

"Also, Signor Tempesta. Under your contract with the New Orleans Opera, failure to sing at a performance, no matter what the reason, is grounds for default. Therefore, the New Orleans Opera will not be paying you any portion of your fee. We consider you to be in default of the contract. Thank you for your understanding."

And with that, she hung up. Giovanni was red with anger. He told Salvatore what she had said. Salvatore assured him that he would do whatever was necessary to get a portion of the contract price turned over to him for the time spent at rehearsals since the reason he did not sing was not due to his fault. As for Mrs. Voelker, Salvatore said, "I was afraid of that. People were upset that she was named director. She has her own agenda. She wants to split with the past. Anyone that Signora Prandelli supported probably will never sing here."

Giovanni sat in his bed, fuming. That was it. He didn't care what Alfredo told him when he got home. He was never going to be a singer. He was tired of chasing a dream that was impossible to achieve. It was finished. And along with his operatic dream, he knew his hope of one day being with Isabella was useless. He didn't even want to call her now. Why keep up the charade. He would return to Milan and find a job, a real job, like Signor Toscano had told him to do months ago. Slowly, Giovanni drifted deeper and deeper into a depression.

Except for a very short conversation he had with Isabella later that day, he did not call Alfredo or Isabella and avoided their phone calls for the remainder of his stay at the hospital.

---

ON JULY 17TH, Giovanni and Anna were brought to the New Orleans airport by Hermann. The Dantonis were there to send them off. Giovanni thanked them for all that they had done. They wished Giovanni and Anna the best of luck and invited them back to New Orleans anytime.

As the plane lifted off the ground, bound for Atlanta and then Milan, Giovanni thought how different everything had turned out. Just a short time ago, everything was so promising. But now it all looked bleak.

America had closed it's doors to him. He had no connections there anymore. Italy had never opened its doors. He was tired of trying to chase a dream that was impossible to attain. He had given it his best try, but it was now finished. The fire to keep pursuing his dream had been extinguished.

## A TEACHER'S REQUEST

*W*hen Giovanni arrived back in Milan, he spoke very briefly to both Alfredo and Isabella. Alfredo tried to argue with Giovanni not to give up his dream, but Giovanni would not listen. Alfredo begged him not to turn his back on his God-given talent and his destiny, but Giovanni could not be persuaded. His mind was made up. He would no longer pursue a singing career.

As the days since his return passed, Giovanni slowly recovered from his accident. However, at the same time, he slipped further and further into a depression. Since he no longer considered having a career as a singer feasible, he no longer would accept the financial support Alfredo had been providing. He would go find a job.

Anna was concerned about her son's growing depression. She tried to convince him to speak to Angelo about getting his old job back, but Giovanni said he no longer had the heart to sing. Anna found herself praying every night for Giovanni to find happiness again. She also noticed that Giovanni and Isabella were growing apart. Anna knew that Isabella brought happiness to her son. She prayed that their relationship would last through these hard times.

After a few weeks, Giovanni started to look for a job. With the help of Anna, he found one as a salesman at Babeto's. His father had held the exact same job. Giorgio Babeto offered the job to Giovanni on the spot.

Giovanni started his job on August 6th. Once he started working, he spoke to Alfredo and Isabella less and less. He devoted all of his time to his work as a salesman. He even stopped listening to opera around the house.

During the same time, he was looking for a job, Isabella came to see him. After arguing back and forth with her father, she had finally agreed with her father's "advice" to go to the University of Bologna to study pre-law. She went to see Giovanni, hopeful that he would give her a reason to stay. None was forthcoming. His depression was so low that he gave Isabella the impression he didn't care whether she went or not. In his mind, he began to believe that her father was right. He was a nobody. Giovanni had lost all confidence in himself.

When Isabella left him that day, she was certain that their relationship was over. She would go to Bologna and try to forget him, if at all possible. Giovanni did not speak to her again before she left for Bologna in mid-August. She saw no other alternative or any reason to stay. Giovanni didn't even attempt to see her before she left. She knew she still loved him, but he had changed so much since New Orleans. Perhaps, with time, she could forget him.

As for Alfredo, Giovanni's talks with him became shorter

and shorter and less frequent. They soon stopped altogether. Giovanni had shunned all that he loved and dreamed.

———

IN LATE AUGUST, Giovanni arrived home from work around 7:00 p.m. He sat down and ate dinner with his mother and sister. Right after he finished, there was a loud knock at the front door. Giovanni got up and was surprised to find Alfredo del Monte standing on his doorstep. Alfredo had a deep look of sadness on his face.

Giovanni asked, "Alfredo, how did you get here?"

Alfredo responded very quietly, "I got a nurse's aid to bring me. She will be back for me in an hour. I must talk with you."

"Sure," was Giovanni's response.

In the meantime, Anna had come into the front room and told Alfredo hello. Alfredo asked her if she minded if he and Giovanni went for a walk. She told him that would be fine. Alfredo and Giovanni went out into the street.

As Anna closed the door behind them, she peered out into the street. Giovanni was leading Alfredo by the hand. They were talking very quietly. Anna shut the door and prayed that Alfredo would bring happiness back to her son.

Alfredo told Giovanni to walk with him to the *Piazza del Duomo*. They made the short walk over to the Piazza and sat on a bench there. All was quiet except for cars passing along the *Corso di Porta Romana*. Once seated on the bench, Alfredo said, "Giovanni, I have missed seeing you."

"I have missed seeing you also. I have been very busy."

Alfredo nodded his head in feigned agreement and then

said, "Busy selling clothes. Why have you given up your dream?"

"I have not given up my dream. It has given up on me. I realized after New Orleans that it is hopeless."

"It is not hopeless, as long as you don't give up. You have turned your back on everything that you love: opera, Isabella and me."

Giovanni sighed and said, "What do you want of me, Alfredo? I tried. I gave it my best effort. *Lasciami*."

Alfredo lifted his finger and said, "I will not leave you alone. I want you to be happy. I know you are not. I beg of you to please don't make the mistake I made."

"What mistake?"

"I know Lydia told you how I lost my eyesight. I wanted nothing more than to sing at La Scala. But when I lost my eyesight, I gave up all hope and quit on life. I became depressed and felt like I had nowhere to go. Maestro Prandelli and his wife, may she rest in peace, came to me and tried to convince me to continue to sing. An operatic stage career would have been very difficult. But a career on the concert stage and studio recordings might have been achieved. I would not listen to them. I wanted nothing to do with it anymore. I moved on and went deeper and deeper into despair. Since that day, I live with regret. I had a calling, but because I thought the fates were against me, I didn't want to pursue it. Please, *amico*, don't give up. You can still achieve your dream as long as you don't turn your back on it as I did."

"But you didn't turn your back. There comes a point where you must move forward. You did so because you were blind. I did so because I don't want to chase something I can never become."

"And what about Isabella? You gave up on her as well. She loves you."

"It's useless to see her. Her father won't have me. She doesn't need me. She will find someone else."

Alfredo rose up from the bench and said, "Giovanni, is that how you will live the rest of your life. Anything difficult that arises, you give up. That is not the person I first met when he wandered into the *Casa Verdi*, a young man filled with a passion for life and determined in fulfilling his life dream." Alfredo sat back down and said, "As you know, I love to tell stories. Have you ever heard of Josef Schmidt?

"Alfredo, I'm not in the mood."

Alfredo, ignoring Giovanni, continued, "He was a Jewish tenor from Germany. He started singing in the 1930's. He was very talented and the possessor of a beautiful voice. The only problem was, Schmidt was not even 5 ft tall. Thus, his chance of ever singing on stage was hopeless. Yet, he never stopped pursuing his dream. He started singing on radio, and in concerts.

"Prior to Hitler prohibiting Jews from appearing on the radio in Germany, he was broadcasting complete operas on the radio. Schmidt was invited to sing in America, where he was billed as 'The Pocket Caruso'. In 1940, he finally reached his goal. He performed in *La Bohème* on stage in Brussels. You see, you can never let your dreams die."

Giovanni said, "I have never heard of him. What happened after that?"

"In 1942, he was captured while trying to flee the Nazis.

He was imprisoned in a camp where he died. Right before he died, he was singing."

Giovanni ironically said, "That's a great story, Alfredo. Follow your dream, and you end up dead."

"No! He achieved his dream. It's better to die without regret than to die with it. All I'm trying to tell you is not to give up. You have lost the ability to hear background music. You have lost the passion. Get it back somehow and live again. Take it from someone who knows. Someone who went down that path."

Giovanni stood up and told Alfredo, "You don't know what you are talking about. Come, I will take you back to my house."

As they walked back to the house, they didn't speak at all. When they reached the house, Alfredo quietly said, "My name is Alfredo del Monte. I am a teacher in need of a singer. Can I teach you?"

Those words stopped Giovanni in his tracks. He turned to Alfredo, who had tears welling up in his eyes. Giovanni pulled Alfredo close and said he loved him. The nurse's aid pulled up just then. Giovanni went inside his house as Alfredo, with help from the aid, made his way to the car. He hoped Giovanni would change his mind.

Giovanni tossed and turned when he retired to bed early that night. He could not sleep. Alfredo's words hung heavy in his heart. Suddenly, the door to his room was opened and his mother walked through the door. She sat on the bed and said, "Giovanni, I was hoping you were awake. I need to tell you something. When people support you, your response should be to give them back one hundred percent. Alfredo has supported you all these months. Don't quit on him. I know you are unhappy. You are a singer. That is the only thing you ever wanted to be."

"Mamma, I tried. I have given it my best shot. But it's useless."

"Nonsense. You are very good. Someone will give you a break. All you have to do is keep working at it. Alfredo, Isabella and I believe in you."

Giovanni said, "Please don't mention her name. It's over between us. I was stupid to think I had a chance with her."

"Isabella loves you, and I know you love her. She brought you happiness."

"Mamma, it's over. She can find someone else. Someone to make her father proud and happy."

"Don't say that, Giovanni. I know she will hate me for telling you this, but the funds Alfredo gave you actually came from her. She was secretly supporting you. She made Alfredo vow to never tell you."

Giovanni sat in bed, stunned. He finally said, "She did that for me?"

"Alfredo and Isabella devoted themselves to you. You must do the same for them."

With that, Anna left the room. Giovanni thought about what she said and about his conversation with Alfredo earlier. Alfredo and Anna were both right in one regard. He was unhappy. He hated selling clothes. He was a singer. That is what his father wanted him to be. That is what God wanted him to be. That is the only thing he ever wanted to be. He had a gift, no matter what other people thought. He had sung in public, and people liked his voice. That was his destiny and the only dream he ever wanted to pursue.

At that moment, he suddenly realized that Alfredo's

lessons all these past months were not only on how to become a better singer but even more, how to become a better man. Alfredo had taught him to not quit when life got hard.

He sprung from his bed, got the keys to his mother's car, and left. When Anna heard him drive away from the house, a huge smile came to her face as she lay in bed. Perhaps he would try again. Hopefully, he was on his way to see Alfredo.

Indeed, that was exactly where he was going. When Giovanni reached the *Casa Verdi*, he went straight to Alfredo's room, where he found Alfredo sleeping. He entered the room, bent down next to the bed and whispered, "Alfredo. Alfredo. *Senti*."

Alfredo sat up in bed with a start. Giovanni tapped him on his shoulder and said, "Alfredo, it's Giovanni."

"Giovanni, *come va*?"

"*Molto bene.* I have a singing teacher. I want to be a singer. Forgive me. I have been a fool."

Alfredo smiled broadly. "*Grazie a Dio.* We can start tomorrow after you get off of work. Our first priority will be to find somewhere for you to sing. I have an idea and I will let you know tomorrow. I am so happy." He hugged Giovanni tightly.

Giovanni left the *Casa Verdi*, happy once again. Tomorrow, he would be doing what he loved. However, to be truly happy, he knew there was one thing he had to do. He got in his mother's car, entered the highway, and started the little less than the two and a half hours drive to Bologna.

# A SCHOOL SERANADE

*D*ay by day, since coming to school in Bologna, Isabella had tried to put Giovanni out of her mind. Every day she failed at this task. Since starting school, she had ventured out on a few dates. Doing so only reinforced in her mind that Giovanni was the one. There was no one like him. It was as if he was born in the wrong century, the way he treated her with a nobility and a romantic vein that no longer existed in society. He lived his life lost in his dreams of characters from the operas he so loved. He always spoke to her about opera and music. He would sing or quote lines from operas to her to let his feelings be known. And yet, at the same time, Giovanni always showed an interest in Isabella's dreams. He was the kindest and most intelligent person she ever met. She loved him but was positive she would never see him again.

Giovanni arrived at the ancient university city of Bologna around 1:00 a.m. Bologna is an attractive, old city located between Milan and Florence. The University of Bologna is one of the oldest schools in Europe.

Giovanni exited his vehicle and walked into the main quad area of the University. He asked a passing student for directions to the women's dormitory. The student pointed it out to him.

The dormitory was five-stories high, with windows overlooking the quad. A few of the windows were open. Giovanni made his way to the front door.

Giovanni entered the front lobby of the dorm and approached the desk in the lobby. A pretty young student was working behind the desk. She picked up her head and asked Giovanni if he needed help. He said he was there to see Isabella Monterone. The young girl batted her eyes at Giovanni and told him that no visitors were allowed in after 9:00 p.m., and no one was allowed to call the rooms after midnight.

Giovanni walked out of the lobby and back into the quad, determined to see Isabella. He needed to speak to her. He looked up at the windows of the dormitory. For a moment, he remembered that first night when he had sung to Isabella under her balcony. Just then, an idea hit him. He walked into the middle of the quad, below the windows of the dormitory, and began to sing. Background music was alive and well in him again. Alfredo was correct that he had lost it, but now it was back.

He sang the aria "Cielo e mar" (Sky and sea) from *La Gioconda* by Ponchielli, a teacher of Puccini.

As he began to sing, the girls in the dormitory ran to the windows and peered out. Soon almost all of the windows were open, with the girls listening to that wonderful voice. All of the girls were wondering who he was singing to.

At last, Giovanni saw her. On the fourth floor, at the left corner of the building, a window opened, and Isabella was looking out. Giovanni walked to that corner, went to one knee, and finished the aria. The girls realized that he was singing to Isabella. Giovanni sang with great emotion

*Qui nell'ombra, ov'io mi giacio*
*Here in the darkness where I wait*

*coll'anelito del cor, vieni, o donna, vieni al bacio*
*with longing in my heart, come, sweet girl, come to*

*della vita, sí, della vita e dell'amor!*
*the kiss of life, yes, of life and love!*

*Vieni, o donna, qui t'attendo*
*Come, sweet girl, I await*

*coll'anelito del cor, vieni, o donna,*
*with longing in my heart, ah, come, sweet girl, ah,*

*vieni al bacio vieni, vieni, vieni al bacio,*
*come to the kiss, come, come to the kiss,*

*vieni e dell'amor, si, dell'amor.*
*come to the kiss of life and love, yes, love.*

*Ah vien! Ah vien!*
*Ah, come! Ah come!*

When he finished, all of the students applauded. He blew a kiss up to Isabella. She was crying in the window. The girls in the dormitory were yelling for her to go out to the quad. Without a gesture, she closed the window. Giovanni wondered if she was on her way down or did she close the window to never see him again. He stood up and looked up at the window again.

Just then, from out of the lobby, Isabella came running out into the quad in her nightgown and into the arms of Giovanni. The girls erupted in applause again. A few of the girls who knew Isabella guessed that this was the true love that she had spoken about so fondly.

Isabella was crying in his arms, telling him how glad she was that he came. After a few moments, she went inside to put on some clothes. As she made her way back to her dormitory room, the girls on her floor of the dormitory came out of their rooms and were congratulating her.

After quickly changing her clothes, she came back out, and strolled with Giovanni, out the front gates of the University, down the winding streets of Bologna.

The University was close to the *Piazza del Nettuno* with its charming fountain of Neptune. Giovanni and Isabella held hands walking into the piazza. Since it was so late, there were only a few people around. They sat out in the piazza at a table near the fountain. Giovanni apologized to her for his attitude the past couple of weeks. He missed her the whole time and just needed a crack on his *"testa dura"*. He went on to tell her about Alfredo coming to his house and that he had decided to try to sing again.

She said, "You owe Alfredo so much."

"I know. He brought me back to you. If you will have me? I also owe a lot to you. I love you so much."

She leaned across the table and kissed Giovanni, assuring him that she was hoping for this day. "I'm the luckiest girl in the world. Those girls in the dormitory are going to be so jealous. No one gets serenaded to anymore."

Giovanni grew serious and said, "*Ti amo,* Isabella. I am so sorry if I hurt you."

"Giovanni, I love you. I have always loved you since that first night you stood below my balcony and sang to me. My father has no control over me. I have grown up these few short weeks. I will not lose you again."

They spoke for a little while longer about how much they meant to each other and had missed each other. They then got up from the table and slowly, arm in arm, walked across the *Piazza del Nettuno,* under the bright moon overhead.

# MAESTRO MASSIMO TORCELLI

*A*nna could tell the next morning that happiness had returned to Giovanni. She was overjoyed when Giovanni said he would be home late because he had to train with Alfredo after work. She asked him why he was so late last night and was thrilled to hear about his trip to Bologna. Giovanni was so happy to know Anna approved of Isabella. If only there were some way Judge Monterone would approve of him.

When Giovanni arrived at the *Casa Verdi* that afternoon, Alfredo was waiting for him in the second-floor salon. Alfredo had a huge smile on his face. Giovanni asked him what he was so happy about.

"*Siediti*, Giovanni. I'm waiting for someone." Giovanni sat down, and the two men made small talk. Giovanni was extremely tired from his excursions last night but was very interested in what ideas Alfredo had on furthering his chances of singing somewhere. But Alfredo was very silent on the subject. He instead spoke to Giovanni about how exciting it was for him, when he was a young singer, to be in a new city, preparing to perform an opera. He missed that feeling.

Their conversation was interrupted by the sound of footsteps coming up the stairs toward the salon. Alfredo said, "*Eccolo che arriva.*" (Here he comes.)

Giovanni's face almost hit the floor when in walked Maestro Massimo Torcelli, the director of La Scala. Giovanni and Alfredo stood up when he entered. Alfredo was the first to speak and said, "Giovanni, I would like to introduce you to Maestro Massimo Torcelli." Giovanni, as if in a dream, extended his hand. He no longer felt tired.

Maestro Torcelli shook his hand and said to Giovanni, "My young singer, you have some very persuasive supporters." Giovanni had a look of confusion on his face. Torcelli continued, "I'm sorry to hear about the events that took place in New Orleans with Signora Prandelli. She was a fine lady. She loved your voice and would have done wonders for your career. However, you didn't need her for that. You have Alfredo del Monte.

"This morning, upon arriving at my office, I was met by Alfredo, waiting to speak to me. He had brought along a friend of his, Giuseppe di Stefano. Your teacher assured me that you are ready to make your debut. I have heard you on two occasions and agree with that assessment. Alfredo also informed me of your problems with finding a house willing to let you sing. At La Scala, I am the judge and jury. No one, and I mean no one, can tell me who can sing there." He looked right at Giovanni, winked, and said, "Not even a Milanese Judge."

Giovanni smiled while Torcelli continued, saying, "Signor del Monte and Signor di Stefano were both persistent this morning at my office that I give you a chance. Di Stefano was perhaps the most popular tenor La Scala ever had in its stable. La Scala owes him. La Scala also owes Alfredo a favor. He saved the life of the greatest costume designer La Scala has ever had. I have granted Alfredo his wish."

Giovanni sat back in his chair, shocked. Torcelli said, "We open this season with Verdi's *Aida*. I have already booked a tenor to sing the lead. However, as is my practice, I hire two leads for every part. Neither singer knows who will win the role until the end of rehearsals. Based on how they do, I make my decision. One will sing all of the performances. The other will be an understudy and sing if the winner cannot. I have a contract for you. It calls for seven performances of *Aida*, including opening night. There is a clause that gives me discretion to choose who will sing. Your fee is based on that decision. Even if you don't get chosen, the opportunity to study at La Scala and be under contract with La Scala will do wonders in your pursuit of a career. Do you accept?"

Giovanni nodded his head without even blinking. Torcelli handed him a contract and told him to have a legal person review it with him to make sure everything was in order. "Opening night, of course, will be Friday, December 7th, with rehearsals starting in November."

Giovanni thanked Maestro Torcelli for giving him this chance. Maestro Torcelli said to thank Alfredo, not him. With that, Maestro Torcelli left Alfredo and Giovanni.

Once he left, Giovanni turned to Alfredo and tried to speak but could not. Alfredo instead said, "Giovanni

Tempesta, you will beat out that other tenor. You will be making your debut at La Scala. What do you think of that?"

"*Aida* at La Scala. That was the first opera I ever saw at La Scala with my father. Although not Puccini, it will do."

Alfredo laughed and said, "We have a lot of work to do. You must quit your job as a salesman and devote all of your time to get ready. The contract probably gives you a stipend. Do you have someone who can read it?"

Giovanni thought immediately of Salvatore Dantoni. He could send it to him in New Orleans to read. "As for my job as a salesman. Quit? Gladly."

Alfredo said, "Before we begin your training, you must study the role of Radames in *Aida*. I want you to study the libretto and listen to a recording for a week before we begin to train. Immerse yourself into the story. It is a wonderful tale. Come back in a week to begin your training."

Giovanni hugged his teacher and thanked him for all that he had done. Alfredo had even gotten his favorite tenor of all time to speak up for him. That truly was unbelievable. Without Alfredo, he would have probably spent his life selling clothes. Now he would be a singer. He would start his training with Alfredo in a week. But for now, he would study the opera and know it by heart.

Unlike *La Bohème*, Giovanni didn't know *Aida* as well. He knew the story and the arias but not the entire opera. However, by listening to a recording and studying a libretto, he would know it. Giovanni knew just the place to study the opera for a week.

The next day, after Giovanni quit his job at Babeto's, he took the train to Bologna, along with his recording of *Aida* with Zinka Milanov and Jussi Bjorling. Isabella met him at the train station that night and took him to her dormitory. His plan was to study the role while she was in class and enjoy time together with her as well. At night, he would have to secretly sleep there, since there was a curfew for men in the dormitory. She was so happy to see him and was thrilled they would be able to spend time together.

While she went to class the next day, Giovanni studied the libretto sitting out in the quad. He studied all day, sitting under the trees, while students passed him throughout the day en route to their classes.

Sitting under the trees, reading a libretto, made him think of the French opera composer Jules Massenet. Alfredo had described to Giovanni that Massenet while working on his operas, would memorize the entire libretto before writing one note of music. He would then take a walk through the woods, repeating the words from the libretto, allowing inspiration to come to him for the music. When one listens to his music, one feels the peace that was in his soul, walking through the woods. Giovanni hoped sitting under these trees would give him the inspiration to learn the role of Radames.

At 5:00 p.m., Giovanni went back to the dormitory to meet Isabella. He went inside her room and waited for her return. Soon she arrived carrying her books into the small room. She dumped the books on the bed, kissed Giovanni, and went to use the bathroom.

While she was in the bathroom, Giovanni picked up one of the books. Expecting to see pre-law books, he was surprised when he noticed that all of the books concerned childhood education. He asked as she came out of the bathroom, "I thought you were studying pre-law?"

"My father thinks that is what I am studying. I am

studying to become a teacher. I am tired of him leading my life. He wanted me to come to school here, so I did. But I will study what I want. Dating you has taught me how to stand up to him. As I told you, I have changed."

Giovanni asked, "What will happen when he finds out?"

"I don't care anymore. Just like I don't care if he finds out I'm seeing you. I love you and want to be with you. I never want to lose you again." With that, they fell into a long kiss.

---

THE NEXT MORNING, they were awakened by the phone. Isabella picked it up and spoke to the person on the other end of the line. Whoever it was only spoke English, because Isabella was trying to respond in her broken English. She finished speaking and told the person to hold on. She handed the phone to Giovanni and told him, "It's someone for you. Your mother gave him my phone number."

Giovanni picked up the phone and said hello.

"Signor Tempesta, this is Salvatore Dantoni from New Orleans."

"*Ah, consigliere.* How are things in New Orleans?" "*Consigliere*" was the nickname Giovanni called Salvatore, referring to the attorney character in the Godfather movie that had come out a few years before.

"All is well. My father asked how you were doing?"

"I'm doing great. I'm so glad you called. I have mailed to you a contract from La Scala. I have been given the opportunity to perhaps make my debut there."

"That's wonderful news. My father will be thrilled to hear that. Imagine singing at La Scala. I'll gladly look at your contract. I was calling you today to tell you that, first, I have been speaking to the attorney for the New Orleans Opera. They have agreed to pay you $2000 for the time you spent at rehearsals. And secondly, as you know, we have been speaking to the adjuster for the truck company. They are adamant that they want this case settled. They have asked us for an offer. I sent them an offer, as well as your medical records showing the injuries you sustained. I think it is to our best advantage to settle this case before you sing at La Scala. Part of our negotiations with the adjuster was the fact that you lost the opportunity to sing. Our first offer to them was for seventy-five."

Giovanni repeated the figure, "Seventy-five hundred?"

Salvatore laughed, "No. $75,000.00. The adjuster came back to us with an offer to settle this case for $55,000.00, plus medicals."

Giovanni almost dropped the phone. Salvatore advised him he thought that it was a good settlement. Giovanni agreed and thanked Salvatore for the call. After Salvatore took his fee, Giovanni would have over $40,000.00.

Giovanni was stunned by the turn of events. He was getting prepared to open rehearsals at La Scala, he was again training with Alfredo, Isabella was back in his life, and now he would have money in his pocket. Giovanni was sure it was all too good to be true.

He turned to Isabella and told her the good news. She was very happy for Giovanni. Little did she know that his receiving those funds would change her life as well.

# SING WITH PASSION

*A*fter his week of study in Bologna, Giovanni felt very confident about his memorization of the role. He had listened to the recording and had studied the libretto intently. He was very prepared to begin his training with Alfredo.

He was also convinced more than ever that Isabella would be with him forever. The night before he left Bologna, he spoke to Isabella about their future plans. Once he had established himself and had a career, hopefully in a few years, they would marry. His *zio*, Piero, who lived in Parma, could set them up in an apartment. Parma was centrally located between Bologna and Milan, so Isabella could finish school, and Giovanni could continue with his career, with Milan as his base. Perhaps by then, Isabella's father would approve.

The weeks before the start of rehearsals at La Scala went very quickly. Giovanni and Isabella spent as much time as they could together. Whenever Giovanni had the chance, which was not often, he took the train to Bologna to spend time with her. Dating now was a lot easier since she lived far away from the watchful eye of her father. Also, her not living at home allowed Giovanni the opportunity to call her on the phone, which he did every night.

As far as Giovanni's training, it was going very well. Alfredo was a master teaching his beloved Verdi. Giovanni's voice was becoming better and better. And his passion for singing was even better than before. Signora Cantu even helped Giovanni with studying the duets.

Soon, his weeks of training with Alfredo were drawing to a close. It was time to report to La Scala. Alfredo knew that the most important thing he had to do since Giovanni's return from New Orleans was to restore Giovanni's confidence. He was convinced that he had done so.

On the night of October 31st, Giovanni and Alfredo walked outside the *Casa Verdi* and sat out in the *Piazza Buonarroti*. Giovanni looked around the Piazza, and his mind was flooded with memories of that first day when he had come to this place and met Alfredo. Across the Piazza, Giovanni noticed Signor Toscano's apartment. He laughed to himself as he thought how he would love to tell Signor Toscano where to go.

Alfredo broke the silence and said, "*Amico*. Tomorrow you begin what you have worked very hard for these past few months. If you continue to work hard, La Scala will hear a first-class tenor."

"I owe everything to you, Alfredo. I will never forget everything you have done for me. You are a foxhole man."

Alfredo laughed and said, "*Grazie*. You have brought me so much joy. You have a natural talent. All I had to do was provide you with the connections. You already had the voice."

"No, Alfredo. I can tell that my studies with you have improved my voice. You can't deny that."

Alfredo said, "Always sing with passion. When you sing *Aida*, let Verdi live through you. At the heart of the opera is passion. I know you know the role. But feel it. Radames, a young Egyptian warrior, is named commander of the Egyptian army in its war against Ethiopia. He is loved by the Egyptian Princess, Amneris. However, he loves and is loved by the Princess's slave, Aida, who, as it turns out, is the daughter of the King of the Ethiopians. The perfect love triangle is thus established. You must show through the use of your voice the inner turmoil Radames has brewing; love of country or love of Aida. It's a beautiful story when sung with passion."

"I will sing with passion, Alfredo."

Giovanni and Alfredo spoke for a little while longer, and then Giovanni left to go home. Tomorrow he would start the pursuit of his life-long dream.

# PART IV

MILAN, ITALY
NOVEMBER, 1979

# 37

## REHEARSALS AT LA SCALA

On November 1, 1979, Giovanni woke up early and ate breakfast with Anna. After receiving a phone call from Isabella, he made the short walk to La Scala to begin rehearsals for *Aida*.

When he arrived at the stage door to La Scala, Giovanni had to laugh to himself. Across from the stage door was Angelo's. How far he had come. He entered the stage door and was met by a guard. Giovanni's name was on the list, and he was allowed to enter backstage. It was like he was in a dream. He walked along the hallway where the dressing rooms were located. Giovanni tried to imagine all of his favorite singers walking these same halls.

Giovanni was startled when he heard a voice from behind him say, "Signor Tempesta. I am Enzo Fracopoco. I am the stage director for *Aida*. Welcome to La Scala. We will be meeting with Maestro Torcelli in the *Sala Gialla*. I will lead you there."

Giovanni's ears perked up at the mention of the *Sala Gialla*. He thought of Alfredo and the bombing. Enzo led Giovanni upstairs and into the second-floor room. Enzo opened the door to the *Sala Gialla* and told Giovanni, "The others will be coming shortly. I shall return."

Once Signor Fracopoco left, Giovanni looked around the room. The walls of the *Sala Gialla* were lined with photos of the bombed-out La Scala right after the allied raids during World War II. Giovanni looked closely at those pictures and was amazed that Alfredo had even lived through it at all. The damage to the theater was tremendous. La Scala was reopened in 1946, with a gala performance, conducted by Toscanini.

Giovanni then looked around the rest of the room. Just as Lydia had said, the room was windowless. Not a sound from outside could be heard. No wonder Alfredo never heard the planes coming that day, Giovanni thought. A massive table was in the center of the room. Against the far wall was a grand piano. Above the piano was the huge portrait of Arturo Toscanini.

The door to the *Sala Gialla* was suddenly pushed open and in walked Maestro Torcelli and his entourage. He had three assistants, two beautiful women, and a man with him, plus Enzo, and the rest of the cast.

Torcelli made the introductions of everyone to Giovanni. Maestro Torcelli first introduced Giovanni to Signor Gino Fidito, the other tenor under contract for the role of Radames. Giovanni extended his hand to the older tenor. Fidito turned his back and walked away. The contest was on.

Signor Fidito was from Calabria. He was 36 years old and had been singing professionally for twelve years. He had sung at all of the major opera houses in Europe and America and also had a lucrative recording contract. With all of those credentials, he considered an upstart like Giovanni Tempesta, nothing more than a pest. After all, Signor Fidito had already sung at La Scala and was ready to return.

The rest of the cast was very nice to Giovanni. Most were aware that he had never sung before in opera. All of them had sung all over the world, and all had sung at La Scala numerous times. One of the sopranos signed to sing the role of Aida was Christiana Gabodo, a world-class soprano. Giovanni had a few of her recordings. He was mesmerized when he met her.

Maestro Torcelli put a stop to the introductions and was ready to start work. He handed out an itinerary of how the rehearsals would go. Every day would start with vocalizing, then arias, and then stage work. It would be long hours. Today each person would be measured for their costume, but first, Maestro Torcelli wanted to hear each person sing something of their choosing so he could get a feel for their voice.

Maestro Torcelli sat at the piano located in the *Sala Gialla* and called each person, one by one, to sing an aria of their choosing. As each person sang, Maestro Torcelli would rant and rave and scream at the top of his lungs. Maestro Torcelli was a perfectionist. He always gave the impression to a singer that he was not happy with their voice. He thought this would make them work harder. Maestro Torcelli was adamant that the singer had to adhere to how the music was originally written. Thus, if there was an interpolated high C called for by tradition in an aria, Maestro Torcelli would not allow it.

Since the time Maestro Torcelli came to La Scala from the San Carlo Opera House in Naples, his hometown, he kept up his practice of hiring two singers for each major role. Singers hated this because they were never sure if they were going to sing. Yet, it fostered competition and a drive to succeed in the singers. And Maestro Torcelli could get away with it because this was La Scala and singers wanted to sing here.

When it was Giovanni's turn, Maestro Torcelli asked him what he wanted to sing. Of course, Giovanni chose, 'Io conosco un giardino', the same aria he had sung at the picnic in New Orleans. Maestro Torcelli was surprised by his choice. He began to play, and Giovanni sang. While he was singing, Signor Fracopoco leaned over to Maestro Torcelli and said, "You were right. *Bellisimo*."

But Maestro Torcelli never showed signs of liking anything. He screamed at Giovanni that his timing was all off. When Giovanni was finished, he went and sat down next to Signora Christiana. She leaned over and told him, "I hope you win. Your voice is wonderful."

That first day lasted about six hours, dissecting the opera and then getting measured for the costume. Giovanni's costume would be a short tunic with a metal breastplate as the leader of the Egyptian army.

As Giovanni was preparing to leave the theater to go home, Maestro Torcelli came up to him and said, "Tempesta, you did well for your first day. Come with me."

Giovanni was surprised by the compliment. The other singers had mentioned how Maestro Torcelli never said anything nice about their voices.

Maestro Torcelli first brought Giovanni to the stage of the La Scala opera house. The theater was dark. Giovanni stepped onto the stage for the first time and was hit with a flood of emotions. He thought about his father. The view from the stage was spectacular. The silence was broken by Maestro Torcelli, who said, "This is where it all happens. Most of the greatest singers who have ever lived have all sung on this stage."

In Giovanni's mind ran the voices of di Stefano, Caruso, Gigli, Callas, Bastianini, Granforte, de Luca, Ruffo, and Pertile. He also thought of Puccini and Verdi standing on this very stage, accepting the applause of the audience after their opera had been performed. He looked up at the top of the theater and noticed the *loggione,* the most feared place in all of opera. On this very stage, perhaps, Giovanni Tempesta would be making his debut.

Maestro Torcelli then led Giovanni away from the stage and down to the basement. They soon came before two ancient columns. Maestro Torcelli said, "This is all that is left of the original church, *Santa Maria della Scala,* that once stood on this spot. It was knocked down, and in 1778 La Scala was completed. That is how La Scala got its name, after the church."

The two of them descended further down under the stage of La Scala. The entire ceiling was lined with pipes that, through the use of water, controlled the massive hydraulic lifts for the stage. Maestro Torcelli said, "I wanted to bring you down here to show you how we create our magic on the stage up above. Alfredo told me about your knowledge of opera. I doubted it until you sang the aria upstairs. Only someone who has knowledge would have chosen that forgotten song. Young singers today come to me with a wealth of music school training. They attend the great music schools throughout Italy. I will ask them about singers like Pertile, Gigli, de Lucia and Bonci. They look at me with blank stares. But when I say these names to you, I can see through your eyes that you hear their voices in your head."

Giovanni remarked, "I grew up listening to all of those tenors with my father."

"Well, my young tenor, you have a gift. And it is a gift, especially after what Alfredo told me. You can't read music. I have heard you sing now on three occasions. To sing like you do, but not be able to read music, is a gift. But, the fact that you can't read music will be our secret. If Signor Fidito ever found out, and if you do win the role, he would make use of that fact to embarrass you with the *loggione*."

When Maestro Torcelli said the word "*loggione*", he said it with fear in his voice. Even the great director of La Scala feared it. The *loggione* was the beast. Every singer feared it, yet thrived on it at the same time. The opening night at La Scala was usually when the *loggione* was at its wildest. If the *loggione* liked you, it could make a career. If it disliked you, it could end one.

Maestro Torcelli said, "Every day, after rehearsals, I will give you a basic lesson on reading music. It will help you in your pursuit of a career and will make learning a new opera much easier."

"*Grazie*, Maestro. I don't know what to say."

"That was at the request of Alfredo del Monte. He is a wonderful man."

"I know."

Giovanni thanked Maestro Torcelli for the tour and his offer to help him learn to read music. As Giovanni turned to leave, Maestro Torcelli said, "You are a '*terroni*', like me.

Practice hard every day and perhaps your voice will bounce off the walls and be heard by the ghosts of La Scala come December 7th and maybe . . . you shut up the *loggione*."

Giovanni shook hands with Maestro Torcelli, then left the theater. He chuckled to himself that Maestro Torcelli called him *"terroni"*, that derogatory word the Milanese called foreigners. Although Giovanni was born in Milan, the fact that his parents were not, meant he was not a true Milanese. Perhaps since Maestro Torcelli was a foreigner too, Giovanni had a chance. He left La Scala and headed to the *Casa Verdi* to tell Alfredo about his first day of rehearsals at La Scala.

---

REHEARSALS WENT VERY WELL for the next few weeks. Giovanni also worked hard with Maestro Torcelli, learning to read music. Giovanni was well trained by Alfredo, which made him look very prepared at the rehearsals. Giovanni found the acting part of rehearsals to be harder than the singing part. He had absolutely no training in acting.

He brought up this fear to Alfredo on one of his nightly telephone calls to him. Alfredo said, "Act naturally. You have lived with music in your head all your life. Just relate that to the stage."

One night after the first week of rehearsals, Giovanni stopped in Angelo's after practice. The Maenza boys had to get all the scoop on how rehearsals were going. Giovanni asked how his replacement was doing.

Mario chuckled and said, "Angelo has been through two singers already. We have a new tenor starting tonight. You are a hard singer to replace."

Just then, Angelo came over and offered his congratulations. He told Giovanni, "Some of the stage workers from La Scala, who come over here to eat, keep me informed of your progress. They are all very impressed. As well they should be. I miss you, Giovanni."

"I miss you too," he told his old boss.

# 38

## A DEFIANT MOMENT

*I*n mid-November, Isabella's father became aware that Giovanni Tempesta was under contract at La Scala. He went wild. He called a few board members and demanded that a no-name singer from next door at Angelo's should not be singing at the greatest opera house in the world. The board told Judge Monterone that their hands were tied because Maestro Torcelli was adamant that Giovanni would remain under contract. The Judge grew furious.

Around the same time, Judge Monterone ran into the daughter of a close friend of his. She also went to the University of Bologna. During a casual conversation with the young lady, she told the Judge that it was nice being in school with Isabella. They even had a class together, since they were both majoring in education. The Judge made her repeat that statement. His face even got redder with her last comment. She told him how all the girls at school were envious of

Isabella because her boyfriend, who had a wonderful voice, had serenaded her outside the dormitory.

The very next day, the Judge drove to Bologna to confront his daughter. He went straight to her dorm room and found her there. She did not deny seeing Giovanni. As their conversation became heated, she told her father, "I love him and will not stop seeing him."

The Judge yelled, "You will not defy me. I did not pay for your education so you could become a teacher and marry some loser."

They argued back and forth. He finally told her to pack her bags. She would leave school and be transferred somewhere far away next semester, where she would study pre-law. She begged her father not to do this, but he wouldn't hear of it. She returned to Milan with him, totally dejected.

When she arrived in Milan on that Thursday night, she went to her room after another screaming match with her father. After she cried in her bed for an hour, she climbed down the balcony, jumped the fence, and caught a bus to La Scala, afraid to take her car and alert her father that she had left.

She waited outside the stage door at La Scala for the rehearsals to finish. After about an hour, Giovanni came out of the doors and was surprised to see Isabella there. She was crying and said, "Giovanni, I have to speak to you."

They made their way to the bench across from La Scala. Giovanni asked her, once they sat down, "What's wrong, Isabella? Why are you here? Is everything alright?"

"My father pulled me out of school. He found out what I was studying and that I was dating you. He is sending me away next semester to another school to study pre-law. I don't know what to do. He wouldn't even let me take my finals."

Giovanni looked kindly at Isabella and said, "*Ti amo, Isabella.* I have been thinking about us for some time now and where our relationship was going. I believe your father has made our decision for us."

Giovanni stood up from the bench, went to one knee, grabbed Isabella by the hand, and asked, "Will you marry me?"

Isabella was taken aback. She asked, "Are you serious?"

"*Si. Tanto.*"

"But how? How can we? Where will we live? How will we live?"

"Since I've gotten the funds from my settlement, I have thought about how much I wanted to be with you for the rest of my life. As I told you, I have an uncle who lives in Parma. I know he can get us a nice apartment. Parma is only an hour from Bologna and less than an hour and a half from Milan. It will be perfect for us. I can easily get to Milan, and you can finish your studies in Bologna. I will have enough money from my contract with La Scala and my settlement to pay for your education and our expenses since I'm sure your father will not."

"Oh, I know he will not."

Giovanni looked intently into her eyes and said, "I know in my heart and soul that walking through life with you at my side will be both a very gracious and passionate thing. Will you marry me?"

"Of course, Giovanni. Of course," she said excitedly as she melted into his arms and kissed him.

Giovanni said, "I want to get married right away.

Saturday is two days away. Rehearsal will be over by three in the afternoon on Saturday. Meet me right here by four, and I will take care of everything. I have Sunday off, so we can have a one-day honeymoon. I'm sorry we can't have a big wedding or that I don't even have a ring for you."

She smiled and said, "You have given me yourself. That is all that matters."

They kissed again and slowly walked arm and arm through the *Galleria* to get a bite to eat. Giovanni refused to tell her what his plan was for Saturday, mostly because he didn't have one yet. But he did believe that Padre Guardiano, because of his long friendship and fondness for his father and him, would officiate at the nuptial Mass without the need for formal delays.

# THE SECRET GARDEN

*I*sabella was standing outside of her car by La Scala at 4:00 p.m. on Saturday. Giovanni walked out of the stage door and rounded the front of the theater. She looked beautiful in a polka dot sundress. Her hair was pulled back in a ponytail, which made her brown eyes stand out even more.

Giovanni ran over to her and hugged her. As he did so, Isabella said, "I am so happy, Giovanni. I can't believe I'm doing this, but I've never been so sure of anything."

"Me too, Isabella. *Ti amo.*"

She asked, "How do you like my wedding dress?"

"I love it."

She climbed into the passenger seat and told Giovanni, once he got in the driver's seat, "My father believes I went to my grandmother's house for the weekend. I will tell him what I did when we get back on Monday. I'm sure he will be very happy for me," she said ironically. "Can you tell me where we are going? Where are we going to get married?"

"Just you wait and see."

They drove the roads down toward Tuscany. Giovanni, with the help of Anna, had spent all of Friday lining up the wedding ceremony. All in all, he thought he had done a good job in such a short period of time. When he informed Alfredo of his impending marriage, his teacher was very excited for his young pupil.

As they drove, Isabella asked, "Since you're not telling me where we are going, can you tell me where we are spending tonight?"

"We are going to spend two nights in Bellagio, near Lake Como. I hear it's beautiful. My mother worked on getting us a room there."

"Is she happy for us?"

Giovanni looked at her and said, "She is thrilled. She knows how happy you make me. When we come back to Milan on Monday, we will go talk to your father. Then I will go to my rehearsal while you go to Parma with my mother to find us an apartment. By Tuesday, you will be back in school in Bologna, preparing to take your exams, so that you can teach children."

Isabella smiled and said, "I can't believe this. I love you so much. I will try not to think about speaking with my father. I will just enjoy these next two days together and imagine our life together."

Giovanni said, "Our life together. That sounds nice. We will look back at today and will remember this day forever. This is the beginning of an amazing journey for us. There is no one else with whom I would rather be on this journey."

Soon, Giovanni and Isabella were in familiar territory. Isabella asked, "Are we going where I hope we are going?"

Giovanni said, "I don't know where you hope we are going."

"Oh, yes you do. My most favorite spot in the world."

"Vicopelago."

"Oh, Giovanni. You are so romantic. *Ti amo.*"

They soon were by the iron-gate outside the convent. Isabella was surprised to see Anna and Alfredo standing outside the convent gate, waiting for them. As they exited the vehicle, Giovanni told Isabella, "Look. It's your matron of honor and my best man."

Anna came up and hugged Isabella. Alfredo made his way to Giovanni and offered his congratulations.

Anna told them all, "The groom is not allowed to see the bride before the wedding. Alfredo, take Giovanni over to the chapel and see Padre Guardiano."

Isabella and Anna dashed off toward the cloister inside the convent while Giovanni led Alfredo over to the small chapel to meet with Padre Guardiano, the local priest who took care of the property and who had said the funeral for Franco Tempesta. He immediately agreed to do the wedding for Giovanni when he had received the phone call yesterday.

Anna led Isabella inside the cloister. The cloister was dark, yet peaceful. Near the front door was a small room into which Anna led Isabella. The room was once the bedroom for Puccini's sister, the mother superior of the convent. Isabella looked around the little room. It was empty except for an old bed. Isabella noticed a white wedding dress lying on the bed. Anna said, "This is the dress I wore when I married

Giovanni's father. I want you to wear it when you marry my son."

Isabella broke into tears and fell into Anna's arms. She couldn't believe how nice Anna was to her. She thanked Anna for all that she had done.

Anna said, "Well, let's try that dress on. I brought my sewing kit and will fix anything you need done to it. Although you are pretty much the same size I was when I got married."

Isabella undressed and was helped into the wedding dress by Anna. It was a perfect fit. The length needed to be shortened a little bit, but that would be easy for Anna to fix. Anna went to her knees and started to mark off the dress with pins where it needed to be hemmed. She told Isabella to stand up straight and not to move. As Isabella did so, she could look out the window in the little room, which overlooked the courtyard and which provided the light for the room. As the sun was setting, it was a magical sight. Isabella thought about what Giovanni had said in the car and agreed that she would remember this day for the rest of her life.

After the dress was marked off, Isabella disrobed, and Anna started working on the dress, while Isabella put on make-up and fixed her hair. Anna and Isabella spoke the entire time.

Meanwhile, Alfredo and Giovanni were in the chapel, where Gabriella was busy helping Padre Guardiano get the little church ready. Padre Guardiano had spent the entire day fixing up the little chapel. The altar was covered with candles and flowers from the Tuscany region. The flowers were like a burst of spring colors while the candles gave everything a golden glow. The view from the windows located behind the altar of the Tuscan hills was magnificent.

Signor Romano and Signor Montefeltro, from the coffee shop in Milan, had driven up with Anna, Gabriella and Alfredo. Signor Romano would be the photographer for the wedding, while Signor Montefeltro would play the small organ. Giovanni would have loved to have had the Maenza boys come play, but there had not been time.

Giovanni thanked Signor Romano and Signor Montefeltro for all they had done. Signor Romano asked, "How do you like the flower arrangements? We picked those out this afternoon. They are all from Tuscany. While we drove up here with your mother and Alfredo, we stopped along the way whenever we saw a flower we wanted for the arrangement."

Alfredo said, "Giovanni, we made quite a group. Your mother drove. Signor Romano or Signor Montefeltro would yell at her from the backseat, '*Ferma! Ferma!*' They would jump out and grab a flower or two from the fields as we drove. As they did so, I would exit the car and take a leak at every stop. I'm old you, know. Your mother thought we would never get here."

Giovanni laughed and said, "They are beautiful. The whole chapel looks great."

Gabriella came running over into her brother's arms. She was dressed in a beautiful lace dress Anna had made for her at Easter. "You look wonderful," Giovanni told her.

Giovanni also thanked Padre Guardiano for arranging everything. Alfredo called Giovanni over and showed him a bag his mother had packed, as well as the tails she had brought from Babeto's for him to wear. Giovanni told Alfredo, "I wouldn't want anyone else as my best man."

Alfredo said, "As I know I have told you, I got my love of opera from my parents and my love of Verdi from my father. One of his favorite Verdi operas was the forgotten *Alzira*. I know we have spoken at length about the importance of words in opera. The librettist for *Alzira* was Salvatore Cammarano, who also was the librettist for Donizetti's *Lucia di Lammermoor*. Cammarano wrote his opera librettos standing on the porch of the Church of San Francesco di Paolo in his beloved Naples. He would lean against a pillar on the porch and scribble a verse every now and then. When he grew tired, he would just lay down right there on the steps of the church.

"In *Alzira,* he wrote some words for a baritone aria, which were my father's favorite in all of opera. When my father married my mother, he had those words inscribed on a music jewelry box, which plays the tune to the baritone aria from that opera."

Alfredo pulled a small box out of his pocket. He said, "I always intended to give this to my son on the day of his wedding. You are like a son to me. I want you to have it to give to your wife."

Giovanni hugged Alfredo and took the box. He opened it, and the strains of the baritone aria from *Alzira* were heard. Giovanni noticed a gold wedding band in the bottom of the box. The ring had been Alfredo's mother's ring.

Alfredo said, "I want you to give that to Isabella, along with this box. You can get the ring sized at a later time. It would mean so much to me if you would accept it."

Giovanni thanked Alfredo. He then read the inscribed words from *Alzira*:

*E' dolce la tromba che suona vittoria,*
*The trumpet that announces victory is sweet,*

*t'infiamma, t'esalta, un inno di gloria:*
*it inflames and exalts the heart, it is a hymn to glory:*

*Ma innanzi agli altari, agl'uomini, a Dio,*
*But in front of the altar, before men and before God,*

*condurre la donna che avvampa il tuo cor,*
*to lead the woman that set your heart on fire,*

*e dir: questa donna, quest'angelo é mio,*
*and to say: this woman, this angel is mine,*

*di mille trionfi é gioia maggior!*
*is a joy greater than a thousand victories!*

Giovanni turned to Alfredo and said, "This is wonderful, Alfredo. I hated not being able to give Isabella a ring. You are unbelievable. I love these words. Opera librettos have always been like novels to me. *Grazie.* I have never heard this opera before and have never read the libretto. This means so much."

"*Prego.* I wouldn't want anyone else to have it. Now go change." Giovanni quickly excused himself and went to change.

The sun had just reached the very top of the Chianti hills in the distance when Anna and Isabella walked across the courtyard toward the little church. Anna was holding up the bottom of Isabella's dress so it wouldn't get dirty.

When they reached the front door of the church, Anna

told Isabella to stay outside. Anna then went into the church and said very excitedly to everyone inside, "*Pronto.* She is ready!"

Anna, along with Gabriella, came back out by Isabella. Anna told her, "You look beautiful. I am so happy for the both of you. You have made my son very happy." Anna opened the door, and Gabriella walked down the aisle first, carrying a small basket with flowers, which Signor Romano had arranged. Signor Montefeltro was playing Bach's *Jesu, Joy of Man's Desiring,* as Gabriella walked down the aisle.

Giovanni and Alfredo were standing near the altar. Padre Guardiano was standing directly in front of the altar. Signor Romano was busy taking pictures of Gabriella walking down the aisle. Giovanni was beaming near the front.

Anna was the next person down the aisle and took her place on the opposite side of the altar from Alfredo. She smiled broadly at Giovanni as she took her place.

Suddenly, the music changed to the wedding march. Isabella opened the door to the church, and entered. The moment the door was opened, Giovanni knew he would remember the way Isabella looked for the rest of his life. She looked stunning in her wedding dress. Alfredo leaned over to Giovanni and told him she was wearing his mother's wedding dress. Tears came down his face.

As Isabella walked down the aisle, she noticed how beautiful the little church looked. The view she had out the windows behind the altar of the Chianti hills, lit with the setting sun, was truly spectacular. As she got closer to the altar, she smiled at Giovanni. She made her way up by Giovanni, offered him her arm, and together they took their places in front of Padre Guardiano and God.

It was a moving ceremony. Padre Guardiano said some very nice words about Franco and Giovanni and how he got to know them when they would come to the convent over many years. When the ceremony came to a close, Padre Guardiano said, "I would now like to introduce you to Signor and Signora Giovanni Tempesta."

Everyone clapped as the newlyweds made their way out of the church. When they exited the door, both were elated to see what was in the courtyard by the fountain. Some local women, arranged by Padre Guardiano, had set up a table with a cake and some food on it as well as a few bottles of Chianti wine. A three-piece mandolin group was off to the side. They started playing some Neapolitan love songs.

Isabella leaned over and kissed Giovanni as everyone else came out of the church and made their way into the courtyard for the little wedding reception. It was a glorious night and a very memorable evening.

At one point, Alfredo quieted down everyone and said, "To Giovanni and Isabella, two very dear friends, I dedicate this song to you."

The mandolins started to play, and Alfredo began to sing the very famous Neapolitan love song, " 'O sole mio" by di Capua. Anna was surprised by the beauty of Alfredo's voice. Signor Romano and Signor Montefeltro danced together. Giovanni and Isabella joined them. Padre Guardiano danced with Anna.

When Alfredo completed the song, Isabella ran over and hugged him. Giovanni yelled bravo at the top of his lungs. The mandolin players were amazed at how well Alfredo sang.

As the festivities continued, Giovanni approached Alfredo

and again thanked him for the music box. With devilment in his eyes, Giovanni asked, "Alfredo, with such beautiful lyrics in Verdi's aria from *Alzira*, can you imagine the magnificent melody Puccini would have provided for them?"

Alfredo countered by saying, with feigned forcefulness, "Giovanni, you are incorrigible!"

After the little party broke up, Isabella and Giovanni climbed into the car and started the drive to Bellagio. Anna cried as her son pulled away. Alfredo put his arm around her to comfort her. Anna told him, "These are tears of joy. I'm very happy for the both of them."

"I am too. Your son is a wonderful person and a fantastic singer."

"He owes you everything, Alfredo."

Soon, the little wedding group was back in the car, making their way back to Milan, stopping along the way to let Alfredo "water the Tuscan flowers".

———

GIOVANNI AND ISABELLA loved spending Sunday walking around the town of Bellagio. They agreed with the description people had given the town, "The prettiest town in all of Europe."

Bellagio is located at a magnificent site, right on a promontory dividing Lake Lecco from the southern arm of Lake Como. Giovanni and Isabella spent the entire day walking up and down the pretty, steep streets on the hillside and taking in the splendid lakeside gardens of *Villa Serbelloni* and *Villa Melzi*.

Early Monday, they returned to Milan. Giovanni had to

report for rehearsal at 10:00 a.m. Isabella told Giovanni that she would go talk to her father without him. She thought it might be better that way. Deep down, Giovanni was relieved.

The rehearsal went very well. Giovanni was starting to get the hang of acting. He got back to his house around 7:30 p.m. that night. Isabella was sitting in the front room with Anna. Gabriella was sleeping in Anna's lap.

When Giovanni walked in, Anna picked up Gabriella and took her to bed, so that he could speak to Isabella alone. Giovanni asked Isabella, "How was the meeting with your father?"

Isabella broke down into tears and said, "Giovanni, I knew what his answer would be. But it still hurts. He wants nothing to do with me. He told me, 'You are on your own. You are dead to me'. He also told me he will make it very difficult for you when you sing at La Scala. I don't know what he meant by that. I picked up my clothes and went to Parma with your mother. I love our little apartment. Your uncle Piero was very nice and is giving it to us at a very cheap rate. It's already furnished."

Giovanni sat down next to her and said, "I'm sorry for what your father told you."

"You are my family now. I am devoted to you, no one else. All of my love shall be yours until my dying breath. I have given everything up for you. In return, all I ask is that you never leave me."

Giovanni replied, "I've loved you from the moment I saw you at Angelo's. Our hearts are united in love. Nothing can part us, *mio amore*. Not even death. You can rest assured that I will never leave you."

They kissed and spoke until they retired to bed.

Tomorrow, Isabella would be back in school in Bologna, and they would begin their life together in their little apartment in Parma, as Giovanni Tempesta prepared for his operatic debut at La Scala. He wondered what her father meant by making it difficult for him at La Scala.

# 40

## AIDA AND VICINO AL SOL

*G*iovanni worked extremely hard the last few remaining weeks of rehearsals at La Scala. He hoped he had edged out Signor Fidito for the opportunity to open the new season at La Scala.

Isabella was hard at work preparing for her exams; exams in childhood education, not pre-law. Giovanni, after rehearsals, would catch the train and arrive in Parma, usually before eight. He would leave for Milan the next morning around eight.

As rehearsals were drawing to a close, Giovanni had a surprise for Alfredo. He called his old mentor the night before and said he would take a bus from the train station so he could see Alfredo in the morning before he reported to La Scala.

When Giovanni arrived at the *Casa Verdi*, he thought how much he missed coming to the home. He missed seeing all the other residents and listening to their stories while he sat in the salon with Alfredo. But most of all, he missed spending time with his old teacher.

Signora Lydia ran up to Giovanni when she saw him, saying "Oh! I have missed seeing you around here. How are rehearsals going?"

"They are going fine. It's a lot of hard work and long hours."

"Congratulations on your marriage. Alfredo told me the ceremony was lovely. I hope Isabella realizes how lucky she is?"

"I try to tell her every day," Giovanni said, before breaking out into a laugh.

As they were speaking, Alfredo, assisted by an aid, walked into the foyer. "Is that a tenor's voice I hear speaking?"

"Yes, it is," Giovanni said, as he went to hug his good friend. "Today, it is my turn to take you on a field trip."

"Where are we going?"

"La Scala."

Giovanni and Alfredo caught the bus to La Scala. Upon exiting the bus, Giovanni said, "I wanted you to come to a rehearsal. I thought you would like to sit out in the theater."

"I would love that. It's been years since I've attended a rehearsal."

Giovanni and Alfredo entered the old theater via the stage door. Giovanni led Alfredo out into the auditorium and let him sit down, two rows in front of the orchestra pit. Giovanni then left Alfredo as he went to warm up backstage.

Today's rehearsal was a complete staging of the entire first act. At 10:00 a.m., all the singers reported to the stage. The orchestra pit was already filled with the musicians.

A little while later, when Giovanni walked out onto the stage, he looked out in the auditorium and saw Alfredo. Maestro Torcelli called everyone to order and explained what they were going to do today. He then announced the order of the singers. Giovanni felt like jumping for joy when he heard Maestro Torcelli state that he wanted Giovanni to do the walkthrough first. Signor Fidito, on the other hand, was very upset.

When Maestro Torcelli turned to make his way to the pit, he noticed Alfredo sitting out in the theater. He went up to the old tenor and spoke very briefly to him and told him how well his pupil had been doing. Alfredo thanked Maestro Torcelli for giving Giovanni a chance.

Maestro Torcelli took his place in the pit and started the prelude to *Aida*. Alfredo sat out in the auditorium, taking it all in. Oh, how he missed the excitement of the theater world. The creative process at work.

Once the prelude was completed, Maestro Torcelli called for the first two principals on the stage to take their places. Signor Enzo Fracopoco, the stage director, gave some instructions.

The opera starts with two characters on the stage, Radames, a young warrior, and Ramfis, the High Priest, carrying on a conversation. In a very eloquent arioso, Ramfis tells Radames that the Gods have chosen a new leader for the Egyptian army, and he is on his way to relate the name to the king. Radames prays that he be so named.

Giovanni took his spot on the stage. Luigi Grotticelle, the Ramfis, took his spot. Maestro Torcelli began the opera, and Luigi sang his lines, followed by Giovanni.

Once Ramfis leaves the stage, the time comes for "Celeste

Aida", the first aria in the opera. "Celeste Aida" is a very difficult aria to sing, especially because it comes so early in the opera, and the tenor has not had time to fully warm up his voice.

Maestro Torcelli began the recitative. It is punctuated by martial fanfares. Giovanni hit the first lines of the recitative like a ton of bricks.

Giovanni finished the first section of the aria. He had listened to Caruso sing this aria countless times with his father. Giovanni nailed the opening. Alfredo was sitting in his seat, conducting with his hands. Giovanni and Alfredo had worked on this aria for weeks. Giovanni began the opera proper:

> *Celeste Aida, forma divina,*
> *Celestial Aida, divine form,*
>
> *mistico serto di luce e fior,*
> *mystic crown of light and beauty,*
>
> *del mio pensiero tu,*
> *you are the queen of my*
>
> *sei regina, tu di mia vita sei lo splendor.*
> *thoughts, you are the splendor of my life.*
>
> *Il tuo bel cielo vorrei ridarti,*
> *I would like to give back your beautiful sky,*
>
> *le dolci brezze del patrio suol;*
> *the sweet breezes of your country;*

*un regal serto sul crin posarti,*
*place a royal crown on your head,*

*ergerti un trono*
*and erect a throne for you*

*vicino al sol.*
*near the sun.*

Verdi wrote the aria such that, with the phrase, "vicino al sol", the tenor is supposed to sing the last word with a top B flat *pianissimo* and *morendo*. Most singers avoid this and just sing the last note all out in full voice. During rehearsals so far, both Giovanni and Signor Fidito had both steered clear of the pianissimo ending. Although, Giovanni did try it several times while working with Alfredo.

Today, as Giovanni ended the aria, he looked out to Alfredo who had his hand raised and was bringing his fingers inward, which meant for a singer to sing softly, pianissimo. Alfredo had done the same thing at the *Casa Verdi* when they had practiced it.

Maestro Torcelli brought the orchestra to the end of the aria and expected the aria to end with Giovanni hitting the last note at full force. Giovanni hit the words "vicino al" at full voice. However, at the word "sol", his voice lightened up, and in a beautiful pianissimo, he took the top B flat. As he held the note, there was a gasp in the orchestra. When he finished, the entire orchestra erupted in applause. Even Maestro Torcelli was clapping. Maestro Torcelli, who always wanted the music sung the way the composer wanted it, was in awe. Alfredo had a huge grin on his face.

Signor Fidito, sitting offstage, was shaking his head like it was nothing. When everyone settled down, the rehearsal continued. At every break for the rest of the day, people were still talking about that note.

When the first act was completed, rehearsals began again, but this time with the other cast members. Signor Fidito began "Celeste Aida". Giovanni thought his voice was loud, but it didn't have any lyrical quality to it. Alfredo was sitting out in the theater, thinking the same thing. Both Alfredo and Giovanni hoped Maestro Torcelli was thinking the same thing.

When Signor Fidito reached the end of the aria, he was determined to show everyone that he too could sing the aria the way Verdi intended. He hit the final word and tried to sing it pianissimo. The crack that emanated from his voice made it sound like La Scala was being bombed again. A few members of the orchestra laughed.

Signor Fidito stormed off, with Maestro Torcelli yelling at the orchestra to quiet down. Giovanni sat on a chair near the stage, very proud of himself.

When rehearsals ended later that day, Giovanni made his way to where Alfredo was seated. He told his old friend as he sat down next to him, "I knew you wanted me to sing it that way."

Alfredo said, "I felt you had it in you. Your voice was calling to let it out. It was beautiful. Just like Corelli in his recording with Mehta. My young friend, you buried your competition today."

"Do you think so, Alfredo?"

"*Si.* I feel like Caruso going to see Schipa."

Giovanni was confused and asked Alfredo what he meant.

Alfredo said, "When Caruso was living in New York, at the height of his powers, he heard about a new tenor, a great tenor, by the name of Tito Schipa. There were rumors that he might be even better than Caruso himself. Schipa was a gifted lyrical tenor of great refinement. His tone was light and warm, and he sang a restricted repertoire.

"It came to be that Schipa, who in reality could never be compared with the great Caruso, was giving a concert at Carnegie Hall. Caruso, like most tenors, was deathly jealous of losing his place, so he had to go see this new tenor for himself. He settled into his seat with his American wife, Dorothy. Schipa came on the stage and sang his first selection. Caruso sat in his seat and listened. The moment the aria was completed, Caruso turned to his wife and said, *'Doria, andiamo. Non c'è nulla di cui preoccuparsi.'* (There is nothing to worry about), and he left the theater.

"I feel like Caruso today. I have heard Signor Fidito. There is nothing to worry about."

Giovanni laughed and said he had never heard that story and knew his father would have loved it.

Giovanni left the theater with Alfredo and went to get a bite to eat with him, before bringing him back to the Casa Verdi.

---

TWO DAYS LATER, November 26th, Giovanni got off the train from Parma around 9:00 a.m. and made his way toward La

Scala. Little did Giovanni know that after his singing of that note, Maestro Torcelli had made his decision.

As Giovanni approached the front of La Scala, he noticed one of the workers hanging a poster out front. During the opera season, the theater was lined with the brown posters announcing the opera and the cast. Today, the posters for the opening night of the season were being hung. Giovanni walked up to one of the posters already up and stared in disbelief.

*TEATRO ALLA SCALA DI MILANO*
*PRESENTA*
*AIDA di VERDI*
*7 DICEMBRE, 1979*

*AIDA: CHRISTIANA GABODO*
*AMNERIS: ROSINA PICCOLOMINI*
*RADAMES: GIOVANNI TEMPESTA*
*AMONASRO: FRANCESCO CARRARA*
*RAMFIS: LUIGI GROTTICELLI*
*IL RE: VINCENZO PASETTI*

*DIRETTORE D'ORCHESTRA*
*MASSIMO TORCELLI*

*DIRETTORE DI SCENA*
*ENZO FRACOPOCO*

GIOVANNI HAD DONE IT. He would be making his debut at La

Scala. He walked to the bench across from La Scala, sat down, and cried deeply and remembered his father.

After a few moments, he collected himself and walked into the Galleria. He found a phone and called Alfredo. Alfredo had to sit down when he heard the news, unable to speak for a few moments. When he was finally able to say a few words, he congratulated his young pupil and told him it was well deserved.

Giovanni then made his way to La Scala and rehearsals. But this time as a tenor definitely making his debut. He still couldn't believe it.

He was congratulated by the other singers backstage, except for Signor Fidito. He had left La Scala when he got the news. Maestro Torcelli was in his office trying to get a replacement for him to be an understudy to Giovanni, in case he couldn't perform.

Maestro Torcelli came out of his office and sent all of the singers who were not chosen home. The next few days would be intensive training with the principals. And to think, Giovanni was one of them.

When rehearsals were over that day, Giovanni walked out the stage door and was surprised to find the Maenza boys waiting for him. They rushed up to him and hugged him. They had seen the posters earlier that day and couldn't wait to see him. They told Giovanni that all the regulars from Angelo's had been calling the restaurant all day talking about the news.

After speaking with them for a short while, Giovanni went to see Anna and his sister to tell them. Anna held her son tightly for a long time and then said, "Papa would be so proud of you."

"I know Mamma. I know. Even if it is not Puccini."

He then quickly got on the train to Parma, so he could tell the good news to Isabella. She cried when she heard the news, so happy for her husband.

When Giovanni went to bed that night, he reminisced about all that had occurred. He had finally done it. He wished his father could have seen this day. He couldn't sleep at all.

# 41

## DI STEFANO'S PROTÉGÉ

ord spread very quickly throughout Milan that a local boy had been chosen to sing Radames and would be making his debut in opera at La Scala. The phone at Anna's home never ceased ringing. Anna was so proud of her son and gladly accepted the adulation from the well-wishers.

One of the newspapers in Milan, *La Repubblica*, sent their music critic to La Scala four days before the performance to interview the young tenor. Giovanni was excited since he had never been interviewed before.

The critic, Signor Onofrio Baldassini, sat down with Giovanni in his dressing room after rehearsals had been completed for the day and spoke with him at great length. Giovanni first spoke about his family and where his parents were from. He then spoke about his years of singing at Angelo's and how he thought it had provided an opportunity for him to learn his trade.

However, Giovanni saved his most eloquent and passionate discussion for his description of what Alfredo del Monte meant to him. He related how Alfredo had gotten him into the di Stefano competition and also how Alfredo and di Stefano approached Maestro Torcelli on his behalf. He ended the interview with a conversation about the love of his life, Isabella.

The next day, only three days before the opening, Giovanni got off the train from Parma and made his way to La Scala. As he left the train station, he passed a newspaper stand. The headline of that day's paper caught his attention. He bought a paper and read the article while he walked to La Scala. The article was as follows.

---

### DI STEFANO'S PROTÉGÉ TO MAKE OPERATIC DEBUT AT LA SCALA IN AIDA

*Giuseppe di Stefano, the retired tenor who was the darling of La Scala throughout the fifties, where he often sang with the great Maria Callas, has a protégée of his own on the brink of making his debut in opera at La Scala in Verdi's Aida on December 7th. Giovanni Tempesta is from Milan, although neither of his parents were born here: his father, who is deceased, was from Naples; his mother, Sicilian.*

*Giovanni attended St. Matteo's high school here in Milan. Upon graduation, he pursued a singing career and, while doing so, sang at Angelo's Restaurant. Signor Tempesta credits his time at Angelo's as what gave him his musical foundation.*

*His break finally came in the form of Giuseppe di Stefano. Di Stefano allowed Signor Tempesta to enter his local voice competition, which is held every year in Milan. After a successful appearance, Signor Tempesta, through the connections of di Stefano, was awarded a contract to begin his career in New Orleans.*

*But that was not to be. Because of a car accident, Signor Tempesta was unable to sing in New Orleans. He returned to Milan, where di Stefano wasted no time in lining up the contract with La Scala.*

*This critic has not heard Signor Tempesta sing. However, the reports from rehearsals are very encouraging. People are raving about this find of di Stefano's.*

*It is with a great deal of anticipation that Milan awaits to hear the voice of a local son, a protégée of a famous singer at La Scala. We will see if the young tenor can live up to the expectation.*

---

GIOVANNI WAS DUMBFOUNDED. The article did not mention Alfredo one time, even though Giovanni had spoken highly of Alfredo. What would Alfredo think about the article?

After rehearsals that day, before returning to Parma, Giovanni went to the *Casa Verdi*. Lydia told Giovanni that Alfredo was in the salon. She congratulated him on the article in the paper today.

Giovanni said, "They never mentioned Alfredo's name one time. Not once. I must speak to him."

Giovanni left Lydia and made his way to the salon. He found Alfredo sitting on a sofa, listening to a recording of a potpourri of tenors.

Giovanni said, "Alfredo, *come va*?"

"Ah, Giovanni. It's close now. December 7th is near."

"Alfredo, I wanted to speak to you about the article in the paper today. Did you hear about it?"

"*Si*. Lydia read it to me. It sounds as if all of Milan is waiting to hear you. They will hear a first-class tenor."

"Alfredo, you must believe me that when I spoke to the critic, I told him all about you and everything you did for me. I was shocked when I read the article today and never saw you mentioned."

Alfredo said, "I did not help you and work with you so that I could get my name in the paper. I trained you so that you could become a tenor and bring forth the music of the composers. I did it for them and for God, not for myself. But, use today as a lesson. When you have a career, be wary of critics. Most have their own agendas." Alfredo laughed at his own comment.

"Alfredo, you are unbelievable. You are truly wonderful, and I am so glad I have you as a friend."

"The same applies to you. Do you have a few moments? Please sit with me, and let's listen like we used to."

"Sure, Alfredo."

Giovanni sat down on the sofa and listened to the recording of different tenors. Giovanni and Alfredo would try to be the first to pick out which tenor was singing. Neither was ever wrong. Giovanni missed spending time with his old friend.

When Giovanni left the *Casa Verdi* to return to Parma that night, he was still upset about the article. One day, Giovanni would make it up to Alfredo, somehow.

THE NEXT DAY, December 5<sup>th</sup>, Giovanni left Parma, but this time by car. Isabella was with him on the return to Milan. She had taken the rest of the week off of school so that she could be with her husband for his debut at La Scala.

Giovanni had gotten them a room at the Grand Hotel in Milan, located at *Via Manzoni 29*, very close to La Scala. Most of the great singers from the past would stay at the Grand Hotel during their run of opera performances at La Scala.

Giovanni and Isabella arrived early in Milan and checked into the hotel. The same hotel where Caruso had first been recorded; where Verdi had died; and where Mascagni and Ponchielli and many others had stayed.

After checking in at the hotel, Giovanni reported to La Scala for the final complete walkthrough of the entire opera. Isabella, meanwhile, went to the coffee shop to meet with Signor Romano and pick up the photographs from the wedding.

When Giovanni got to La Scala, he felt like he was prepared. He was ready and willing to make his La Scala debut.

On December 6<sup>th</sup>, Giovanni had to attend a short meeting with the cast, Maestro Torcelli, and Signor Fracopoco to go over some last-minute details. After that meeting, as Giovanni left La Scala, the nerves hit him for the first time. He was glad Isabella was with him in Milan. Being with her would comfort him.

That night, Isabella and Giovanni met Anna, Gabriella and Alfredo for dinner at Angelo's. Being a Wednesday night, there was no singing, only recordings being played of great moments from opera.

Some of the patrons at Angelo's noticed Giovanni and came over and offered their congratulations. They asked Giovanni if he had any extra tickets to the performance, but Giovanni assured them that his allotment had already been taken by family.

Giovanni had been given ten tickets by the management of La Scala. He had presented those tickets to Isabella, Anna, Gabriella, Alfredo, Angelo, the Maenza boys, Signor Romano and Signor Montefeltro, and his uncle, Piero. Lydia and her husband had season tickets, so Giovanni didn't have to worry about trying to get them a pair.

Giovanni did buy one single ticket for someone special; it was a ticket to the *loggione*.

After dinner, the group walked across the street to La Scala to see the poster for *Aida*. Anna pulled out a camera and took a picture of Alfredo, Isabella and Giovanni standing in front of the poster with La Scala as the background.

Before Anna took Alfredo back to the *Casa Verdi*, Alfredo told Giovanni, "The next time we are together, you will be making your debut on the stage of La Scala. You will make a sensation. I leave you with the words of the Maestro." Alfredo quoted to Giovanni the opening lines of the famous soprano aria from *Aida*.

*Ritorna vincitor!*
*Return victorious!*

"I shall try, Alfredo. I shall try."

# 42

# A TICKET

*F*riday, December 7, 1979, finally arrived. Giovanni spent the day relaxing as much as he could around the hotel, but he was a bundle of nerves. He tried to avoid speaking in order to save his voice for the performance that night.

At noon, he had lunch with Isabella at Caruso's, a restaurant located in the hotel. Isabella tried to calm his nerves as best she could, but he was still very tense.

After lunch, Isabella went to get her nails and hair done while Giovanni was supposed to go to their hotel room to get some rest. However, he had other ideas. He quickly left the hotel and hailed a cab.

The cab driver took Giovanni to a lonely cemetery on the outskirts of Milan. Unlike the *Cimitero Monumentale* in downtown Milan, where the elite Milanese are buried, such as Arturo Toscanini, Alessandro Manzoni and Ermann

Einstein, father of the scientist, the cemetery Giovanni went to was for the poorer, mostly forgotten citizens of Milan.

Giovanni walked along a crushed stone path until he came to a small crucifix that was one of many stretched across the vast field of small, rolling grassy hills. Written across the crucifix were the words, "Tempesta, Franco. Beloved husband. Devoted father". Here, laid to rest, was his father.

Giovanni knelt down by the grave as tears began to flow down his face. He reached into his pocket and pulled out the ticket he had purchased for the performance tonight at La Scala. The ticket was a standing room only ticket for the *loggione*. The same kind of ticket Giovanni's father had bought for him the first time Giovanni went to La Scala.

Giovanni laid the ticket on top of the crucifix and said, "Papa, this is for you. You will be there tonight. Thank you for all of your help in sending to me Alfredo and Isabella. Also, thank you for teaching me to love music. I will try to make you proud tonight."

Giovanni stood up and slowly left the cemetery and returned to the hotel.

---

AROUND 4:30 p.m. that afternoon, Isabella sent him off to La Scala. She said, "I'll see you backstage after the performance. I'm sure Alfredo will be with me. Don't be nervous. Alfredo trained you well."

"I know. Thank you for all your help. Being married to you has been wonderful."

Isabella said, "All I wanted to do with my life was to teach and marry someone whom I loved and who loved me in return. Because of you, all of my dreams have been fulfilled. Tonight is your night. I am so happy for you."

"*Ti amo.*" They embraced, and Giovanni left the room.

Giovanni made his way to the third floor of the Grand Hotel. He strolled down the hall and passed the suite where Fred Gaisberg had first recorded Enrico Caruso in 1902.

Giovanni then made his way out of the hotel and into the streets of Milan; the city where he was born and the city where he was raised; the city where his father had died and the city where he had met Alfredo; the city where Giovanni had met his wife and soon, the city where he would be making his operatic debut.

The rest of the walk to La Scala had been planned by Giovanni since the first day he had gone to the opera as a boy with his father and decided that he wanted to become a singer. He had always dreamed about this day.

Giovanni first walked to the Duomo. He entered the old cathedral and sat in a pew for a few moments. He prayed to God and his father to help him get through this night.

When he left the Duomo, he walked through the *Galleria Vittorio Emanuele II.* As he did so, he thought about all of the singers and composers who had come before him, all of them who had walked through here on their way to La Scala to perform. The *Galleria* was filling up with people having dinner or drinks before the performance.

As he came out of the other side of the *Galleria*, La Scala, in all its splendor, was straight ahead. It looked ready for another opening night to a season filled with operas performances.

Giovanni made his way to the stage door. Before going in, he looked across the street at Angelo's. Tonight, opening night at La Scala, was always the busiest night at the restaurant. But Giovanni was surprised to see that no lights were on at the venerable, old restaurant. Giovanni ran across the street to see why it was dark.

On the front door to Angelo's hung a sign, which read: "The Caruso of Angelo's sings tonight. Restaurant closed." Giovanni welled up with emotion. Angelo, except for that one week in March, never closed his restaurant. He thought of his old boss and realized how much Angelo loved him and how much he loved Angelo.

Giovanni, very pleased, crossed the street and entered the backstage area of La Scala. He didn't see any of the other singers before he settled into his dressing room. The backstage area was filling up with backstage workers and chorus members. *Aida* uses a large number of chorus, so they were all crammed in backstage. The performance was to start at 7:30 p.m.

At 5:30 p.m., Giovanni heard a loud knock on his dressing room door. Signora Gloria Lambini, the make-up artist for La Scala, came into the dressing room and prepared Giovanni for the performance.

At 5:50 p.m., Signor Vito Ogeto, one of the costume designers, came into Giovanni's dressing room and helped Giovanni dress.

At 6:10 p.m., Signor Maurizio Fissore, a rehearsal pianist, came into the dressing room, sat at the piano located in the room, and played while Giovanni began to vocalize. Giovanni, at first, was worried. His throat was very dry. Signor Fissore advised him that it was due to nerves. But, the longer Giovanni vocalized, the looser and better the voice became.

He was finished at 6:45 p.m. The performance was only forty-five minutes away. Giovanni still hadn't seen any of the other singers or Maestro Torcelli. Giovanni left his room and walked to the dressing room of Signora Christiana Gabado. He knocked, and the door was answered by her assistant. Giovanni asked if the Signora was available. The assistant advised Giovanni that she was not. Over the assistant's shoulder, Giovanni could see the soprano, with her head inside a wastepaper bucket, vomiting. As the assistant closed the door, Giovanni felt a sense of relief. Signora Gabado had sung numerous times, yet she still got nervous. It was all right that he was nervous too.

Giovanni walked to the stage to look out into the theater. The curtain was down, but it had a few peepholes, which allowed Giovanni to look through and see the auditorium. The theater was packed with people. Giovanni looked over to the left of the stage, about four rows away from the orchestra pit, and saw his family. Sitting on the end of the row, with a look of pride, sat Alfredo, dressed, as most men for opening night, in tails.

Giovanni then scanned the rest of the crowd. The fire-red hair on two individuals caught his attention immediately. Standing in the middle aisle, by the orchestra pit, were the Maenza boys. They were busy talking to people around them and pointing into the pit. No doubt, Giovanni thought they were speaking about their father playing the oboe at the premiere of *Falstaff*. Giovanni pressed his golden oboe chain close to his chest.

Sitting down, near where the Maenza boys were standing, Giovanni saw Angelo talking to a young, beautiful woman. Giovanni laughed to himself, as he was sure Angelo would be very busy during the intermissions, meeting the young ladies.

Sitting a few seats back, Giovanni saw Tito Trepidoro, Lydia's husband. Lydia had made sure to tell Alfredo where her seats were so he would know where to find them. Giovanni did not see Lydia. Her husband was sitting alone.

Before leaving the stage, Giovanni made a terrible mistake. His eyes scaled the boxes of La Scala, pass the Royal box, and up to the very top of the theater, the *loggione*. It was packed with people. He gulped hard. The nerves came back again, harder this time. He hoped the beast would be tame tonight.

Giovanni left the stage and made his way back to his dressing room. He was caught in the hall by Maestro Massimo Torcelli.

"*In bocca al lupo,*" the conductor told him.

"*Crepi il lupo.*"

That was all Maestro Torcelli said. Giovanni went back to his dressing room and waited. His stomach was churning. Doubt began to creep into his mind. I can't do this, he thought.

His thoughts were interrupted by a knock on his door. Giovanni opened it and was thrilled to find Alfredo and Lydia. He hugged the both of them. Lydia said, "Your teacher here wanted to see you. Isabella found me and brought me to Alfredo. Since the head guard worked with my father many years ago, Alfredo knew I could get him backstage."

Giovanni smiled and thanked her. Lydia continued, "I will leave the two of you alone. Alfredo, I'll be right outside when you are done." She hugged Giovanni and then left the dressing room.

The moment she left, Giovanni turned to his teacher and said, "Alfredo, I can't do this. I am a nervous wreck. If the *loggione*. . ."

Alfredo cut off Giovanni with just the lift of a finger. In a very calm, soothing tone, Alfredo said, "Giovanni Tempesta, you are prepared. Go out and tell a story. That is all you are doing. Telling a story through music. Somewhere out in the audience tonight, there is a person who does not know the story of *Aida*. Sing to them. Tell them a story. Let the composer live through you. And through you, let music enter their life."

"But Alfredo, *ho paura*. I'm scared."

"Of course, you're scared. You should be. But you are prepared. Every singer must face this fear. You can do this. Sing like only you know-how. Don't worry about the *loggione* and their reaction. Sing like you always have, and in time the *loggione* will cheer you. As my teacher told me the first time I sang in an opera, don't be afraid to make a sensation."

Giovanni smiled and said he wouldn't be afraid. Suddenly, there was a knock at his door, and the voice of Signor Fracopoco saying, "Signor Tempesta, you are due on stage."

Giovanni went to one knee and said a prayer to his father. When he stood up, he turned to Alfredo and said, "Time to go tell a story."

"*In bocca al lupo*, Giovanni."

"*Crepi il lupo*. I owe this all to you, *amico*."

He led Alfredo out of the dressing room and to Lydia out in the hall. She patted Giovanni on the back as he made his way to the stage to make his operatic debut and to make his dream a reality.

# 43

# NESSUN DORMA

 $\mathcal{G}$ iovanni walked onto the stage of the La Scala opera house. The curtain was still down. The stage lights were not on, and it was somewhat dark. The massive first act set of the King's room in Egypt towered over Giovanni. Signor Luigi Grotticelli, the Ramfis, also reported to the stage. He came over to Giovanni and shook his hand without a word and took his spot on the stage.

The house was awaiting the arrival of the conductor in the pit. Giovanni stood on the stage, all the while, his stomach churning with nerves. Suddenly, there was a tremendous ovation as Maestro Torcelli entered the orchestra pit, turned to the audience and bowed. He then turned and started to conduct the prelude to the opera.

As the orchestra played, Giovanni stood rigid in place. He felt like he was going to be sick. Signor Fracopoco walked onto the stage, patted both Giovanni and Luigi on their back, and then took his place off stage, in the wing on the right side of the stage.

After a few moments, the prelude ended, and the orchestra went right into the music for the first act, the conversation between Ramfis and Radames. The curtain slowly was lifted. Giovanni tried to take a deep breath, but couldn't. Through the glare of the spotlights, he could see Maestro Torcelli. Maestro Torcelli pointed his finger at Luigi, who sang the opening lines of the opera.

Maestro Torcelli then pointed to Giovanni. He finally took a breath and then sang his line.

*La sacra Iside consultasti?*
*Have you consulted Isis?*

Giovanni had done it. He had finally sung in an opera. After he sang those few words, the nerves left him. He was a tenor.

Ramfis then ended the little conversation aria that started the opera.

Luigi walked off the stage, leaving Giovanni all alone. The orchestra hit the martial music with full force, signaling the start of the first aria, "Celeste Aida". Giovanni, who had turned his back to the crowd, turned quickly and began the recitative. He messed up on one word but got through it.

Maestro Torcelli gathered the orchestra and started the main part of the aria. Giovanni thought about Alfredo. Giovanni had sung this aria countless times with him. Pretend you are singing just to him, he told himself. He began the aria. Throughout the course of the aria, his voice was strong, lyrical and filled with emotion.

When he got to the end of the aria, he dropped to one knee, and with perfect control he ended the aria with a top B flat, pianissimo. You could hear a pin drop in the theater when he hit that note. As the note drifted into silence, La Scala erupted. Alfredo was screaming "bravo" at the top of his lungs. Isabella and Anna were both crying. The applause was thunderous. However, the applause was slowly drained out by the cries of "Fidito" coming from the *loggione*, yelling for the tenor whom Giovanni had replaced. Then someone in the *loggione* yelled, *"terrone"*. Maestro Torcelli, aware of this, quickly started the music to continue the opera. Amneris and Aida came on stage, and the act continued.

The rest of the act went well, without incident. Aida's aria, "Ritorna vincitor", got a huge ovation. At the end of the first act, the principals went on stage together for a curtain call. Giovanni was holding Signora Gabado's hand. They received a nice round of applause. However, from the *loggione*, the word *"terrone"* came cascading down. Someone even yelled, "Tempesta, go back to the café. Bring us Fidito." Signora Gabado squeezed Giovanni's hand tight, before the principals walked off the stage and went to their dressing rooms.

When Giovanni returned to his dressing room during the first intermission, he found Maestro Torcelli waiting for him. "That ending was perfection. It took balls to do it."

"*Grazie*. I was a nervous wreck."

"Giovanni, don't let the *loggione* scare you. Keep singing like you are singing, and you will win them over."

After Maestro Torcelli left, Giovanni couldn't just sit in his dressing room. He was too worked up. He went back to the stage and looked out through the peepholes in the curtain.

The theater was filled with chatter. Some members of the

audience had gone out into the lobby to stretch their legs or get something to drink during the intermission. But a majority were still standing in the aisle by their seats, talking about the opera. Giovanni looked up into the *loggione*. It was still packed. Every few seconds, a person standing up there would yell something with regard to Giovanni, like *"Terrone go home"* or "Go back to Angelo's."

Giovanni's eyes locked on something, which made him fully understand what was behind the reaction of the people in the *loggione*. Standing among a group of people up there, talking very excitedly, Giovanni saw the one person in this world who hated him, none other than Judge Pietro Monterone. That bastard was instigating the whole thing, Giovanni thought. That was how he planned to make it difficult for Giovanni's debut.

Giovanni returned to his dressing room. He was nervous that the further along the performance went, the worse the actions of the *loggione* would become.

The second act began.

The La Scala crowd clapped wildly after the Triumphal March, with most of the audience singing along. Giovanni sang the lines at the end of the act with great emotion and passion. Still, the *loggione* whistled when he came out to take his bow with the rest of the principals at the end of the act.

The second act hadn't required a lot of singing from Giovanni, nor was he on stage a lot. During the second intermission, Giovanni just sat in his dressing room. He didn't want to go out and look at the crowd anymore. The next act was a big act for him. He had a huge duet with Aida. As many a singer before him, he began to fear the *loggione*. He dreaded being called out to the stage.

The third act began.

Both Signora Gabado and Signor Carrara sang the duet very well. Both received a very warm round of applause at the end of the duet. The act continued, which leads to the great duet for Aida and Radames along the Banks of the Nile River.

Giovanni sang the duet beautifully, but it was very hard to hear him over the raucous yelling from the *loggione*. By far, this was the loudest they had been all night. A few times during the duet, Giovanni had even looked up toward the *loggione*. The *loggione* knew he was succumbing to the pressure. They were in control. Blood was in the water, and the beast was swarming. Alfredo listened intently and could hear fear in the voice. He buried his head into his hands. Giovanni was losing it. His nerves were rattling him.

The concluding part of the act was reached.

After Radames tells Aida to run away with her father, he is left on the stage alone. Giovanni turned his back to the audience, and his hands were shaking from nerves. The music swelled into action, as the Egyptian leaders, led by Ramfis, came to arrest Radames for freeing Aida's father.

When they rushed onto the stage, Giovanni turned to the crowd and drew his sword. The music built up to the concluding lines of the act, sung by Radames when he gives himself up to the High Priest of Egypt, Ramfis, to be arrested. As Giovanni waited for his cue from Maestro Torcelli, he thought momentarily about Alfredo. Alfredo would never be intimidated by the *loggione*. Alfredo would tell him to sing for the composer and God. Make a sensation. Giovanni had worked too hard and had come too far to be reduced to fear. With all the emotion and passion in his body, he threw down his sword and attacked the final line of the act:

*Sacerdote, . . .*
*Priest, . . .*

He hit the initial note very well.

*io resto a te!*
*I am staying with you!*

The first three words required high A's to be sung at the conclusion of each word. Verdi had written the music to then go down on the word "te" and the singer to end the note at a lower range. That was not to be tonight. Giovanni sang the first three words as written. However, when he sang the word "te", he hit a high D, a very difficult note for most tenors to hit, and held it a long time.

To this day, there are some members of the audience, true opera aficionados, who say that the note sung by Giovanni Tempesta was, without question, the single greatest note ever hit at the old theater.

When Giovanni hit the note, Alfredo stood up out of his seat, and under his breath, he said, "Yes, Yes! Do it! Go for it!"

The moment Giovanni completed the line, pandemonium broke out in the theater. Bravos were yelled throughout the theater. Giovanni walked over to Ramfis and knelt before him as the curtain came quickly down to end the act. Before the curtain had come all the way down, someone in the *loggione* yelled, "*Viva Tempesta.*"

It was soon picked up by everyone in the *loggione* as well

as the entire theater, all except one, Judge Monterone. He kept yelling *"terrone'*, but could not be heard over the applause and bravos.

When the curtain was completely down, Signor Luigi Grotticelli, the Ramfis, knelt down and grabbed Giovanni and said that his singing was unbelievable. The other singers all came up to him and congratulated him as well. Then all the principals went outside the curtain for the curtain call.

*"Tempesta, Tempesta, viva Tempesta,"* greeted them as they stood on the stage. Giovanni was smiling broadly. Out the corner of his eye, he could see his family and Alfredo. All were cheering and crying. Anna leaned over to Alfredo and asked, "What does all this mean?"

"Anna, your son, has made a sensation."

In the *loggione*, Giovanni's name was being called out over and over again. Judge Monterone looked on with disgust and yelled insults toward Giovanni at the top of his lungs, but he could not be heard over the noise. The Judge stormed out of the *loggione* and out of La Scala.

Giovanni made his way back to his dressing room. He was congratulated by chorus members backstage. When he reached his dressing room, he found Maestro Torcelli again waiting for him. Giovanni walked in and was struck by Maestro Torcelli's baton, which had been thrown at him. Maestro Torcelli was laughing and said, "Toscanini hit Lauri-Volpi like that when he tried that ending and refused to conduct the rest of the opera. I should do the same, but cannot. You have won them over. Listen, they are still screaming for you out there."

"Maestro, forgive me. A long time ago, Alfredo had told

me that story. I forgot about it until tonight. I knew I needed to do something good to calm the *loggione* down."

"Something good. I say what you did was something spectacular. I have never heard a more perfect note. If Verdi had heard it, he might have changed the way the music was written."

Maestro Torcelli then left Giovanni alone in his dressing room. There are some people who credit that night as what changed Maestro Torcelli. After that performance, he no longer insisted that singers sing the music as written.

Giovanni sat in his dressing room, very pleased. But he still had to sing the final act. He had to stay focused and finish strong. If he could do that, he would win the evening completely.

The final act began, which is divided into two scenes.

Giovanni sang his part very well. It was as if Giovanni was singing in front of another audience. They cheered at every opportunity. The first scene is dominated by Amneris, yet it was Giovanni who received most of the applause.

At the close of the opera, Radames is condemned to death and is sealed up in a vault, left to die. Aida secretly had hidden herself in the tomb to die with him. Giovanni took Aida in his arms, and in a beautifully sung duet, they ended the opera as the stone was rolled over the top of the tomb, sealing their fate.

*O terra, addio, addio, valle di pianti!*
*O earth, farewell, farewell, valley of tears!*

*Sogno di gaudio che in dolor svani!*
*Our dreams of happiness melt into sorrow!*

*A noi si schiude il ciel, e l'alme erranti*
*Heaven is opening for us, and our wandering souls*

*volano al raggio dell'eterno dì.*
*will fly in the light of the eternal day.*

As the curtain slowly descended on the scene, and the last strains of music died away, the crowd applauded again and started cheering Giovanni's name.

When the curtain was completely down, Signora Gabado turned and kissed Giovanni. "*Magnifico*," she told him.

"You were wonderful," he replied.

All of the principals then walked in front of the curtain, holding hands, bowing to the audience. They then retired behind the curtain and awaited their turn to take a solo bow.

While Giovanni awaited his turn, he was congratulated by backstage workers and the other singers. Giovanni was to take his bow second to last, right before Signora Gabado. She came up to Giovanni and told him, "I know this is improper, but tonight is your night. You go after me. You will remember this day for the rest of your life. Your sensational debut at La Scala."

Before Giovanni could say a thing, she brushed by him and went out on the stage to thunderous applause. Giovanni took a deep breath. Her words made Giovanni think about Alfredo. Alfredo never had this chance. The chance to stand on the La Scala stage and accept the applause of the audience. Signora Gabado reappeared behind the curtain and said, "Your turn, Giovanni."

Giovanni stepped in front of the curtain and received, by far, the largest ovation of the night. Giovanni bowed deeply.

When he came out of his bow, he was smiling. He had done it. He was officially a singer. He owed it all to Alfredo. He looked over to his right and saw his mother. She was beside herself with emotion. Gabriella was holding tight to Anna, afraid of all the noise. Giovanni looked further down the row, but could not see Alfredo and Isabella.

He again bowed to accept the applause. When Giovanni came up out of his bow, he was momentarily blinded by a flash from a camera. Right in front of the orchestra pit, in the middle aisle, Signor Romano was standing with his camera. When Giovanni could see again, he noticed Signor Romano and realized the illegal photographer was he.

Giovanni bowed again to accept the applause. He then straightened up, waved to the crowd, and turned to walk off the stage, glancing one more time to see if he could see Alfredo, but he could not. As he made his way through the curtain, he finally saw Alfredo and Isabella, standing backstage in the wing. Alfredo just had to be the first person to congratulate Giovanni. Isabella had helped him backstage just as the opera ended. The security guard, who had allowed Alfredo and Lydia backstage before the performance, allowed Alfredo backstage again, but this time with Isabella.

Giovanni saw his teacher and stopped before coming all the way through the curtain. It was repayment time. He turned and walked back onto the stage through the curtain. The crowd applauded again. Giovanni stood on the stage, waving his hands above his head, trying to get the crowd to be quiet. Slowly, the crowd quieted down. Everyone was confused. It looked as if the tenor wanted to say something. No one ever did that at La Scala. People started yelling to be quiet. *"Silenzio,"* they screamed. *"Silenzio."* The crowd became quiet.

Giovanni put his hands down and said, *"Signore! Signori!* I want to thank you for your kindness here tonight, and I am glad you enjoyed the performance. I would like to thank the person who is most responsible for my standing here tonight. He is the great tenor and my teacher, Signor Alfredo del Monte."

Most of the serious opera goers at La Scala knew who Alfredo was and his story. But they had no idea this was his pupil. Isabella led Alfredo through the curtain and out onto the stage. As he came through the curtain, La Scala erupted in applause. The orchestra members stood up and gave the old man a standing ovation. Giovanni hugged Alfredo and led him to the front of the stage. He leaned over to Alfredo and said, "You have stood on the stage of La Scala, *amico."*

Tears came rushing down Alfredo's face as he extended his hands and received the warm reception. The clapping lasted a few minutes. Giovanni then grabbed Alfredo's hand and began to lead him back through the curtain. The clapping died down.

Suddenly, Alfredo let go of Giovanni's hand and walked back to the front of the stage. Giovanni, who had already walked through the curtain, was turning around to get him but was stopped by Isabella, who hugged him from behind. *"Aspetta,"* she said. "Wait."

Alfredo stood on the stage and began to sing.

*Nessun dorma!*
*No one shall sleep!*

*Nessun dorma!*
*No one shall sleep!*

Giovanni leaned back into Isabella and began to cry. He said, "He's singing the aria from *Turandot* by Puccini, the opera he was supposed to sing here when he was injured."

The crowd had become totally silent. Most were standing, listening to the old man sing from the stage. Then, a member of the orchestra, a solo violinist, picked up the melody and joined Alfredo as he sang.

More and more orchestra members joined in and played the aria. The audience was in awe at the beauty of his voice.

At the word *splenderá*, Alfredo's voice melted into a beautiful and splendid pianissimo. Many in the theater now realized who taught Giovanni to sing the last note of 'Celeste Aida' with that glorious sound.

The entire La Scala orchestra had now joined in. When the aria reached the part where the chorus sings offstage, the audience members, as well as the chorus members from *Aida* backstage, started to sing along; after all, this was Italy.

While this was happening, Alfredo turned toward the curtain from where he came onto the stage and waved with his right hand, beckoning Giovanni to join him on the stage. Giovanni didn't know what he wanted him to do. He walked on stage and stood next to his mentor. When the chorus part was over, Alfredo, with great emotion, hit the final part of the aria perfectly and reached the triple climax.

*"Vinceró!" (I shall win!)*

Alfredo's voice thundered.

Alfredo then nodded to Giovanni, who then guessed why his mentor had called him to the stage. Giovanni stepped forward and hit the next note perfectly: *"Vinceró!"*

Alfredo then grabbed Giovanni's hand, raised it up, and in perfect unison, with the full La Scala orchestra playing, the two of them sang the final high B to the aria: *"Vinceró!"*

"I shall win." Indeed, Giovanni had. As a matter of fact, both Alfredo and Giovanni had. At the conclusion of the aria, pandemonium broke out in the theater again. Everyone was standing and screaming. There were few dry eyes in the house. The orchestra members stood up and cheered. Alfredo stood on the stage, still holding Giovanni's hand up in the air. Tears were coming down both men's faces. Both Alfredo and Giovanni bowed to the crowd, over and over again. Anna was crying out in the audience.

Signor Romano took another illegal picture, this time of Alfredo and Giovanni standing on the stage of the La Scala opera house, hand in hand, with their arms raised high above their heads. This picture would one day find its way to the wall of glory at the *Casa Verdi*, the rest home where Alfredo del Monte, a singer who had sung on the stage of the La Scala opera house, was a resident.

The audience refused to quiet down. Alfredo leaned over to Giovanni and said, *"Grazie, amico.* I have sung on the stage of La Scala."

"No, Alfredo. Thank you."

Some members of the audience stood in the aisle near the stage. Giovanni waved to them. He laughed when he saw Signor Montefeltro throw a huge Tuscan sunflower on the stage. Other people were throwing roses on the stage.

Giovanni waved to Angelo, who had his arm around a

plump woman, Angelo's own age, whom he had met during one of the intermissions. She definitely did not match the usual type of young, gorgeous women he always chose. She soon would become Signora Angelo Basta.

Giovanni also waved to the Maenza boys, who were both beaming. Now, when they related the story of their father, in the same breath, they would forever mention the name of Giovanni Tempesta.

Then he saw Lydia and her husband, Tito, both yelling bravo to the two of them on the stage. Tears were coming down Lydia's face. More so than anyone there, she knew what this night meant to Alfredo.

Giovanni turned and looked through the curtain where Isabella was standing. She smiled back at Giovanni with a look of utter love.

He then turned and looked at Alfredo. For the rest of his life, he would never forget the look of pure joy on his old teacher's face. Giovanni had repaid the debt he owed his friend.

Finally, after a few minutes, Giovanni and Alfredo waved to the crowd one last time, turned, and walked through the curtain. Isabella ran up to them both and hugged them.

Alfredo turned to Giovanni and said, "Your Puccini is ok."

Giovanni laughed and replied, "Your Verdi's not half-bad, either."

At that point, teacher and student hugged. They were mobbed by the other singers, chorus members and stage workers. Maestro Torcelli, who had made his way backstage and had forgone his solo bow, was spiritedly clapping for the duo.

Giovanni, Alfredo and Isabella, arm in arm, walked

amidst the crowd, who were cheering wildly, on the way to Giovanni's dressing room. The dressing room of Giovanni Tempesta, Tenor.

Giovanni Tempesta had always dreamed of becoming an opera singer. That night, Giovanni had finally achieved his dream.

# AUTHOR'S NOTE AND ACKNOWLEDGEMENTS

The convent in the novel is loosely based upon the *Monastero della Visitazione*, an actual Augustinian convent, located in Vicopelago, Italy. The opera related stories told throughout the novel about the historical composers, conductors and singers of opera are based on opera lore.

In the telling of this story, portions of the lyrics of opera arias and Neapolitan songs are used to assist in helping one understand the importance of the words used by the composer in crafting their stories.

Signora Giuseppina "Pinuccia" Cellini, the wife of the late Italian opera conductor, Renato Cellini, provided all of the English translations of these arias and songs at my request.

I remember fondly the time spent at her home one rainy afternoon in New Orleans. We looked over her photo books of all the famous singers that her husband had conducted at the Metropolitan Opera as well as with the New Orleans Opera. We also spoke at length about her father-in-law, Enzo

Cellini, who was a stage director for the great conductor, Arturo Toscanini. We then worked the rest of the afternoon on the translations in the novel over a bottle of Chianti. Pinuccia, I truly thank you for those wonderful memories and for making my novel sing.

In large part, due to my parents, Vincent and Lynda LoCoco, and my older sisters, Pam and Beth, I grew up in a house surrounded by music. My earliest memories of falling in love with music were watching Mario Lanza movies and hearing that glorious voice that he possessed. I also have vivid memories listening around my home as my father played recordings of Korngold movie music, who was and still is the greatest Cinematic composer who ever lived – in my humble opinion, of course. When I got older, I still cherish the many nights my family had Kirk Redmann, who was to become the youngest tenor to ever make his debut at the Metropolitan Opera, come over for dinner, and he would ultimately have to sing along with my father's Giuseppe di Stefano records.

Back then, opera was something that I knew some of the arias, but it had not touched my soul. Then, one day, I purchased a *Tosca* recording with Jose Carreras, conducted by Herbert von Karajan. As they say, that was that. I was hooked.

---

Thinking back to my childhood, I was raised in almost a different world. Yet, it was not a different world, just a very unique place. New Orleans was that place. Without a doubt, it's large Sicilian-American community was one of the reasons for its uniqueness. Being of Sicilian heritage, Cefalù and Monreale, I understood very quickly that to live, one had to live with passion. Passion for family, food, wine, opera, Saints football, Mardi Gras, and God. I am blessed to have been born and raised here, met my New Orleans girl here, and that my children are being raised here as well.

---

There are certain people I need to mention by name who contributed greatly to this book. They are my parents, sisters, and all of my extended family, including all of the Hemel family. I also thank John Gehl, George Weaver, Allain and Judy Andry, Heather Neff, my aunt, Janet LoCoco, and Glenn Noya.

To everyone else who contributed to this book in some way, whom I do not need to mention as you all know who you are, all I can do is say *"grazie"* and raise a glass of Chianti in your honor for a job well done.

To my children, I thank the both of you for the inspiration.

Lastly, but certainly not least, I thank my wife, Wendy. For ten years, Wendy was the administrator of a nursing home in New Orleans. My depiction of the nursing home in this novel was aided by her assistance in helping me create the atmosphere. Since this novel concerns music, it seems appropriate that mention should be made here about us making beautiful music together for the last 15 years, but since that would only make her embarrassed, I will instead just say thanks for all your support and love.

*Tutta la mia vita.*

Chip LoCoco

## LISTEN TO THE MUSIC OF
## TEMPESTA'S DREAM

Do you want to hear some of the music that appears in the novel, sung by some of the greatest artists the world has ever heard? We have put together a Spotify Playlist with music from the novel as well as a few other operatic selections to help give a reader sense of this passionate music. Be sure to follow it to get updates.

The Spotify Playlist can be found as:

**THE MUSIC OF TEMPESTA'S DREAM**

# ABOUT THE AUTHOR

Vincent B. "Chip" LoCoco, an estate planning attorney, lives in New Orleans with his wife and two children. His novels, *Tempesta's Dream – A Story of Love, Friendship and Opera* and *A Song For Bellafortuna* have became Amazon bestselling novels and both have been named as a Top Rated Novels in Italian Historical Fiction. He is currently at work on his next novel, *Saving the Music*, which is book 2 in his Bellafortuna Series. It is set to be released in Spring 2020.

facebook.com / Authorchiplococo

twitter.com / VincentBLoCoco

amazon.com / author / vincentlococo

# MORE INFORMATION

If you would like to let others know about this novel, please consider leaving a review on Amazon.

If your group or book club is interested in inviting Mr. LoCoco to discuss his novels or the writing process in person or by Skype, please use the contact form on his website at www.vincentlococo.com.

Made in the USA
Columbia, SC
14 September 2023

22853099R00221